Long Tan

The Start Of A Lifelong Battle

Harry Smith (Vietnam 1966/67)
With Toni McRae

16pt

Copyright Page from the Original Book

Copyright © Harry Smith

First published 2015

Copyright remains the property of the authors and apart from any fair dealing for the purposes of private study, research, criticism or review, as permitted under the Copyright Act, no part may be reproduced by any process without written permission.

All inquiries should be made to the publishers.

Big Sky Publishing Pty Ltd
PO Box 303, Newport, NSW 2106, Australia
Phone: 1300 364 611
Fax: (61 2) 9918 2396
Email: info@bigskypublishing.com.au
Web: www.bigskypublishing.com.au

Cover design and typesetting: Think Productions
Cover photograph: Jack Kirby and Harry Smith firing captured Russian Goryunov medium machine gun made famous at Stalingrad in WW2.
Printed in Australia by Ligare
National Library of Australia Cataloguing-in-Publication entry
Creator Smith, Harry A., author.
Title: Long Tan : the start of a lifelong battle / Harry Smith with Toni McRae.
ISBN: 9781922132321 (paperback)

    Smith, Harry A.
    Australia. Army. Royal Australian Regiment. Battalion, 6th.
    D Company--History.
    Soldiers--Australia--Biography.
Subjects: Long Tan, Battle of, Vietnam, 1966.
    Vietnam War, 1961-1975--Australia--Personal narratives.
    Vietnam War, 1961-1975--Veterans--Australia.
    Other Creators/Contributors:
    McRae, Toni, author.
Dewey Number: 959.704342

TABLE OF CONTENTS

DEDICATION	i
FOREWORD	v
FOREWORD	viii
PRELUDE TO BATTLE: 18 AUGUST 1966	xi
ONE: BEGINNINGS IN TASMANIA	1
TWO: CANNON FODDER TO GO	40
THREE: MURDER IN MALAYA	67
FOUR: BODY PARTS AND BATTLING COMMOS	81
FIVE: BATTLING RUSHES OF BLOOD TO THE HEAD AND HEART	110
SIX: THESE BOOTS ARE MADE FOR WALKING	123
SEVEN: VIETNAM: SUICIDE MISSION	166
EIGHT: BATTLE BEGINNINGS	181
NINE: INTO BATTLE: A 'RORKE'S DRIFT' IN THE RUBBER	223
TEN: AFTER THE BATTLE: UNCOVERING THE TRUTH	307
ELEVEN: COMMANDO ACTION, SAILING AND DIVORCE	356
TWELVE: A BATTLE WITH A PARACHUTE: PLUNGE TO EARTH AND CRASH OF DREAMS	403
THIRTEEN: BATTLING THE BRASS: AUSTRALIA'S SHAME EXPOSED	445
FOURTEEN: ANOTHER WAR: THE BATTLE FOR RECOGNITION	498
FIFTEEN: BATTLES IN LIFE BEYOND ARMY	548
EPILOGUE	607
ACRONYMS AND ABBREVIATIONS	621
BACK COVER MATERIAL	627

DEDICATION

The Battle of Long Tan on 18 August 1966 was a savage action in which 108 men of my former Delta Company 6RAR, supported by artillery, fought off an enemy regiment of four regular Viet Cong and NVA battalions. My company sadly lost 17 killed and 23 wounded, but the enemy's casualties were in the order of 500 killed and 800 wounded. The battle was applauded as the most savage company action of the Australian involvement and was later selected by the Vietnam Veterans Association of Australia as their icon of the war. But the gallantry awards recommended by my officers and me were reduced by half. So began another battle which is still being fought 49 years later, the battle for the proper recognition of my men. This book is my life story and the story of my ongoing battle seeking proper recognition of my men.

I dedicate this story...
To the officers and men and women in the Armed Services, especially those of 1 and 2 Commando Companies, the

Parachute School and the RAN Diving School who at various times, since I was a School Cadet in 1945, set me on a course which led me to achievements that had a profound effect on my most unusual military career in the Infantry Corps and Special Forces.

To my officers and soldiers who fought the Battle of Long Tan and all those who helped me to train my company, which led us to survive the battle. And to those who have supported me in my battle for awards justice, particularly Dave Sabben MG; Bob Buick MM; Bill Akell (MID – denied an MM) and Bill Roche (denied an MID).

To my three children Deborah, Sharon and Brett, and sisters Bev and Joan. May this story help you better understand your father and brother.

This book was originally intended as my life story for my family, but I was persuaded by journalist Toni McRae to expand it to include more of the Battle of Long Tan and its legacy. Toni helped me compile my story until she lost a battle with health in 2014. I also dedicate this book to her memory.

Now age 82, I can say I have had a wonderful life in the Army and in my sailing exploits. I have some regrets about my early personal life but I thank my present partner and wife of 17 years, Felicia, for all her support through my long fight for proper recognition for my officers and soldiers and for her love and company on our many sailing cruises up to lovely Lizard Island, Far North Queensland.

In my story about the fight for proper recognition of my men at Long Tan, where the number of recommended awards was cut in half and half of those remaining were downgraded, I quote the Vietnam Official History 1993, which states: 'The awards were little short of insulting for the heroism displayed.' I make no excuses for criticising the former senior officers who managed the Vietnam awards system which saw those furthest from the action claiming awards which should have gone to those who fought in combat with the enemy. I acknowledge the 1974 Military History Association Australia book by Ian Barnes, *Australian Gallant and Distinguished Service, Vietnam,* which has provided me with facts, information and philosophy about the questionable awards system in Vietnam.

My battles include my personal battle with my private life, the battle against the enemy at Long Tan, the battle against the bureaucracy for awards justice, my battle with prostate cancer at age 75, and the battle against critics who would 'cut down tall poppies'.

While I have, as yet, not been completely successful in the battle to get my men recognition, along with those who supported us, I hope that those who read this book will be provided with a greater understanding of their courage – in itself a recognition, even if not official.

FOREWORD

From June 2005 I had the honour to serve as the Shadow Minister for Veterans' Affairs and then as Minister from late 2007 until September 2010. Over that period of more than five years I was privileged to gain an insight into our defence forces, past and present, the men and women who have served our country, their families and the price they have all paid for that service. I learnt of tremendous courage and sacrifice, as well as the tragedy of war. I have also seen the injustice of war, both at home and abroad.

Throughout this time there were many complex issues that came to my attention. Some were resolved, some could not be, others continue to be a matter of public debate. One such issue was the question of gallantry awards resulting from the Battle of Long Tan. The iconic nature of Long Tan has ensured it will always have a special place in the history of our nation's war in Vietnam. The scale of the battle, the number of casualties, the heroic defence in the face of overwhelming opposition have meant this is so.

However, Long Tan's significance has extended beyond the battle itself. It has become symbolic in ways that do not reflect well on the operation of our military in times past. This goes to the very question of how a nation should honour and recognise those who have given so much. It is true that war is a brutal endeavour and those who are rightly recognised and honoured only account for a percentage of those who should be. It is also true that many factors come into play in deciding who is honoured, and 'luck' in many ways plays its part. However, the fact that many who should be honoured are not, because the circumstances do not allow it, does not excuse us from properly honouring those whose valour is recognised and put forward for appropriate decoration. It was this injustice that led my colleague and friend Graham Edwards MP to raise this matter in Parliament and ensure that I and others understood the need for action.

The work of Harry Smith and his men to ensure that those who performed extraordinarily in the rubber plantation at Long Tan are properly honoured has highlighted the manifestly unfair operation of the awards system at the time and the unwillingness of many of those in authority to deal with this issue since then. Harry's story is one of stubborn and dogged determination to right a wrong – an unwillingness to give ground borne of a fierce commitment to stay the course for a just outcome. The character he has displayed in seeking a fair result for his men is no more than what those of us who know him would expect. As he showed throughout his military career, Harry remains a man who will always fight for what he believes in and will always stick to his guns. Although I have not always agreed with him, I have always respected him and always known he will keep facing forward, no matter the cost!

Alan Griffin MP
Former Minister for Veterans' Affairs

FOREWORD

Graham 'Stumpy' Edwards lost both legs to a mine in Vietnam in 1970. He was instrumental in obtaining the Tanzer Review in 1999 which upgraded six awards approved in the 1998 Review and was always supportive of a review of Long Tan awards. He is currently (2015) a Member of the Australian War Memorial Board.

As a young man growing up in Australia I had a strong belief in the concept of a *fair go for all.*

Nothing tested my childhood belief as I grew older more than the disgraceful treatment of bravery awards for those who fought in Vietnam.

Many diggers who served there were overlooked or bypassed as statutory medals were handed out to senior officers for a *job well done.*

None were treated more unfairly than Harry Smith and those who fought with him and supported his actions during the Battle of Long Tan.

It makes an interesting comment on our system of bravery awards when the highest awards for that battle went to officers who arrived at the ground after the last shot had been fired.

Harry Smith has fought the good fight ever since the records were revealed to show how his recommendations for bravery were downgraded, scrubbed or just ignored.

Is it any wonder a bloke like Harry has been back in the fight with authority on behalf of those whose bravery was ignored in that iconic battle which demonstrated the highest traditions of our ANZAC heritage.

I was pleased to support Harry in his battle during my time in the Federal Parliament. Veterans Affairs Minister Alan Griffin also picked up the cudgel on Harry's behalf because we recognised that this was a man still fighting for justice on behalf of his diggers.

I stood next to Harry during a recent closing ceremony at the Australian War Memorial. It was a sad occasion and I watched Harry during that brief ceremony. For a brief and fleeting moment Harry let his guard down and I saw a man in the emotion of the moment. A man still moved by the fierce battle in which he fought and led with great courage and tenacity. A man still feeling the loss of the soldiers around him but determined to fight for justice for those who survived. A man burdened and saddened by the death of those he commanded. A man who felt his diggers were let down by those who turned their backs on a *Fair Go*.

You are a man, Harry, and I cannot pay a higher Australian compliment than that.

Graham Edwards AM
Former ALP Member for Cowan, WA

PRELUDE TO BATTLE: 18 AUGUST 1966

BY TONI MCRAE

The soft swish swish of the 2-m tall elephant grass brushed against their sweaty wet greens; it was the bloody red mud sucking at their boots and the consistent slashing of 12 Platoon's alternating lead section's machetes that made the soldiers' 3000-m trudge to Long Tan punishing.

In the blistering heat the 108 travelled in single file. They were sleep-deprived. On 13 August they had been ordered out on a long patrol, which included the Long Tan rubber plantation to the base of the large hill named Nui Dat 2, which was just to the northwest of where an enemy regiment arrived on 14 August and was waiting to attack the Nui Dat Australian Task Force base. Then, barely back at base, without warning in the very early hours of the steamy morning of 17 August came the blast of enemy 82mm mortar bombs, 75-mm recoilless rifle 'rockets' and 70-mm artillery shells, fired into the base for more than 22 minutes. Silence fell as suddenly as it had been broken. Weary, the men stood to, on lookout until dawn for an expected ground attack which never came. They had been rostered on picket duties that same night.

But now they had to move swiftly.

That morning the big brass sitting somewhat safely at Nui Dat Task Force HQ had ordered Delta Company to relieve Bravo Company's men who had been sent out at dawn on the 17th to look for the enemy who had fired the mortars, not anticipating contact, the enemy thought long gone, and having ordered a late breakfast. There Bravo had uncovered vacated enemy mortar positions and were ordered to continue searching; to be relieved the next day. Bravo's 80-odd soldiers had spent the day and night unmolested at the edge of the Long Tan rubber plantation, east-southeast of Nui Dat HQ and just east of the Suoi Da Bang River.

Not an enemy soldier had lingered to be fingered. Already at dawn 48 soldiers had returned to the base for local leave; no danger perceived by the company commander, the battalion commanding officer or the task force commander.

After relieving Bravo the 108 were to track down the enemy who had shelled the base – probably 30 to 40 Viet Cong, maybe 'a weapons platoon and protection' that had 'shooted and scooted' and were now long gone, slipping into their familiar jungle bases.

That was the most the Delta lads had been told anyway.

This was Operation Vendetta – so named by their nuggety carrot-top company commander Major Harry Smith, as revenge for the mortaring of Nui Dat; a mission that would be short, swift and nothing more, lads. No big deal.

The soldiers had kitted up for an operation of five days, these finely honed and tuned super-fit young men; 68 Aussie Nashos and near 40 tough Regular Army, and with them three well-practised New Zealand Artillery Battery Forward Observer party who had served with the 1st Battalion Group at Bien Hoa.

On this stifling morning the men carried 40 kg on their dripping backs and around their belts, including 110 rounds and water bottles. Some also lugged 200-round belts for the M60 machine guns, along with heavy PRC 9 VHF radios and spare batteries.

Through the undergrowth and over two creek crossings of the Suoi Da Bang, their Armalites, SLRs, M60s and Owen guns held high and dry, the 35-degree sun and clammy stickiness polished the sheen of their youth.

As infantry you are primed for death that arrives without warning or conscience. Hopefully the other guy's, after you send the first bullet. But it is enduring and infinite in your psyche that you could be next. You live from day to day. That is your training.

Yet on this monsoon morning of 18 August 1966 as Major Harry Smith, your nuggety Green Beret commander urges you on through the unrelenting terrain, could you ever foresee the epic David and Goliath battle waiting for you, just a few hours east of the Nui Dat base in the Long Tan rubber plantation?

No fucking way, mate.

Shit, a Yankee Budweiser would go down well right now. Plenty of them back at base. The Delta boys regularly traded their distinctive slouch hats for Buds and Schlitz.

Stay focused, son. This is your life lurking here in the long grass. Meanwhile this afternoon's treat of the eagerly awaited base concert with Aussie rocker Col Joye and his Joy Boys and that nicely rounded Little Pattie was now dead meat. 'Can Do' Delta Company had been called to duty to perhaps make holes in a few D445 Gooks in black/khaki pyjamas, although the Cong were surely gone by now.

Bugger about missing the concert as they marched to the beat of the different drum, the pulsating thump thump of Col Joye's decibels of bass resonating behind them.

But you focus, son.

'Here's the blood.'

It's 1pm and just inside the Long Tan rubber plantation. Delta Company has reached its destination. Bravo Company's boss, Major Noel Ford, briefs Delta Company's Major Harry Smith near the enemy firing positions. Funny meeting up again like this; they'd been roommates at Officer Cadet School, Portsea, in 1952.

Noel, Harry and a security group of men look around at the evidence of discarded empty mortar and rocket ammunition boxes, pieces of bloodstained clothing and Ho Chi Minh sandals.

'And more here; a trail, see. They had bullock carts and took their wounded – or dead, hopefully. Our artillery counter bombardment must have got some of 'em,' announces Noel.

The men brew up and share Delta's hard rations. Bravo had been sent out without calculating they might need to stay overnight and although they'd been resupplied with some rations by a platoon of Charlie Company yesterday afternoon, their provisions were thin. Charlie's platoon had searched the rubber south of Bravo Company and, finding nothing, returned to Nui Dat.

'Harry the Ratcatcher' – which they'd secretly called him since he'd busted a clandestine card game in his time serving in Malaya in '55–'57 and triumphantly announced, 'Gotcha, you rats' – looked at the trails leading north, south and east; the slow trail of the wounded. To the north the surviving enemy soldiers' foot trail was already 36 hours old and would, he knew, be heading to where Alpha Company was already patrolling.

Radioing to his battalion CO, Lieutenant Colonel Colin 'Mousey' Townsend, Harry suggested that despite tracks to the north, east, and south, his gut feeling was to patrol east through the rubber to a secure jungle base for that night and on to the artillery gun range limit – another 3km – tomorrow. And as he had learned in Malaya, jungle is more secure and has far fewer mosquitoes than rubber plantations.

The Ratcatcher's gut feelings had served him well in his 33 years. Twenty-five of those with guns in his hand. He was not an indecisive man. Some even called him ruthless when he took on a particular military mindset.

'On the toss of a coin, go east, young man!' the young career major quipped into the radio frequency.

But at that fateful moment Harry Smith did not know the unpromising truth. In fact no-one from Nui Dat base knew the truth other than the task force commander, Brigadier Oliver David 'OD' Jackson, and just three of his officers. Jackson was London-born, a graduate of the Royal Military College, Duntroon, had done World War II service and now 'Nam.

Incredibly Jackson had already been given crucial information by the top-secret 547 Signals Intelligence Unit at Nui Dat and the Australian Army Training Team Liaison Officer, Commando Captain Mike Wells, based at 10 ARVN Division Sector HQ, Ba Ria.

It was, Jackson was told from Morse code radio intercept, more than likely the 5th Division's 275 Regiment and support units were resting in jungle just east of the Long Tan rubber plantation, with another major force, Regiment 274, somewhere to the north.

And more ... that D445 battalion was probably near Xa Long Tan to the southeast of the rubber plantation.

Local D445 were the very adept band of local soldiers who regularly recruited villagers at the point of a rifle.

They were likely the meeters, greeters, guides and feeders for 275 Regiment when it arrived from the far northeast on 14 August – and all this was reported promptly to OD Jackson sitting pretty at Nui Dat.

But what did the brigadier respond with? 'Oh, the radio is probably just a 275 Regiment HQ doing a reconnaissance.' Reconnaissance for what Brigadier?

So Jackson ignored the critical information available. After being handed this vital classified evidence by Captain Trevor Richards, OC 547 Signal Troop at Nui Dat, OD chose to tell only three fellow officers.

Thus in a heartbeat, in dispatching Harry and his 108 men of Delta Coy and NZ Artillery to Long Tan that risky day of Operation 'Vendetta', the brigadier had unintentionally fitted them up for a possible death sentence.

But what the enemy was to discover was that the indomitable Harry Smith and his courageous soldiers were unerringly programmed to win.

The determined Tasmanian was a driven perfectionist and commanding this titanic unforeseen battle, the thought of losing didn't even waft onto the rim of his radar.

The Ratcatcher may have been feisty, demanding and at times rebellious but he was also ex-Commando and a trainer of Commandos and in the frightful monsoonal battle that was soon to engulf the men of Delta, not even a colossal 2000 enemy VC and North Vietnamese Army were going to stop Harry's men from securing perhaps one of the most impossible of our ANZAC victories.

ONE

BEGINNINGS IN TASMANIA

Harry Arthur Smith my parents christened me, their only son, after I was born on 25 July 1933 in Hobart, the historic waterfront Tasmanian town. I may not have shown the early physique of a future war commander but as a kid I sure as hell could handle a gun.

Although my parents were not at all religious, I was named after a World War II family friend, Padre Harry Thorpe, and my second name is from my grandfather Arthur Ronald Smith.

My father, Ronald Arthur, born in Hobart in 1909, an only child, was a disciplinarian. He'd served in the part-time Citizens Military Force (CMF) 40th Battalion from 1927 to 1930, was promoted to corporal and awarded a marksman's crossed rifles badge. He worked at Cadbury's as an office boy from age 14, rising to production manager, until World War II when in 1942 he joined the Australian Imperial Force (AIF). He moved into the cumbersome General Grant American M3 tanks as a sergeant in the 2/9th Armoured Division on the Atherton Tablelands and the Brisbane Line in Queensland.

My mother Annie Isabel also born in Hobart, in 1910, raised me alone from 1942 to 1944. Dad came home on leave once or twice in his khaki uniform and beret. By then I was running around the yard with a pick handle over my shoulder because it looked and felt like a gun, which I loved. I also played soldiers in an air raid shelter which Dad had built in the backyard after he joined the AIF. He returned to work at Cadbury's just before the war finished because of a government policy that made his job at Cadbury's a 'reserved occupation' in an industry which had to support the armed forces. So he never went to Borneo with his squadron, which landed there in smaller Matilda tanks near the end of the war. I suspect he regretted being left behind.

My Dad Ronald.

Dad had a German 9-mm Luger pistol, which he carried instead of his issue .38 revolver, and while I got to fire it now and then in the bush it was stored, unknown to Mum at the time, on top of my high builtin bedroom wardrobe. I had visions of it passing on to me when I was older but Dad was forced by Mum to get it out of the house when she discovered it, so he passed it on to a mate. A similar situation with Mum arose a few years later. I had brought home as souvenirs of the Vietnam War a Chinese 7.62-mm Tokarev pistol I'd taken off a dead North Vietnamese Army officer, along with three other weapons; an almost mint AK47 Kalashnikov assault rifle; a US Army Garand rifle; and a US Army M1 carbine, which we landed in Brisbane in our 'Delta Company stores', exempt customs inspection.

I donated the Garand and M1 carbine to a private military museum in Sydney but kept the other two weapons. I'd been involved with that museum in the early 1960s when I was stationed at Ingleburn, helping the Infantry Centre museum curator at night to set up what became the largest collection of military weapons in the southern hemisphere.

When I left Commandos in December 1969 to go to Staff College in Victoria there was no armoury so I took the Tokarev and AK47 home to Coffs Harbour to my parents' house. Dad put the guns up in the roof with the idea that they'd be safe and they stayed there until I joined the Parachute

School in 1973. Then Dad rang me to come up and take the guns away because Mum had found out they were hidden in the roof and didn't want them in the house.

Although I had originally indicated I would give the AK47 to my 12 Platoon commander Second Lieutenant Dave Sabben, new gun rules prevented that and I found a home for it with one of my warrant officer parachute jump instructors who was a licensed private collector. Although I had a licence via a pistol club, in 1999 I gave the Tokarev to the War Memorial in Canberra where it was reconditioned and displayed on the wall in the Post-WWII Conflicts area Long Tan Display.

My mother was the daughter of a Hobart family involved with the racing of trotting horses but she was mostly ostracised by her family because of her marriage to a Cadbury's executive and I had nothing to do with her family except for Aunty Ethel, who lived at Old Beach over the river. But Mum did a lot of good work in the community with Red Cross and garden clubs and was eventually very highly regarded by her siblings.

I can't say I had a loving relationship with Mum. Mum was Mum; she cooked our meals and did our housework. Growing up, we didn't spend a lot of time together. Frankly, I was away from home at every opportunity.

In my earliest years we lived at Glenorchy, 10km north of Hobart, in a very modest cottage on the corner opposite the Club Hotel. My grandparents on Dad's side resided just two houses along the street in a house that adjoined their old general store and I used to enjoy investigating the corridors and empty shelves. Grandmother used to make lovely fruit mince pies and other delicacies in her wood oven and when I had asthma attacks she would nurse me in front of a hot fire so I could breathe more easily. Grandad, who wasn't particularly warm towards children, was a good carpenter and had a wonderful range of hand tools, all kept immaculate, as was his treasured 1928 De Soto sedan, never taken out in the rain. I guess some of his woodworking skills passed on to my father and then on to me. I also recall the weekly night cart arriving with its 'forty pisstins and flies', as was sometimes remarked.

Dad worked in Cadbury-Fry-Pascall chocolate factory at Claremont where he became the production manager. It was pretty impressive as careers go in those years. He worked for Cadbury's for 48 years, beginning as a 14-year-old office boy in the 1920s and progressing to become the production director for Hobart and then Melbourne when Cadbury's bought out MacRobertson's Freddo Frogs factory at Ringwood, just east of the city.

One of my memories of his work at Cadbury's is of him bringing home from work a briefcase full of chocolates and putting them on his desk. He would meticulously taste each one of them and write a report. We were never short of chocolates at home. I still like chocolates.

He received an Order of the British Empire (OBE) for services to the community in June 1966, the same year I was awarded the Military Cross (MC) in Vietnam after Long Tan. Although we'd hoped we might receive our medals together, he received his in Hobart in September 1966 and although I received the ribbon at Nui Dat in January 1967, my MC medal was presented in Saigon by our Ambassador in May 1967.

Dad, like his father, used to go to regular Masonic Lodge meetings. He said nothing about them, but would leave the house with a briefcase and purple scarf. All very secretive.

Dad and Mum.

Sadly he and I had very little rapport at home because he was so busy at work. On rare occasions he displayed a sense of humour and I recall him laughing when sister Joan spilt her green peas all over the table, saying 'Joan you have pee'd on the table'. By the time I needed a father he had already risen to that all-consuming management role. He did however push me to be independent, and he gave me a copy of the 1899 *A Message to Garcia* essay that spoke of using one's initiative – of living the dream. The final paragraph sums it up:

> My heart goes out to the man who does his work when the 'boss' is away, as well as when he is at home. And the man who, when given a letter for Garcia, quietly take the missive, without asking any idiotic questions, and with no lurking intention of chucking it into the nearest sewer, or of doing aught else but deliver it.

I recall Dad telling me that, like Garcia, when given a job to do, I shouldn't ask the boss how to do it, but should seek out what was required and do it.

Dad's encouragement to use my own nous led to me becoming fairly good at military appreciations in the Army – being able to assess the aim, facts and options, and quickly come up with the best plan. It also contributed to me being a loner. Dad always believed in fair play, even to writing to manufacturers about faulty goods, usually obtaining apologies and replacements. I recall he once wrote about a packet of broken biscuits and received a whole carton in reply. His perseverance inspired me to seek justice for my men after Long Tan, a battle for recognition that began in 1996 after the official 30-year secrecy period imposed on 1966 records, and which, despite some success, is still unfinished business in 2015.

In their own way my parents set out to make a good life for my two younger sisters, Joan and Beverly, and me. On their limited income they provided us with a good upbringing in the best way they could. Dad helped me with buying parts for radio sets I used to build as a hobby. He had a mate at Cadbury's who was an amateur radio operator and he got me interested in making my first crystal set and then small valve radio sets. Dad instilled in me a number of rules for life, most of which I've followed, such as making sure everything is done properly. He also had a major thing about waste not, want not. He taught me to turn the lights off if I wasn't using them – and I still do that to this day.

By 1942, we were living in Rosetta on the western shore of the Derwent River about a 15-minute drive north of Hobart's CBD. My parents had built a nice brick home on the main road with views of the river. It had a steep driveway that had a long wire alongside it on which our much loved British bulldog Tiny used to travel up and down. When I was young sometimes I used to sit on his back. He was sadly missed when some low-life dropped a bait onto the drive and poisoned him. After he died, one of my sisters brought home an unwelcome cat. Dad put it in the car and dumped it 80km away – only to see it return a week later.

Another tale of the steep driveway was later told to me by Joan, about an event after Beverly and I had moved out of home, Bev to nursing and me into the Army. Once Dad had become production manager both he and Mum drove Holden company cars. One day Mum drove up that driveway and parked her car in the garage while she removed her shopping, forgetting to apply the handbrake, to then see it run backwards down the drive, over the main road, down an embankment, and onto the grass verge of the railway line, not hitting anything on the way but upsetting the suspension by hitting the rails. By the time Dad arrived home at 6pm, the car had been towed away and an identical one was in the garage. 'Mum' was the word, and Joan was sworn to secrecy until Mum passed away.

Looking back on my childhood there is no doubt that my grandfather, father and mother were total disciplinarians, and when I left home, I guess I rebelled against that. As a child, I wagged Sunday school from St Paul's Church in Montrose – which we attended even though Dad happened to be a self-confessed atheist – to go fishing for small trout in a creek near home and, later, I wagged night school classes to go ice skating.

I remember Mum finding empty tins of condensed milk and tinned fruit under my bed, tins that I had nicked from a stock in her kitchen larder, and there was the memorable time she accidentally trod on my big toes. Trouble was I hadn't told anyone about my two ingrown toenails. After two unsuccessful 'V' cuts into the nails, I ended up having the nail beds removed in hospital, with the flesh turned over and sewn up – no big nails to cut or in-grow ever again.

My most vivid childhood memories are the wonderful school holidays with my grandparents who had a galvanised iron shack, aptly named 'The Patches' at Bicheno on the Tasmanian east coast north of Swansea. In those days this was a quiet coastal holiday town sought out by campers who liked throwing in a line. Many residents were fisher folk who had their boats moored in a channel known as the Gulch, from where they indulged in excellent fishing for crayfish and barracuda. I went out with the fishermen and I often caught cod and mullet by myself in the Gulch. I recall breaking Grandad's prized cane fishing rod hauling in a big fish, which did not please him. In the trumpeter season I used to row a heavy timber boat for one fisherman, Neil Potter, often all night, while he netted trumpeter fish in the Gulch, and my reward was a whole sixpenny piece. That was a lot of pocket money in the early forties.

Me in Bichenno.

At the rare times when my parents were there, Dad used to take me into the bush shooting rabbits, which we skinned and used for crayfish bait, tied by a cord to a long pole and dangled in the kelp off the rocks. We'd then take the crays back to the shack to be cooked in old square kerosene tins on a wooden fire. We had plenty of tins as we used bulk kero for the fridge and lighting. Local fishermen were very friendly and they would often give us one of the huge ocean sea crabs that had got caught by a leg in their cray pots, thought a nuisance then, but now marketed commercially.

Two of my holiday girlfriends were Neil Potter's daughters, Una and Ina. By then I was 12 and starting to realise that boys and girls were different. We used to go down onto the beach in summer time and swim but it was mostly cold so we played games, running round the sand hills – and engaging in other harmless activities – to keep warm. I also fell in love with an older girl with whom I played tennis but the friendship remained platonic. I didn't lose my innocence until I was 20 – and that was with Kathleen, my future wife.

I was not a really good swimmer in spite of spending a lot of time on the ocean beaches, and getting sunburnt, with no 'slip, slop, slap' or hats in those days. I very nearly drowned one year in the Derwent River near Risdon when I capsized my 12-ft Rainbow dinghy in a big wind gust. I'd built it with my father's help in our backyard at Rosetta.

That day on the Derwent I stupidly jumped overboard to swim after my good rain jacket when it blew overboard. The fast current was running the other way and a fisherman came out from shore to rescue me. All I can remember is trying to save this damn jacket, getting exhausted and being very frightened and wondering what was going to happen. It took a long time before I jumped off a boat again into a fast current and that was when anchored at Palm Island north of Townsville in 2001, to retrieve a remarkable empty Nautilus shell floating by, home to one of the planet's most amazing creatures. I again had some trouble against the current with one hand occupied holding the shell but I eventually got back to our moored yacht, with wife Felicia about to up-anchor our yacht and chase me. Although I was not a good surface swimmer I could stay under the water all day with diving gear and enjoy it.

    The dry hot Tasmanian summer sun took a toll on my fair skin – I was then a freckled red-head – and one year I recall going to school with large blisters, no doubt the start of my problems with skin cancer in later years. A large blister on my back broke in school and the water ran down my back. The class laughed when I put my hand up and asked to go home to change my pants. I had to change my pants another day after I had eaten too many green tomatoes from the Rodman farm near our house in Glenorchy. 'Rodman's Reddies' were the very best tomatoes grown in Tasmania. My sister Bev later married a Rodman, Lynley. Bev was just 17. The marriage broke up a few years after daughter Trudi was born; Bev never wed again and now lives at lovely St Helens on the Tasmanian northeast coast. After two marriages Trudi lives in Melbourne and is an executive in a firm that supplies movies and associated equipment to hotels.

The childhood sun damage was aggravated by many years in the sun while in the Army where in such places as Malaya and Vietnam the dress on base was shorts and no shirt, and of course I can add 35 years of too much sun while sailing up and down the Queensland coast.

Catch of the day.

Ironically, in 2010, Defence issued a policy that soldiers were no longer to wear berets to avoid facial skin cancer problems, but it was too late for me, having worn Green and Red Berets in Commando and Airborne for some 10 years before leaving the Army in 1976. To date, I have had over 20 excisions for basal and squamous cell carcinomas, plus one small melanoma, and I underwent surgery on an ear canal skin cancer by a plastic surgeon in Townsville in 2011. It just goes on and on as they cut bits of me away.

Nevertheless, I have enjoyed an outdoor and very adventurous life under the sun. My dermatologist tells me, yes, it all started in childhood and will continue even if I stay out of the sun, but that if I can put up with the nitrogen freezing and excisions then I can go ahead and enjoy life on the water, which I am still doing. Sailing and messing around in boats remains my ongoing passion.

The sailing passion began when I was very young. While on school holidays at Bicheno one year at age eight or nine my father took me to a friend's home near a lake – just before he enlisted in the Army – and introduced me to sailing in a very basic dinghy with a single mainsail. While my parents and sisters were not interested in boats, I took to sailing like a fish to water. In Hobart my father placed me on a friend's large A-class yacht as cabin boy, and later I was able to race each weekend as crew, the mainsheet hand and bailer boy, in the traditional Cadet Dinghies off Battery Point. Our PT teacher Billy Lawrence had a Derwent-class yacht and took us out often, and sometimes on a heavy-weight Sharpie. I became obsessed with sailing, moving on to crew on a Sandridge Sharpie dinghy owned by Brian Stevens, then onto Neil Tate's Rainbow-class dinghy. When I was 15 Dad funded and helped me build a new Rainbow. He got bits of cut dressed timber from Cadbury's workshops and I made the hull frames. He built a stand and I did most of the work under his guidance. That boat cost us just £22, including the mast and sails. These fast 12-ft flat-bottomed square-nosed racers were based at the Sandy Bay Dinghy Club.

In the gusty winds off the hills on the Derwent River I developed an instinctive ability to get the best out of a yacht upwind and the next year my *Samba* won the Tasmanian Rainbow Championship and in the National series came second to a lightweight West Australian yacht *Epic,* an upmarket boat with a light alloy mast and centreboard, rather than a heavy timber mast. I always seemed to achieve good results in racing right up to 2009 when I sold our Cavalier 395, and bought a traditional Fleming 39-ft timber cruiser, *Melaleuca,* which I finally sold in late 2012 in favour of, again, a racing yacht, Sydney 36 *Mayhem,* my latest toy. Even when in the Army I managed to spend time sailing. In Melbourne in 1964–65 I sailed a Surf Whaler with a Commando crew. In Sydney in 1968–69 I sailed with the RAN in Bosun dinghies.

In West Australia in 1971–72 I sailed 5-m Corsairs, taking out the State title, then skippered the 15-m Rolly Tasker *Siska 1.* In the United Kingdom in 1973, I was able to sail on a Nicholson 43 at Beaullie. Since then I have always had a yacht or boat of some kind. And, except for the timber cruiser where I lost money, I have always been able to buy quality boats, albeit often rundown, restore them with my own labour, and sell them on for a profit to buy another, and upgrade. I could write a book about my sailing exploits alone – my 12 different boats have provided me with many good stories.

Sailing a Corsair, Perth 1971.

One such story was from 2004 when we were in Gladstone Marina en route south and moored near friends Rob and Gay on their yacht *Dancing Dolphin* with two Tonkinese cats. We enjoyed a barbecue with them and other yachties and next morning Rob helped us cast off when we left to sail 50km down the shipping channel then east to Pancake Creek. Felicia, my wife, noticed cat paw prints in the 'Gladstone snow' coal dust on our deck which indicated a cat had been on deck. Around noon we received a radio call asking if we had a cat on board. No sign of a cat that day or night but next morning when Felicia was sitting up in the front berth sipping her coffee she exclaimed, 'We have a cat down the back quarter berth cabin – I can see a tail waving.' I coaxed the cat out of the stored sails. Luckily it had not made a mess. Then, after relieving its bladder on paper in a large plastic tray, it took over, investigating all our cupboards and growling at any other passing boats. I radioed the marina office and asked them to tell the owners we had their missing cat but they would have to sail to Pancake to get it. The manager said something like, 'You are lucky it wasn't a big dog, Harry.'

I retorted, 'Oh there's nothing like a bit of pussy', which I am often reminded went out over the VHF radio repeater on Mt Larcom to hundreds of boats along the Capricorn coast.

Later that day Rob and Gay arrived in their yacht and recovered their cat which would have been quite happy to stay with us, but animals and boats don't mix, especially with all the new marine park rules which prevent animals being taken ashore on beaches attached to national parks. Some yachties, who had more regard for their pets than their fellow human beings and the native wildlife, flouted the normal convention of not leaving poo where others swam. So then everyone was penalised – the usual bureaucratic system.

Another sailing tale comes from Cid Harbour in the Whitsundays in 2009. Felicia asked me to take a letter in our inflatable dinghy to another yacht, Ken Johnson's Swanson 36 which was going back to Airlie Beach. The water was mirror-calm so I stood up and steered the dinghy with a new extension handle on the 8-hp outboard, not taking hold of the painter rope. As I neared the other yacht at a very slow pace I thought I was turning the revs down but inadvertently turned the new extension handle the wrong way and all 8 hp went into play. Up went the nose of the dinghy and over the back and down under went me. On surfacing, still with cap and sunglasses, I saw the dinghy going around in circles at 15-knot full speed and I swam to Ken's yacht to get out of its way lest the prop cut off an arm or leg. Eventually, amid the laughter of crews on some 30 other yachts moored nearby, it ran softly into another yacht, *Judet*. Its owners, Paul and Valerie, caught the dinghy and killed the engine. No damage done but a wet me made sure that in future I had the motor cut-off key attached to my wrist and that I held on to the painter rope and sat down. Several years later old friends still talk about these events and recall others who have been severely injured by similar outboard motor accidents.

But back to Tasmania. I was fully committed to School Cadets and sailing, and romance was not on my agenda when I was at school. My two sisters and I were closely watched by our parents, and forced to lead very protected lifestyles. I am sure we were supposed to marry into money but, alas, we disappointed by marrying partners without social status in our parents' eyes. My parents objected to me marrying my first wife Kathleen. Had I listened to their warnings about getting married so quickly and so young, it may have spared Kathleen and me some unhappy times. The bonus was our three beautiful children. The downside was that we quickly fell out of love.

Of we three kids it is only Joan, who won a Rotary Scholarship to the United States when she was a teenager, who has remained with her husband Ian throughout. He became an expert in oil refinery pipelines and fittings and even after retirement is still sought after as a consultant. Ian and I get on well as he is also a yachtsman and a car buff with a collectable Porsche and MG in his garage.

Mum was left at home when Dad travelled to England in Sunderland Flying Boats and then Constellations in the course of his business. But in later years they both often went to Japan for Cadbury's and Mum learned how to grow bonsai trees, eventually teaching the specialist gardening art around Hobart.

Me with my sisters Joan and Bev.

When I turned 16 Mum and Dad let me go to dances in Hobart once a week, where I developed an eye for one special girl, but I was required to be home on the last train by 11pm. One night I went to sleep on the train, and found myself at New Norfolk, 30km up the line, getting back to Rosetta well after midnight. That story was not believed and I was banned from further dances. Compared to the stories of romance my older schoolmates boasted of, I was a novice and I still had not had a relationship when I left school at the end of 1950. Happy with sailing my Rainbow and riding my bike home on hilly roads some 12km after racing, I was always too tired or had homework to do. And unlike in later years, beer and cigarettes were absolutely not on the menu.

As a teenager I was conned into going to Mrs Donnelly's Dance School at night, learning waltzes and the like and I didn't particularly take to it. Mum said it was the done thing for children to go to dancing school. I never learned to master rock and roll very well either but I do admire people who can dance. I also avoided piano lessons although my sisters both played well.

After we moved to Rosetta I enrolled at Claremont State School. But I couldn't wait for the weekend when I'd ride down to Sandy Bay to go sailing. It kept me busy in between high school homework after my parents sent me to Hobart High at age 11. I had begun primary school at age five and qualified for entrance to high school in grade six so was one of the youngest. Hobart High was actor Errol Flynn's old school. We remembered the swashbuckling Hollywood screen legend for many interesting things but the one that tickled us most was the tale of his shoving a potato up the headmaster's exhaust which prevented the car from starting. Errol was definitely our hero and after he beat several rape charges we kids also learned the fashionable phrase 'In like Flynn'.

By the time I reached 15 I had matriculated but wasn't allowed to leave school to go to university so I stayed on for another 12 months until I reached the legal leaving age of 16. I didn't mind that much because I was still involved in Cadets and sailing. I took on new subjects like French and maths, which I detested, but I managed to do exceptionally well in social studies, geography, geology and history.

I played cricket but wasn't particularly good at it. My father said to me, 'It doesn't matter how good you play son, just wear white trousers and pullover and you'll look the part.' I also played Australian Rules – with mediocrity – but I wasn't too bad as a rover and at basketball in the school gym. One time I recall an older and much bigger player saying to me, 'You've never had a screw, Harry. You wouldn't know what it was like to have butterflies coming out of your arse.' I never forgot that and, a few years later, quite a few, I discovered what he meant.

It was at Hobart High, a co-ed school, that my life changed dramatically. I signed up for School Cadets and fell in love – with guns and the military life. I stayed with the Cadets for five years. Within months I became an ace marksman and even though still a teenager I handled an issue BSA .310 and then a .303 with confidence. Guns and I were destined to bond.

I rose to be a cadet officer: first corporal, then sergeant and finally cadet lieutenant. I loved the Cadets without reservation, even having to take orders.

But along came a pretty serious glitch. I was around 14 when I was discharged for pinching about 20 .303

rounds after a Vickers Machine Gun range practice to go and shoot rabbits in the perimeter paddocks of Brighton Camp, 27km north of Hobart. The temptation was too much for me. Next door was that great big paddock alive with fleet-footed furry creatures and before breakfast I'd take out my .303 rifle, which in those days we kept in our barracks during camps. Range practices weren't allowed out of official training time but I often put a few rounds in my pouch and went for the bunnies.

My father got stuck into me very verbally and told me I'd heaped disgrace on the family's good name. Mum was horrified too. Six months later, after I had spent all this sudden free time doing even more sailing, the Cadets took me back – and promoted me. At age 15 I became cadet officer and started to enjoy giving orders instead of taking them.

My knack of being able to work with other soldiers began in Cadets. They seemed to respect my ability to do things well such as shooting, map reading and marching. I wouldn't say though that I was a born leader. I just refused to fail. I'd die rather than fail. It's been the same for me winning yacht races. You get nothing for nothing. I didn't understand that when I was a child. I just did the best because I wanted to win.

My father was a very good marksman in his day and now his Army Marksman's Badge resides in the Maryborough Military and Colonial Museum on Queensland's Fraser Coast. I think I inherited the skill from him. I was a very good shot. It was a matter of being able to hold the rifle properly and steady and line up the sights, then carefully squeeze the trigger without disturbing the aim. It was a very competitive system shooting on that Brighton range to see who could get the best score and I certainly felt good when I hit the bullseye, often at ranges up to 700 m.

My School Cadet days. Me leading the Royal Hobart Show Guard 1951.

    I'd enjoyed shooting using Grandad's .410 shotgun to shoot rabbits when I was eight. But the high note was with the Vickers machine gun. It was wonderful to sit behind one and fire belt after belt. Our Cadet unit had six of them, supplied by the Army. Noel Mulcahey was our Regular Army captain. I used to admire the way he took the time to educate us in military matters and at the same time keep his cool. The bonus was you went to school in your khaki uniform and beret. Cadet days were once a week and they were more important to me than any other activity at school except sailing on sports days.

Even though I rose in the ranks I still did not have my sights on a full-time career in the military. And my parents had other ideas for their single-minded young son – even though it is doubtful they ever fully understood me.

When I matriculated for the second time in December 1950, Dad wanted me to go to university but another four years of academic study did not appeal to me. I said a firm no. Dad then chose a job for me as a laboratory assistant and apprentice trainee with Austral Bronze, manufacturers of copper, brass and bronze sheeting, pending a night school diploma in metallurgy, a seven-year course. I always liked geology, but seven years? My work involved three eight-hour shifts seven days or nights each week, in which I had to take samples from rolled metals and test them for hardness and chemical composition at various stages along the production line. I found time to learn ice skating at the Derwent Park rink, graduating from basic figure skating to racing in long speed skates called flats and I did quite well at team racing. We dyed our long johns and singlets to make ourselves a distinctive uniform. It was an exciting sport and I revelled in it.

There was a lovely girl at the rink and I used to take her home after skating and even occasionally visit her home when her parents were at night movies. The relationship was serious but never developed into anything more than a kiss and cuddle, and so when I was called into Army National Service in January 1952 I was still innocent at age 18. Not only had I been warned by my parents about the pitfalls associated with girls, but sailing left me little time for romance. Later at Brighton doing National Service I confess I had motives of seducing this girl and bought a packet of condoms just in case but I had no car to get to Hobart when I had time off, which was not very often. Mum found them in my greatcoat one day when I stayed at home, and there was hell to pay. I told Dad that we had to take them from the Regimental Aid Post when we went on leave and asked him to tell Mum to note the packet was still unopened!

Australia had been fighting in the Korean War since September 1950 and that had inspired the introduction of National Service under Prime Minister Robert Menzies. All Australian men aged 18 were made to register. Army was 176 days' training – 98 days of that full-time and the rest as two years' part-time weekends and nights in camp as part of the Citizen Military Forces (CMF) system. Those in the Royal Australian Navy and Royal Australian Air Force served their 176 days in one hit.

Five years in Cadets laid the groundwork for National Service training so when I was called up in the second intake in January 1952, I was promoted to temporary lance corporal, then to corporal by the end of the 90-day intake. National service was an extension of what we'd done in cadet camp. We were in the same buildings that we'd occupied in Cadets. Only the corporal instructor who lived in a room at one end had any privacy. It was go go go, being taught all aspects of Army work from 6am to lights out at 10pm. We marched regularly the 8km from Brighton Camp to the rifle range at Pontville although there was often so much fog you couldn't see to shoot – we would have needed horizontal post-hole borers to see to fire at the targets. So we would hang around until the fog lifted and work on weapon training lessons.

Apart from the cold and fog everything about the Army National Service was good, including the odd weekend leave breaks to keep up sailing with mates, although Dad had sold my championship Rainbow for me for £45, a 100 percent profit on the cost of parts not including our labour.

Fate played its hand. When I went to return to my laboratory work after the 90 days, my job had gone, despite government policy that required employers to hold the positions for those called into National Service. I was not that unhappy and told my father I wanted to join the Regular Army, which did not please him but I won out, enlisting on 24 April 1952 at the recruiting office at Anglesea Barracks,

Hobart. And back I went to Brighton Camp as a Regular Army private.

TWO

CANNON FODDER TO GO

Now in the Regular Army, I was placed on a non-commissioned officer (NCO) course then promoted to temporary corporal as a National Service Section instructor responsible for the basic weapons and drill training of 10 or so men for the three-month intakes. There were three such sections in each of nine platoons at Brighton Camp's 18 National Service Training Battalion, each platoon having an officer and sergeant in its headquarters to instruct on broader subjects, do the administrative tasks and supervise live firing practices.

It became a wake-up call – literally. During each three-month intake we were required to be in the lines at reveille at dawn to get the soldiers out of bed. The usual call was 'Hands off cocks, hands on socks!' or sometimes 'Wakey, wakey, hands off snakey'. We were also required to front up for lights out at 10pm after working all day. So we were caught up in long days and long weeks with little time for any social life. All this discipline in icy winter weather very quickly sorted out the men from the boys. And in the Regular Army NCOs' canteen I was to start smoking and drinking for the first time, socially required across the ranks and definitely the accepted behaviour.

In May 1952, Dad and Mum were concerned at my future social status as an NCO and suggested that if I was to stay in the Army I should go to the new Officer Cadet School (OCS) at Portsea, Victoria, and obtain a commission – to be an 'Officer and Gentleman, if only by Act of Parliament', so Dad said. I agreed to apply for the second six-month course starting in July. I was accepted after the fairly probing interview by a panel in Hobart, and departed for Portsea, Victoria, in late June via train to Devonport and then ship to Melbourne.

OCS Portsea was the newly created officer promotion academy to provide officers for cannon fodder for Korea. Duntroon graduation would have taken four years. So Portsea was definitely that fodder route – just six months. But a few months after I graduated as second lieutenant in December that year, Korea finished. Who knows, maybe I got lucky. Maybe I needed to learn more before I faced war.

For once taking Dad's advice and getting myself a commission at the newly raised Officer Cadet School at Portsea, I discovered that six months at OCS was a bit like being in prison. Discipline was very strict and if you were awarded extra drill and physical training punishment for small things like a dusty light shade (checked by Regular Army instructors wearing white gloves) or clothes not folded in regulation sizes and shapes, it was difficult not to incur further punishment. There was never the time available to do the extra drills and get things right before these meticulous morning room inspections.

My roommate was Noel Ford, who was later to be a fellow company commander in Vietnam in 1966–67. He commanded Bravo Company 6RAR but went back to Australia in December 1966 to go to Staff College. Noel bizarrely disappeared (some say he did a Harold Holt) at Bondi Beach in December 1967 en route from Queenscliff Army Staff College to 6RAR Townsville, posted as the second-in-command. I gather he was near the top of the course and, just recently, in 2014, his son Duncan got in touch with me and sent a photo of Noel holding him as a baby. I sent photos from OCS back to him. Noel's car and clothes were found at Bondi Beach. No body was ever recovered. Rumours suggest he has since been seen in New Zealand, but I am happy to believe he drowned. Noel was an academic and, while I excelled in field and weapons work and was promoted to cadet corporal, he took the big prizes for essays and the like.

On graduation in December 1952, Noel won the Staff Prize while I was awarded the Field Prize and second place in the Staff Prize; both of us winning medallions for best results over the course. Overall I came seventh out of 70. For our graduation night ball, I invited my parents and my skating girlfriend over from Hobart, although I then moved on to the School of Infantry at Seymour, Victoria, for three months Infantry Corps Training and when I later went back to Tassie she had another boyfriend and I never saw her again.

Graduation parade December 1952. Officer Cadet School at Portsea. Corporal Smith centre, Noel Ford far right.

The OCS commandant, Colonel James Harrison (later Major General Sir), interviewed us on our final day and he soberly told me that I had achieved good results but, in the opinion of the staff, I was a 'happy loner, independent, and not requiring or seeking company'. I have never been sure whether this was a compliment or a reprimand but it didn't change me. A brand-new and proud second lieutenant, I was asked for my preferred choice of corps, to which I replied 'Armour', hoping to follow in my father's footsteps in World War II tanks. Never ask for want you want in the Army; you'll be sure to get the opposite. A couple of days later I went to check my name on the list on the noticeboard and saw I had been allocated to Infantry Corps – grunts, as the Yanks called us in Vietnam, foot sloggers – and I was ordered to report to the School of Infantry after Christmas leave. Oh well, Infantry would have been my second choice and I was to enjoy work at Seymour.

Others at Portsea were dispersed to a variety of schools and corps such as the School of Armour at Puckapunyal, and the School of Artillery at North Head in Sydney. At the School of Infantry I was one of the smallest men there and maybe that spurs you onward harder and faster. With Cadets and National Service background experience, it was fairly easy to qualify well in all subjects, which included map reading, tactics and field work with weapons such as pistols, rifles, machine guns and mortars.

Classroom discussions were thought-provoking. We used cloth models of landscapes, including rivers, streams and the like. These days the Army conducts exercises of that ilk in fibreglass and foam. There were little model tanks and toy soldiers to move around in the mock-ups. All this exercised the brain so hopefully we would be able to make an expert appreciation of any given military situation. I found that usually I was able to come up with the best answer in the shortest possible time. Map reading was my favourite subject, an art where you could figure out complicated terrain and work out exactly where you are. We had no such luxury as GPS in 1953.

For whatever reason, maybe my background in rural Tasmania, maybe my Cadet and National Service training, or maybe an inherent sense of direction, I had the ability to come out spot on, over and over. I also liked drawing things. As a youngster I had enjoyed art at school and found myself sketching cars and boats at random. I got hell from Mum and Dad once when I drew an anchor on our dining room table, actually carving it into the highly polished wood. My ability to draw accurate lines aided my map reading skills where one had to take three compass bearings to known points and carefully draw the back-bearing on the map. Normally there was a triangle of error but mine was always very small, if any. This skill has been supplemented by GPS these days, but soldiers and sailors still have to be familiar with chart work in case the GPS system fails, to avoid situations like that experienced during the Israeli war when most boats could not work out where they were because the GPS system operated by the USA Defence system had been switched off for several days. I topped the Infantry courses out of about 30 of us. My parents were pleased.

From Seymour's fairly spartan 4 ha, 100km from Melbourne in the scrub, we wandered over the local farming countryside concentrating on Tactical Exercises Without Troops (TEWTs). We had little to do with the nearby village. But we used to go to Melbourne for weekends. One of our senior instructors, Major Max Thirwell, owned a big old Jaguar coupe and he used to drive three or four of us young second lieutenants down to Melbourne to stay at the YMCA from Friday to Sunday nights, and he'd drive us back Monday mornings. We had a ball every time checking out the local pubs and clubs.

One of our instructors, and a good one, was a Warrant Officer who was regularly trying to catch me out on map-reading tests. I usually won with the correct answer. In Vietnam in 1966, he was with the Australian Army Training Team Vietnam (AATTV) and often visited Nui Dat. He came to my company base to renew friendships. I did not know he was involved in a money-laundering scam whereby he recruited soldiers going on leave to places like Hong Kong to change large amounts of Vietnamese piastre he gave them into US dollars, which could only be done at the Army Pay Office prior to going on leave. He would then sell them on the open market in places like

Vung Tau and Saigon for double the piastre he had paid the soldiers, making a very handsome profit which he would re-invest in more US dollars, so compounding his profit. He was caught out and court martialled. People get sucked in by money and, in today's world, by money and drugs. I didn't waste money and I managed to save a bit in Vietnam and luckily drugs weren't around for us. I was not aware of any of my soldiers doing drugs in 1966–67, but in 2014 'Doc' Dobson my Vietnam Medical Corporal named just one of our soldiers who had experimented with drugs. Instead of drugs we took our ration of cheap whisky and cigarettes down to Vung Tau, often called 'Vungers', and traded them with Momma-san for free drinks with lovely bar girls.

    Near the end of the Seymour course we were asked where we wanted to serve. Still not having learned the game yet, I asked for sunny Queensland and was – wouldn't you guess it – allocated a posting back to Brighton as a National Service platoon commander/instructor – back to the bloody cold weather. But there was worse. I was to be a young officer-in-charge of former Regular Army NCOs who had been my National Service instructors, and new second lieutenants were regarded as the lowest form of officer animal, paid even less than a sergeant. To make it even more dismal for me, two of the January 1952 First Course OCS officers posted there before my arrival had not impressed. One was sacked for homosexual behaviour with Nashos, the other dismissed for drunken misconduct. Consequently OCS officers were not held in high regard.

I got on with my work without incident, apart from a disagreement with a drunken Regular Army driver (his foul abuse led to formal charges rather than a fist fight). I was made well aware by a Duntroon graduate, Commanding Officer Major Jim (Poodles) Norrie, who replaced the first commanding officer (CO), Major Dick Newman, that I was essentially of servant status. My mission in military life as the most junior officer was to pour coffee for all senior officers in the Mess after lunch and evening meals. That continued for six months until a new junior officer arrived and he then poured my coffee – a welcome change. Major Norrie had been to Korea and was quick to air his knowledge and war service with quizzes about tactics and weapons at coffee breaks, but it kept us alert. Later promoted to general, he was my remote boss in Sydney when I became CO/CI of the Parachute School from 1973-76. He retired into the horse racing industry to be replaced by Major General Bill Henderson DSO, a former commanding officer of 2RAR after our Malayan tour 1955-57, and a Brigadier Task Force commander in Vietnam 1970-71, who often visited my Parachute School.

My lot in life from April 1953 to December 1955 was intake after intake of National Servicemen – the same routine each time. But there was something satisfying about seeing each intake moulded into teams of well-trained soldiers, in spite of the freezing weather in winter. In mid-1954 CO Major Jim Norrie called me to his office and told me I was going on a parachute course at RAAF Williamtown NSW, just north of Newcastle. He said,

'Jumping out of a plane sorts the men from the boys, and we will see if you have the guts to do it Smith. All infantry officers should get their wings.' So, over to the mainland by ship I went, up to Newcastle by rail and was driven to the Parachute School at the RAAF base. As the vehicle approached the base I could see this huge 30-m tower, the Polish Tower, rising up over the buildings and hangars, with another smaller tower, the Fan Trainer, alongside. I thought Shit, what am I doing here? But I have to qualify, failure was not on the agenda. So, as the only officer on the course, when the day of the first jump out of an old Dakota came, I was last out, number 20. And I recall the first 19 circuits where one parachutist jumped each time – 'Red on, stand in the door', 'Green on, go'!

Early life Guard 2IC at Government House Hobart Guard of Honour for HM Queen in 1954.

My adrenaline count went up at each successive circuit and exit, the old Dakota grinding around in a circle at 1000 feet (300 m), until it had lined up on the final run 19 times and it was my turn in the door, looking dead ahead until the 'Go', and then I went. We had done so many training runs in the hangars and off the towers in the past three weeks that there was no time to think about failing; when they said 'Go' you went, it had become instinctive. The chute was pulled out of its pack by a webbing strap called a static line (freefall parachutists called this 'dope-roping'); and then there you were, riding softly under a parachute, and a great view from about 290 m. We did eight jumps, including a night jump, and then we were presented with our wings. The RAAF tailor sewed them onto our uniforms and I wore them back to Brighton, making the point of marching into the CO's office, saluting and proudly saying 'No problem, sir'. In later years I was to thank Jim Norrie for my wings, as they led me into a career with 1 and 2 Commando companies, overseas training with UK, US and Canadian airborne forces, and then as commanding officer of the first Army Parachute School in 1973.

One National Service intake which appreciated my work presented me with a young bulldog, which I had to leave behind when I went to Malaya. I don't recall where he went to, or what I did with a personal small 9-mm pistol I took to Malaya, or with a small motorcycle I had at Williamtown in 1974. I recall I had bought it for young son Brett to ride during his infrequent visits, and I often chose to ride it from married quarters to my office rather than use the khaki green Army station wagon. The RAAF wagons all had white roofs, air-con not being standard in those days. I think it took me six months and six letters to get the roof painted white, lowering the inside temperature by 20 degrees in summer. But where the dog, bike and the pistol went is lost. The memory often plays interesting tricks on us, perhaps small things being pushed aside by more serious matters, like the horrors of war.

It was back to reality at Camp Brighton. It was bloody cold; even the water pipes were constantly freezing up so we couldn't have a wash. We had flannelette pyjamas and we pulled our service uniforms over them many days of the week when we marched to Pontville rifle range just past the town. Those marches were 8km with full pack and carrying our .303 rifles. I was lucky I was so fit at age 19. At school I had run the 100 m in almost record time before my large toenail beds were removed, reducing leverage.

Years later, in 1978 when I sailed to Airlie Beach on my yacht and was walking on the shore with Tom

Williamson, a lovely old gentleman who'd won a Sydney–Hobart race in *Struen Marie* and sailed his latest Taiwanese-built cruising yacht up from Sydney, he looked at my ugly big toes and said, 'Harry what in goodness have you done there?' I couldn't help myself. I told him I'd been captured and tortured by the North Vietnamese when in Vietnam and they'd torn my toenails off.

'You poor bastard,' responded a naive Tom. Then I told him the truth.

The bad side at Brighton was serving under Duntroon officers who treated second lieutenants as shit – the lowest form of animal in the Army system. However, it taught me to soldier on and get ahead of others in the practical performance of Army work. I was to excel at practical work and was not too bad at theoretical examinations either – much to the disgust of my contemporaries. I also learnt not to suffer fools.

I became very aware of the wide gap between RMC and OCS graduates, the latter being considered 'six-month wonders' compared with the Duntroon 'four-year professionals'. That prejudice against OCS graduates was to continue for the next 24 years of my Army service, albeit waning as some OCS officers reached brigadier rank. The old school tie RMC Club syndrome was to adversely colour the careers of many OCS graduates, even though most excelled in practical command, having served with soldiers in the field for three plus years while the RMC students had only served in their Duntroon classrooms. I had served with soldiers and on active service in Malaya for over three years by the time my contemporaries graduated from RMC Duntroon as largely academics, often with little practical ability.

In Vietnam many RMC officers were disparagingly referred to as 'Duntroon Wankers' by the 'ordinary' soldiers, quoting Paul Ham's Vietnam book. However I have personally known, and still know, some very fine men who graduated from Duntroon; a credit to the military and to their country, like our former Governor-General Mike Jeffery AC, AO (Mil), CVO, MC; Major General Steve Gower AO AO (Mil) and

Major General Peter Phillips MC, to name just a few. And these days we have had generals come up through the ranks and OCS who have made their mark, such as Major General John Cantwell AO, DSC and Lieutenant General David Morrison AO, former Chief of Army, who retired in May 2015, replaced by 2RAR Malaya 1955 Lieutenant Wally Campbell's father, Lieutenant General Angus Campbell DSC AM.

In late 1953 I took a liking to Kathleen Burke, an attractive young stewardess in the Officers' Mess at Brighton Camp. She was about a year younger than me. While things have all changed in 2014, with husbands and wives both serving, fraternisation with other ranks of the Women's Army Corps was forbidden in those days, but forbidden fruits were tasty and she educated me in the spice of life for the first time.

My father had bought me a used but rather nice 1950 Morris Minor convertible for £500. With a small side-valve engine it would only do 60 mph flat chat on level roads and, unbelievably, one of Dad's friends, artist Harry Kelly, whose watercolour of Bicheno Gulch is on my wall today, dobbed me in for speeding, maybe 40 mph, through Oatlands, a historical village on the shores of Lake Dulverton, 84km north of Hobart. That did not go down well after I had previously been caught doing 35 mph in a 30 mph zone on the deserted road just south of our home, which led to a police fine, delivered to home by the boys in blue, horrifying my mother. Leadfoot Harry! In 2015, unable to locate a good used Nissan 370Z, I now drive a Toyota 86, having had all the early Datsun and Nissan Z car models, albeit second-hand, from the 240Z to 260Z, 280Z, a grey-import twin-turbo 300ZX, and a 350Z! But I mostly drive slowly, with only one speeding fine in the past ten years, 52km in a 40 zone.

On one of my early morning return trips to Brighton camp I successfully ran the Morris Minor under the tray of a truck, which I thought was turning right but which then turned left as I was starting to pass on the left. Instinct caused me to duck and the tray took off the soft top, converting it into a topless model and just missing my head. About this time my grandfather passed on and left me his 1928 De Soto sedan, still in mint condition with beautiful velvet upholstery, so I had wheels while the Morris was being repaired. Not long after, when I was posted to Malaya, Dad sold the De Soto for me for about £100. These days the pristine veteran car would be worth thousands of dollars. Dad also eventually sold the Morris Minor.

We hear about all the Army sex scandals at Duntroon these days, but while we didn't have computers and wireless links to show and play to others 'sacred and secret' downloads, I can say that Kath often used to visit my quarters at night and we never got caught or filmed. There was a charming local pub at Bridgewater where we also used to meet. I was obsessed with the young lady and against my parents' and senior officers' objections we married in late '54 in a very military wedding at St Paul's Cathedral in Hobart. We moved into a small flat at the back of a house in Derwent Park, which I visited about once a week on our only leave nights.

Grandpa, Grandma, Mum me as a baby and the treasured 1928 De Soto.

Not long after we married I realised we really had little in common. My parents had pleaded with me not to get married when I was so young and so innocent, and not to marry a girl whose family was lacking in social status, and I came to realise they were right. I was too young, too inexperienced, too deeply involved in the Army, and I had fallen for the first girl who opened my eyes and anatomy to love. Brighton was demanding: physically, mentally and in terms of time. Unless you were in a base desk job, military life in field units made it pretty impossible to look after a wife and family when you were absent for weeks and months on exercises, or a year on active service. I was also regularly away on all sorts of courses. I really did not want to be tied down by marriage and we often argued.

Add to all this the poor pay we were getting, which led to conflict over money when we were eventually bringing up three young children. I never sought money from my parents even though they were reasonably well off. When I was a second lieutenant I was earning 17 shillings and 6d a day. After 24 years in the Army when I retired as a Lieutenant Colonel in 1976, I was only getting $22,000 a year, including parachute pay (around 75 cents a day). In Vietnam we got 75 cents a day combat pay. Soldiers in Afghanistan now get $245 a day combat pay over and above their tax-free salary. A private soldier is on about $45,000 p.a. plus a similar amount of combat pay for six months. Mind you, they are sent back too frequently on tour and they sure earn it!

While I have participated in writing stories about the Army and my cruising experiences, I have always been reluctant to write about my early life, especially about my first two marriages, partly for the sake of my children. But in my younger days, especially after separating from Kath, I had a good time. Harry Smith ... what an unlikely name! When I booked into motels with young ladies, I would normally get the smug retort from the desk clerks, 'Yes sir, we have 70 Smiths staying here tonight, which one are you?'

In more recent years, with my third wife Felicia, I have become closer to my three children, two who have also had failed marriages and can now understand there are usually two sides to the story – and, of course, the human species is not perfect!

An unexpected pregnancy led to a miscarriage, but Kath fell pregnant again just as I was to be posted to war service in Malaya. We had agreed we should have a son to carry on the family name in case I was killed. I was destined to be a platoon commander with 2RAR in the Malayan Emergency in January 1956. All those years of training to mould me into cannon fodder were finally to become useful.

I was posted to 9 Platoon, Charlie Company. Second Lieutenant Brian McFarlane, First Course OCS commanded 7 Platoon, and 10 years later in Vietnam he was to be my neighbouring Charlie Company Commander while I led Delta Company 6RAR. Brian and I were always good mates. He never married, finding other ways to invest his salary. After Malaya he bought a huge Buick coupe and I remember him driving me down the highway south of Holsworthy at 100 mph-plus one morning. We still get on well in the fairly regular communications we have. He wrote a very good book based around his Vietnam experiences with his Charlie Company: *We Band of Brothers,* published in 2005. In 2015 he now drives a white Nissan 370Z!

When I went to Malaya I had to leave Kathleen at home, with few friends and an unhelpful mother-in-law, until about May 1956 when she was able to come up to Penang Island and live first in a hotel and then in a nice British Army married quarters house complete with female servant or 'amah'.

Kathleen soon gave birth to a daughter – not a son – on 19 June 1956 and we named her Deborah Anne. Fifty-seven years later Debbie went back to Penang with sister Sharon and presented the local museum with old photographs of her birthplace. I was away on patrol hunting Communist terrorists when Debbie was born. I was regularly away on jungle patrols on the mainland. We usually only got home once a month for two days, other than at major leave breaks like Christmas if not rostered for duty at forward bases on the mainland. Luckily, the amah looked after my wife, as her neighbours were mostly RMC families and the wives followed the Duntroon philosophy of not fraternising with OCS wives. Thankfully one or two of the OCS wives in the village were helpful – I recall Wyn Hands. In the US Army, wives usually wore their husband's rank badges on dresses, so that Mrs Major would be aware of Mrs Colonel and would address her as such, and so on. Badges were not worn by wives in our UK system but the rank and RMC Club barriers were still there. It had ever been thus in the military, even as far back as the days of the Roman Empire. But such inherent class barriers of the 'them and us' ilk certainly don't make for a better military.

THREE

MURDER IN MALAYA

HISTORICAL BACKGROUND

The Malayan Emergency between 1948 and 1960 was, in fact, a war. The Emergency, so called because rubber plantation and tin mining proprietors couldn't collect insurance claims on Lloyds if it had been a 'war', was the longest unbroken military commitment in the history of Australia. It lasted 13 years. Thirty-nine Australians were killed in Malaya, of which 15 were operational deaths with 13 coming from the Army. Twenty-seven men were wounded. Malaya provided near-perfect practice for the Vietnam War – especially the counter-insurgency techniques introduced by the British under its Briggs Plan, developed by General Sir Harold Briggs, the British Army's Director of Operations in Malaya.

It was on 16 June 1948 that the first clear act of the Malayan 'war' took place. Three European estate plantation managers were murdered at Sungai Siput in Perak, Northern Malaya.

Scottish-born farmer A E 'Wally' Walker, the manager of the Elphil Rubber Plantation, was the first to be shot – in his office. A few hours on, wounded World War I soldier John Munt Allison of Phin Soon Estate and his assistant Captain Ian Christian, who had served with a Gurkha regiment, were executed. The High Commissioner Sir Edward Gent declared a state of emergency in Perak and Johor, later extending it nationwide.

The men were killed by guerillas from the Malayan Communist Party, known to our soldiers as the MCP, although the Malayan National Liberation Army, MNLA, also known by other names, was its military arm. The organisation was a product of the anti-Japanese guerilla movement, which had blossomed during World War II. The MCP had been ordered to go on the offensive in accord with Soviet global dogma and strategy.

Even though the MCP never had more than a few thousand members, it was able to draw on the support of disgruntled Malayan-Chinese, upset over unfulfilled British promises of a smoother path to full Malayan citizenship. The Chinese were not allowed to vote in elections, had no land rights and were largely poor.

The Communists' support was mostly centred on some half million of the three million ethnic Chinese. They were tagged 'squatters' and most of them were farmers eking out a meagre living on the rim of the jungle where MCP fighters had based themselves.

This, coupled with a plummeting economy, made the MCP's work relatively easy. The withdrawal of Japan at the end of World War II had left the Malayan economy dislocated. There was unemployment, low wages and high levels of food inflation, way beyond the two to three percent so-called 'healthy' rate. Significant labour unrest ruled and many strikes occurred between 1946 and 1948. The British administration was trying to fix Malaya's economy; revenue from Malaya's tin and rubber industries was critical to Britain's own post-war recovery. Protesters were severely dealt with via arrest or deportation. Not surprisingly, the protesters grew even more militant.

Slow to initially react to the MCP the Malayan Government waited until March 1950 to counter the insurgency by appointing a director of operations. The new director had a two-fold plan: to address the core economic, social and political problems confronting the Chinese community, while at the same time bringing government control to the peripheral areas where the MCP was getting substantial support.

A good plan but useless unless implemented. The British High Commissioner was murdered in October 1951. The attack roused the British into meeting the MCP threat. The Malayan Government ramped up counter-insurgency tactics and sustained operations began against the Communists in an all-out effort to extinguish their local support base and force them into the jungle where it would be hard for them to get vital supplies. The MCP thus outlawed, police were given the power to jail, without trial, Communists and those implicit in helping them.

Interestingly, the MCP was led by a very smart, very driven young Chinese-Malayan, Chin Peng, later to pop up as a major Communist strategist for Vietnam. During World War II Chin had fought with the Malayan People's Anti-Japanese Army, for which he received an OBE for his contribution to the British war effort. But Chin had already embraced Communism in 1939 and by 1948 he had become Britain's official enemy. As Secretary-General of the Malayan Communist Party he was made the leader of the guerilla forces during the Emergency.

On 31 July 1960, when the Malayan Government declared the state of emergency was over, Chin

Peng left his exile in southern Thailand for Beijing where he was accommodated by the Chinese authorities in the International Liaison Bureau, the party's political greenhouse for growing and nurturing Communists and where many other Southeast Asian Communist Party leaders were also housed.

    Chin led the forming of the MNLA, also called the Malayan Races Liberation Army (MRLA), and the Malayan People's Liberation Army (MPLA). The MNLA was structured into regiments and each incorporated all forces operating in a specific region. Each regiment had a political section, commissars, instructors and secret service. In the camps the soldiers attended lectures on Marxism–Leninism and produced political newsletters to be distributed among the locals. The MNLA also stipulated that their soldiers needed official permission for any romantic involvement with local women.

    Tin mines and rubber plantations became their primary targets along with the sabotaging of installations and razing of transportation and infrastructure.

The twenty-three-year-old determined anti-colonialist knew exactly what he was doing. It seems he never got back to Malaya in spite of several legal attempts. He ostensibly died in October 2011 in Bangkok although he was photographed in that same month having lunch with friends at a city hotel – and he looked fighting fit.

Chin Peng, Bangkok.

At the beginning of the Emergency the Brits had 13 Infantry battalions in action including seven partially formed Gurkha battalions, three British battalions, two battalions of the Royal Malay Regiment and a British Royal Artillery Regiment that was used as Infantry.

All this was too small a force to efficiently meet the threat of the Communist Terrorists (CTs) and more Infantry battalions were required. Soldiers from units such as the Royal Marines and King's African Rifles were hurriedly brought in. The Special Air Service was re-formed in 1950 as a specialised reconnaissance, raiding and counter-insurgency troop.

The conflict involved up to 40,000 British and Commonwealth soldiers against 7000 to 8000 Communist guerillas at their peak force.

In the years following World War II most Australians were wary of overseas military enterprises. In April 1950 the British Government asked whether some RAAF units could be sent to assist in the Malayan

Emergency. The Australian Prime Minister, Robert Menzies, vacillated. Menzies was intensely pro-British and anti-Communist and he responded that he was 'deeply conscious of the serious position in Malaya'. But he was also concerned that voters wouldn't want to 'commit Australia to a militaristic policy'. Menzies was unsure whether the British could win.

The British Commissioner-General for South-East Asia, Malcolm MacDonald, brought Menzies' dilemma to a head. MacDonald arrived in Australia in early May 1950 and found our local media somewhat in favour of entering the Emergency. However, there were some anti-British rallies and Cabinet was sceptical of MacDonald's requests.

On 19 May 1950 Menzies displayed his superb political nous by announcing an RAAF unit would be sent to Malaya but it was to be only a transport squadron, not bombers. No 38 Squadron RAAF arrived in Singapore in June – a very modest start to what was to evolve into

Australia's longest immersion in an overseas military engagement.

It was the invasion of South Korea by the Communist forces of North Korea on 25 June 1950 that convinced the Australian Government that there really were Commos under the bed – and probably as close as the next room.

Two days after the invasion Cabinet decided that No 1 Squadron Lincoln bombers would head for Malaya along with a select unit of Army advisors and intelligence officers. The sortie was named the Bridgeford Mission.

In late 1954 Australia joined the newly formed Southeast Asia Treaty Organisation (SEATO) and backed the establishment of the British Commonwealth Far East Strategic Reserve (BCFESR) in Malaya. This coincided with the return of Australian Army units from Korea.

From 1955 Australian Infantry battalions and Artillery batteries did two-year tours of duty in Malaya as part of the 28th Commonwealth

Brigade. From 1958 RAAF bomber and fighter squadrons at Butterworth, and the RAN ships involved in the Emergency, were also part of the BCFESR, which provided the organisational structure for our involvement, including 7000 soldiers.

The first Australian ground forces to arrive in October 1955 were from the 2nd Battalion, Royal Australian Regiment (2RAR). 2RAR left Malaya in October 1957 and was replaced immediately by 3RAR, later followed by 1RAR.

At age 22, I arrived as a platoon commander serving with the 2nd Battalion, which was initially based on Penang Island. The battalion had crossed to the mainland on 1 January 1956 to begin operations. It mainly operated in the northern areas of Kedah and Perak, which had been centres of guerilla activity. Although there were few contacts with the guerillas when the battalion patrolled, a significant action took place in June 1956 in the Pipeline Ambush, in which three Australians of Alpha Company 2RAR were killed.

In that same year, the RAAF extended Butterworth air base, from which Canberra bombers of No 2 Squadron, replacing No 1 Squadron and CAC Sabres of No 78 Wing, launched ground attack missions against the Communists. RAN destroyers Warramunga and Arunta had already joined the force in June 1955. Between 1956 and 1960, for periods of three to nine months, aircraft carriers Melbourne and Sydney and destroyers Anzac, Quadrant, Queenborough, Quiberon, Quickmatch, Tobruk, Vampire, Vendetta and Voyager were committed to the Commonwealth Strategic Reserve forces.

By late 1959 operations against the Communists were in their final phase and many had crossed Malaya's northern border into Thailand. With 3RAR leaving Malaya in October 1959, 1RAR arrived, but even though it operated in the border region the soldiers made no contact with the enemy and were ordered not to move into Thailand, where the presence and location of Communists was known.

The Malayan Government declared the Emergency over on 31 July 1960. 1RAR stayed in Malaya until October 1961 when 2RAR returned for a second tour. In August 1962 the battalion was deployed to anti-Communist operations in Perlis and Kedah and finished its tour in August 1963.

Along with air and Infantry forces, Australia also provided Artillery and engineering support and an airfield construction squadron built the main runway for the RAAF base at Butterworth.

In the long conflict, security forces killed 6710 MRLA guerillas and captured 1287. Some 2702 guerillas surrendered and around 500 more did so at its conclusion. Thirteen hundred and forty-five Malayan troops and police died in the conflict, as well as 519 Commonwealth citizens. An estimated 2478 civilians were killed, with another 810 documented as missing. The Commos did not return prisoners alive. Australia lost 39 killed and had 20 wounded of the 7000 who served in the Malayan Emergency.

The engagements in Malaya and Vietnam have been compared many times and historians question how a British force of 35,000 triumphed when more than 500,000 US soldiers were unsuccessful in a smaller region.

Like Korea, Vietnam was a war that could not be won. It is the same in Afghanistan where politics and the rights of the people and all the regulations relative to Rules of Engagement prevent the various NATO forces from taking the fight to the enemy who have defeated all-comers, from British regiments to the Soviet Army.

Additional sources: Maryborough Military and Colonial Museum and Australian War Memorial histories.

FOUR

BODY PARTS AND BATTLING COMMOS

The first time I encountered human body parts, lots of them and freshly dead, was on a train from Kota Tinggi, just north of Singapore, while I was heading back to my Charlie Company 2RAR base at Sungai Siput in Malaya.

As a second lieutenant I had found myself posted to 9 Platoon Charlie Company and was later sent to Kota Tinggi just north of Singapore for a British Army jungle warfare course. I was returning by train from that tough but exhilarating four-week course.

The high-speed Singapore Express hit a UK Army Saracen Armoured Personnel Carrier (APC) which had stalled on a crossing. The collision opened up the large APC like a can of sardines, killing all eight soldiers on board. All of the army passengers on the train were told by the railway staff and local police to walk back along the railway track and pick up the bloody pieces of bodies, scattered personal items and equipment.

I had never before seen blood and gore, let alone a mutilated dead person up close, and I had to grit my teeth to pick up arms, wrists with watches attached, heads and other parts of about eight soldiers killed in the horrific accident. The memories plagued me for many weeks until I became involved in platoon operations against the Communist terrorists and had to focus 100 percent on the enemy. Over the years, however, those APC carnage memories often returned and, as with the horrific Long Tan carnage less than a decade later, I have had to just try and blot them out of my mind and get on with life. But as one gets older the memories return more often, and more vividly.

These days I would have had to undergo counselling and perhaps be diagnosed as having Post Traumatic Stress Disorder, but such services and medical conditions were not on the agenda in 1956, nor 1966, and we just had to get on with life, mainly by devoting our thoughts to seeking out and killing the enemy and relaxing with mates when in base.

The Malayan Emergency became my training ground for Vietnam. Without Malaya it is possible I might not have trained my soldiers so seamlessly for jungle warfare. Senior officers largely drew their experience from World War II and the cold climate combat of Korea. Malaya was also where I killed my first enemy.

It was in late December 1955, just after two and a half years serving as Platoon Commander, 18 National Service Training Battalion at World War II Brighton Camp north of Hobart, that I was flown to 2RAR Malaya as a reinforcement officer. After arrival at the Penang Island 2RAR battalion rear administrative base I was trucked to the mainland on the ferry and south to the Charlie Company base at Sungai Siput.

The rear base was in lovely old British colonial barracks on stunning Penang Island, the fourth-largest island in the country, taking up an area of 293 square kilometres. Many early settlers succumbed to malaria on Penang, earning this beautiful isle the undesirable epithet of White Man's Grave.

Sungai Siput was a pretty town famous then for Lion Hill, an eye-catching peak standing sentinel on the settlement's edge. Some 80km south of Butterworth, Sungai Siput was also known for abundant ground nuts – the simple peanut that grows into a pod under the earth – and for the incident that led to the Malayan Emergency.

The Battalion Operational Headquarters was further south at Kuala Kangsar, acknowledged then as the Royal Town for the fabulous palace of the Sultan of Perak that had been built there in 1903. In 1954 the palace had been turned into a school.

On arrival at Sungai Siput base I was kitted out with UK greens, jungle hat, jungle boots, webbing and a light US .30 calibre carbine that could be tucked neatly under the arm while map reading. I was ordered to get a Charlie Company crewcut by my company commander, Major L C Chambers, who, for obvious reasons, was nicknamed 'Elsie'. He was Army Service Corps, seconded to Infantry, a tall, happy, likeable man who had the idiosyncrasy of acknowledging anything and everything said to him with 'Seen'. Or using the word when seeking an understanding of his orders or instructions, such as, 'Smith, you will patrol to the hill over there. Seen?' 'Elsie', who saw service with our Logistics Support Base at Vung Tau in Vietnam, died in 2012.

With my head suitably sharpened, I was driven to the Company forward operational base some miles north, which sat in a collection of open rubber-tapper huts in a rubber plantation, with huge mature trees milked for their white latex; we named them 'condom trees'. The monkeys used to play in the high treetops and every now and then one would fall off his female mount, all the way to the ground, pick himself up and go back up again, to the hearty and encouraging cheers of the soldiers below. I met my platoon soldiers and fellow officers, who, all except RMC graduates 'Elsie' and ex-Korean War second-in-charge (2IC) Captain Dave Mannet MC, were one-pip second lieutenants. These were Brian McFarlane, Brian Gosman and Warren Meredith, all OCS officers. In other companies most were recent Duntroon full lieutenants – two-pipper graduates as we referred to them.

I had been ordered before leaving Australia to learn some Malay so that I could converse with locals. So I studied a cheap Malay dictionary and learnt a few simple words and phrases, unaware that most people spoke English anyway. Early my second morning there, leaning out of the open window frame, I saw a young Malay boy walking along a dirt track towards the hut, carrying the usual tapper's pole over his shoulder with two buckets of latex rubber. Smart-arse me greeted the kid with the Malay version of 'Good morning' – *'Selamat Pagi'*.

He looked up at me with his big shiny eyes and bright smile and said, 'Good morning, sir' in very clear English. That was the last time I used Malay. And, even more delightfully, all the bar girls spoke good English.

I started soldiering work right away. We would spend four weeks patrolling in the jungle hills or searching villages, with a weekend break back in Penang. And you couldn't wish for better than a weekend in Penang. On patrol we carried up to ten days' rations, UK one-man ration packs, better than the Bully Beef and Biscuits which our generals claimed would be 'just fine' for us as that was good enough for them in New Guinea in World War II. The diet was a staple during World War I. The UK Army took pity on our old outfits and had replaced our khaki uniforms, tan boots, slouch hats and .303 rifles with jungle greens, jungle hats, light jungle patrol boots and the Fabrique Nationale Belgian 7.62 mm NATO rifle, produced after 1959 at the Lithgow Small Arms factory as the self-loading rifle (SLR). It was also our main rifle in Vietnam. Some soldiers had learned how to niftily file the trigger sear pin down to make it smoother and easier to pull the trigger and also automatically fire like a light machine gun, albeit hard to control the recoil.

Malaya 1956. From left to right 2LT Smith, 2LT Brian McFarlane, Major LC Chambers and 2LT Meredith.

On one of the Penang leave breaks I went into town with four or five fellow officers and we were drinking with some bar girls when the Momma-san yelled, 'You go – Red Caps come!' She was referring to the UK Military Police approaching in a Land Rover. We then realised we were in an out-of-bounds area and took off, confident that in our suede desert boots, also called 'brothel brogues', we would outrun the police with their heavy boots by scooting down back alleys. While we did manage to outrun them we then got caught in a dead-end alley and finished up in their vehicle and behind cell bars while our ID was checked out. They released us – after a report to our unit for whatever action was deemed applicable.

Next day we fronted the commanding officer who could have charged us and put us on a plane back to Australia. But Colonel Jim Ochiltree, 'Gentleman Jim' as he was fondly called, let us off with a severe tongue lashing and a pointed warning 'not to get caught' in any future ventures into town, which was just what I tried to tell one of my young officers in Vietnam.

Me in Malaya, 1956.

I was then sent to Kota Tinggi for the jungle warfare course where we went through the mill with very good UK instructors, who had seen considerable active service in the previous years of the Malayan

Emergency where both sides suffered major casualties in bloody conflicts until the British forces resettled local residents into fenced villages.

My company sergeant major in Vietnam in 1966–67, the late Jack Kirby, was to serve at Kota Tinggi as an instructor 1963–65, then joining 6RAR in Brisbane. Jack would have handled the role well, as he did in Delta Company.

At weekends we were given leave from Kota Tinggi to nearby Singapore and that was my introduction to Change Alley markets: bar girls and cheap clothing, where you could have a tailormade suit finished in a day. Beautiful exotic girls lured us into bars with, 'You buy me drink' and Momma-san served them tea for the price of expensive spirits. Relaxed after a few drinks, and after a week of hard work in the jungle, it was hard for soldiers to resist when the lovely little Asian ladies asked 'You want boom boom?' But gonorrhoea was rife in Malaya; later in Vietnam it was better controlled. In Malaya we often had young soldiers return from Penang with a dose of the disease which appeared about four days out.

Local doctors had a scam for soldiers returning to jungle bases who thought they may have caught venereal disease (VD). The soldiers were asked to urinate in a glass, which was held up to the light by the doctor, who then poker-faced announced, 'Yes, you see it is has particles in the urine so you need a $50 injection.' The injection was probably just water. The soldiers later discovered that urine held up to sunlight always has fine particles in it.

I had the misfortune to have to conduct 'short arm inspections' before long patrols – it was not much fun inspecting penises of all shapes and sizes, and asking uncircumcised soldiers to roll back foreskins. I also had the task of trying to educate soldiers that if they did succumb to the charms of the bar girls, they had to immediately urinate and wash themselves rather than going to sleep. Such was the lot of a young platoon commander in Malaya.

My medical orderly carried penicillin. After four to five days when the disease appeared I had the pleasure of injecting penicillin into culprits' backsides. I'd say, 'Serves you bloody right', and whack in it went. I had no medical training of note but there wasn't a lot of skill required with injections. I think the soldiers were wary of my skills and perhaps the thought of their platoon commander rather than the medical orderly giving them the injections might have kept some of them on the straight and narrow. I recall one of my soldiers was hospitalised with a bad dose of piles. He claimed he had fallen asleep on the brothel toilet after sex and they fell out.

We didn't seem to have the same problem with VD in Vietnam. I think the local girls in Vung Tau and Saigon were given regular health checks by the government. But unlike Malaya, I delegated any treatment to my medical corporal, Doc Dobson, and wasn't told who had what and where from. I am aware the US Army had major problems caused by the local Vietnamese men not taking a full course of antibiotics due to the cost and so each type of VD eventually became resistant to all known antibiotics. Rumour had it that a US hospital in Hawaii was full of soldiers rotting away from incurable forms of VD.

I had been promoted to full lieutenant in December 1956 after the normal four years' service and was selected to lead the Charlie Company patrol of 30 men that was to last six weeks along the top of steep mountain ridges on the Thai border. Called Operation 'Eagle Force', our mission was to set ambushes along ridgeline tracks which ran across the top of towering mountains on the Thai border, as part of a force of five similar patrols, one from each company, including the Support Company, normally a heavy weapons company with Vickers machine guns and 3-inch mortars, but converted to a rifle company in Malaya.

Agents were sending in reports that Chin Peng the leader of the Communist Terrorist (CT) organisation, was moving into Malaya. Chin had been forced into exile over the border in Thailand but occasionally crossed back to visit villages for money and food and/or to murder village chiefs to enlist village support via his ruthless fear tactics.

Chin Peng circa 1956.

We had no luck finding him, but Support Company patrol did have a successful contact, though not with Chin Peng, for which the patrol sergeant, Des Kennedy, was awarded the Military Medal (MM). Talking about medals in

Malaya, Lieutenant Wally Campbell's platoon leading section was ambushed on a track along a pipeline near Sungai Siput and three men were killed. Wally and his headquarters ran forward, killing one escaping CT on the way. He was awarded the Military Cross (MC). Another RMC lieutenant, Claude Ducker, was to get an MC the next year when his small patrol led by trackers killed three CTs sitting around having lunch.

Sometime after I shot a Communist Terrorist, a senior officer told me that if I had been an RMC officer I would have got a Mentioned in Despatches (MID). That's a blatant example of the immature snobbery that then existed between Duntroon and Portsea in all the years up until about 1980 when Portsea officers started reaching colonel and brigadier rank.

Up on the Thai border we set our ambushes along tracks and made a HQ area at some distance away, where those not on duty could rest, mostly playing card games of Five Hundred to pass the long hours. We carried heavy packs with all our rations, ammunition and water bottles and often were resupplied by parachutes out of British or New Zealand cargo aircraft. We very conscientiously protected the UK-issue 2-litre rum bottles from breaking by catching the parachute load before it landed on a rock. We then cut up the parachutes for light sleeping bags.

Part of my job was to decant the rum issue into two extra water bottles on my belt and each night at Stand-To I would go around the platoon perimeter, checking my men were equipped and alert, and doling out a capful of rum into my soldiers' hot chocolate as a night cap. Coffee was not in ration packs in Malaya and it only became a normal drink after Korea, following American habits. To avoid any spillage I developed a very steady hand when it came to pouring the rum!

Routine work included short and long-term patrols and in country that varied from villages surrounded by flat wet rice paddies, to long and hot grassy areas and to high jungle mountains, as in more than 1500 m high, where animals, enemy patrols and our own patrols were mostly limited to moving along the narrow ridgeline tracks.

Tigers and elephants inhabited some of the jungle areas, and although I never saw any there was ample evidence of their presence by large mounds of manure on the tracks. A soldier in another company was injured by an aggressive tiger and later in Borneo an SAS soldier was gored and killed by an elephant in similar terrain. And we saw the odd python – huge reptiles, some at least 6 m long and 30 cm across. Mosquitoes plagued the lowlands but not the jungle, where leeches were a constant problem, especially near creeks. Our defence was to soak our trouser leg bottoms, shirt sleeve cuffs and frontal trouser fly with issue mosquito repellent, but that was always a source of acute irritation in the rain, although better than having a leech get into the old fellow's tube, as happened now and then, with the soldiers needing to be evacuated to hospital. The leeches were able to crawl around undetected but if they got up into the urethra, they would suck blood and expand and only surgery could remove them. At rest breaks you would see soldiers burning leeches off with cigarette tips and carefully checking their trouser fly areas.

While we did not smoke when patrolling, at rest breaks we put sentries well out and enjoyed a clandestine smoke now and then. In those days most of us smoked, and we were given a tin of 50 'Rear Divs' cigarettes weekly through the UK Army rationing system. It was much the same in Vietnam, though with no cigarette (or rum) ration, but a packet of cigarettes was pin money at the canteen; a packet of Camels cost almost nothing.

Searching villagers at checkpoints for food and weapons which could have been handed over to terrorists in the jungle was a daily ritual when not out on jungle patrol, and we often used Saracen APCs supplied by UK transport units to move to and from villages and jungle patrol start points.

While some argued about the relationship between Infantry and Armour in Vietnam, there was no argument in Malaya. Irrespective of rank, the Armoured carrier commander was in charge while on the move, and might provide fire support with his machine gun when the Infantry dismounted. I always cooperated with the crew commander, even if he was a corporal. I had the esteemed rank of second lieutenant, then full lieutenant, in those two years in Malaya, but my rank never came into it in those situations, plus I knew little about UK APC operations and tactics. Later in Vietnam there were bitter and unnecessary arguments about who was in charge of the 10 APCs of the belated Reaction Force moving to reinforce my company at Long Tan. The Infantry captain passenger claimed he was senior in rank and thus in command, but not so. All he did was cause problems with the APC crews which, I might add, still linger all these years on.

When we wanted fresh water other than the rain we collected off our small poncho tents – if we were able to have tents as such, often just digging hip holes on mountain sides – we patrolled down steep hillsides to locate creeks, filled up our special UK issue 20-litre water bags in our packs, then climbed back up, hand over hand on vines and tree roots. Water is heavier than rations. These forays made for a good workout and were somewhat reminiscent of Tarzan.

Every afternoon we got soaking wet with the regular monsoonal rain. We always went to bed in wet greens. We did not wear underclothes as they chafed; just shirt and trousers. 'Crutch rot' as it was called, from continually wet greens, was rife. Most of us had to be painted with the old purple Gentian Violet, but it was not really effective. A liquid medication bought from chemist shops – I think it was called TCP – was the best cure, and our groins were not so brightly coloured or itchy.

There was not a lot of action on patrols in Malaya. But on one night-ambush that we'd set on a track between two villages we fixed trip flares across the trail which were covered with two Bren guns (light machine guns), one each end, and firing along it. It was known that communist terrorists often came into the villages at night to collect food and money and visit families and girlfriends. We were waiting for them.

As happened later in Vietnam, villagers were either sympathetic or coerced into helping the local guerillas; otherwise they and their families suffered pretty dreadful atrocities. Most ambushes were uneventful – a drag, until this night.

I was trying to prop my eyelids open and ignore the incessant mosquitoes. It must have been about 9.30pm when a trip flare went off, the light almost blinding us, but revealing a figure riding a bicycle along the track. As briefed, the two Bren gunners immediately opened up and killed the man, who turned out to be an old village elder, heading home late after having drunk too much rice wine at another village 8km away. Ambush sprung, we reported the kill by radio and sat around until first light.

Just after dawn the local police arrived and took his body and the next day a group from the battalion, including my ambush party, attended the village funeral and paid respects. Unlike all the fuss about killing civilians in Afghanistan along with debatable Rules of Engagement, the law in Malaya was quite clear: anyone outside the 6pm to 6am village curfew was enemy. You shot to kill. No questions asked.

Some weeks later my platoon was ordered to go into the jungle with two Iban trackers from Borneo to try to find a CT who had been reported going up a certain hill by loyal local people. I moved up front just behind the trackers and after several hours of climbing up the ridgeline track on the hill they pointed to a figure hiding behind a bush 20 m ahead. Armed with my US .30 cal carbine, I carefully moved forward to investigate. At about 5 m away I shouted and indicated he should get up and put his arms in the air, but he just moved an arm, appearing to be about to throw a grenade, so I shot him rather than have a grenade killing or wounding my soldiers or me.

I must confess that I fired too many rounds in my first personal kill but in hindsight I just wanted to ensure he was dead. I guess it was kill or be killed. Sadly perhaps, there was no grenade or rifle. He was unarmed, with an earlier wound, a clean hole in his chest that exposed his heart, which I could clearly see. He had obviously been picking rotting flesh off the wound. There was an unofficial policy that a dead enemy was better than a wounded enemy. Indeed my company commander had said to me 'Smith we need a kill. Seen!' I guess it was like the US Body Count policy in Vietnam – bodies being the status symbol of success. In hindsight, probably because I had spent much of my earlier life shooting kangaroos and rabbits, it did not affect me at the time.

Even now, almost 50 years after the Long Tan battle, critics are still complaining about a couple of 6RAR soldiers, including one of mine, shooting two mortally wounded enemies after Long Tan. Their brains and intestines were hanging out – the shootings were complete acts of mercy and they may have already been brain dead. I must be considered equally guilty from my kill in Malaya? I did what I had to do and have to live with it. But, yes, I often think about it when similar discussions occur. I just have to put it out of my mind and turn my thoughts to more pleasant things.

We carried the man's body down to the local road and it was taken by the police and hung up outside the police station for two days with a sign warning this was the fate of those who supported the Communist push.

The incident was recorded in the Malayan Emergency Official History as a 'well-planned and executed operation'. Executed was right! I am not really proud of that, even though my company commander, Major Laurie Chambers, was very happy that Charlie Company had recorded its first 'kill' – much better than a captured 'wounded'.

It was Christmas 1956 and my platoon was ordered to be the duty unit to guard our forward Battalion HQ at Kuala Kangsar while most sub-units went back to Penang on leave. Our adjutant was a strict former expat Scots Guards officer, Captain Donald Ramsay, who used to chastise young officers if their shorts or socks were too short. Mostly, we were afraid of this fastidious and somewhat fierce man with his impressive World War II ribbons, who spoke with a strange accent and would have one 'Sharpen my pencil, Mon' while waiting to speak at his desk.

With a faultless uniform attire, on base parades he would actually measure the distances above and below the knees with his hand and advise what had to be done to observe the regulations of an exact four fingers to the shorts above and long socks below.

Ramsay was every bit the traditionalist and in my short time in the military I'd not seen it taken to this extreme before. The Scots Guards were part of the Guards Division, one of the elite Foot Guards regiments of the British Army. They began as the personal bodyguards of King Charles I of England and Scotland. Their lineage can be traced as far back as 1642, although it was only placed on the English Establishment, becoming part of what is now the British Army, in 1686.

When I reported for duty at the Kuala Kangsar forward Battalion HQ, Ramsay gave instructions that one of my main tasks was to try and locate the soldiers who were loudly drinking and gambling after Lights Out at 10pm.

With my platoon sergeant Alan Seale, who had served in Korea and was my mentor, we patrolled the lines every night after Lights Out but could never pin the blokes who were making the noise. They probably had 'a parrot' (lookout) on duty. But, a week or so after we began searching, the 'parrot' must have fallen asleep and we walked right into the hut making the noise and I announced, 'Gotcha, you rats', and my sergeant joyfully confiscated the grog and cards.

That incident earned me the nickname of 'Harry the Ratcatcher', which was to be revisited in Vietnam by former 2RAR soldiers such as my company quartermaster sergeant Ron Gildersleeve. It wasn't, as has been rumoured, for giving a bonus to my men for catching the large rats that plagued our tent lines at Nui Dat. Courtesy of my blokes, after Long Tan it became 'Harry the Cong Catcher' for a time. But I am happy with 'Ratcatcher' and a nice flag to that effect, which had been made a long time back, was given to the Maryborough Military and Colonial

Museum in 2011 by one of my former soldiers living in Bowen, Private Sting Hornett – a man with a large penchant for humour who had once called me an 'old cunt' at a 1986 company reunion. On presentation of the flag, in adding his thanks, he commented he would not have been alive had it not been for me training the soldiers hard and my able command of the battle.

2RAR Battalion completed its two-year Malaya tour not long after Malaya became the Federation of Malaysia in August 1957 and sailed home on the UK troopship New Australia on a journey that took 10 days, docking in Sydney on 31 October. We ran into a cyclone off Cape York and most were violently ill due to the rough seas and unventilated cabins below deck but I wasn't. I never have been seasick. My wife was with me, as were other soldiers' families, and our second child, daughter Sharon Lee, was born nine months later in June 1958. I put that down to one good night at sea or it may have been the meal of bullock balls, delicately named 'sweetbreads' on the menu, that I had eaten for dinner one night.

In Malaya I had had my first taste of real enemy encounter, logging my first kills. Not at all surprised, I had discovered I liked serving overseas with soldiers on active service.

FIVE

BATTLING RUSHES OF BLOOD TO THE HEAD AND HEART

On arrival in Sydney we went to Holsworthy Barracks where we did well to get married quarters nearby, albeit a cheap old World War II-type home. I was assigned to command the Vickers Machine Gun Platoon in Support Company and in May 1958 promoted well ahead of time to temporary captain. Usually it took four years to make captain, not just 18 months. The (late) Des Kennedy MM was my excellent platoon sergeant and in 1985 I was to meet his Gladstone-based sister Mavis Purcell while cruising in company with her and husband Jim on their Fleming 39 timber cruiser Karee along the north Queensland coast.

As we had a second child I welcomed the higher pay for captain to help with bringing up our two children and buying furniture for the old married quarters. We couldn't afford carpet so we dyed hessian and laid that over cheap underfelt. I had about ten shillings a week for myself and that paid for petrol and bait for a weekend day fishing trip off the rocks at Kurnell, after negotiating rope ladders down cliffs – pretty normal stuff for me anyway. Mind you, ten shillings was a lot of money in those days and I remember the total cost for two trolleys of groceries and items to start off in the married quarters house was a whole £7, now $14, at the local Holsworthy Army Canteen store!

The Machine Gun Platoon was a wonderful command, one which flowed on from the experiences with the Vickers machine gun in School Cadets. I had four Austin Champ vehicles with trailers, two guns and crews to each of three Champs, and one for my HQ, along with reserve ammunition. We were a self-contained platoon group, almost autonomous. Sergeant Des Kennedy was a tower of strength, along with tall Corporal 'Puny' Clarke, noted for his sleek late model BMW motorbike.

Siting the guns behind hill crests for indirect fire via aiming posts and instrument gun sights and seeing the rounds land on the target 3000 m away was a very rewarding task. It was my job to work out the range and angles and watch the fall of shot with binoculars and advise corrections to the guns. We took part in exercise 'Grand Slam' up at Sarina, southwest of Mackay, in 1960, driving our Austin Champs there and back. We normally stayed overnight in smelly showground animal stalls but locals often turned on a dance; all good fun at night, but hard work during the long days in the field or on the road in the hot Queensland sun.

On the battalion's return date, I was held back to conduct a survey of all used and damaged stores, adjudicating whether they be dumped, burnt or stored and completing the always necessary paperwork to satisfy higher HQ to write the stores off ledger charge. Then my driver and I shared the driving back to Greenslopes near Brisbane, where we caught up with the unit before going south to Holsworthy.

One night I 'borrowed' one of our fuel-hungry Austin Champs and drove an hour back to Nambour to have dinner with an attractive local girl I had met at a dance on the way north a few weeks earlier. I paid for the fuel and was able to 'doctor' the trip sheet. I recall returning the jeep into the transport compound at sunrise, and saying good morning to a tired-looking senior officer walking past, also late home from a night out. While I am not proud of my philandering, rushes of blood to the head and heart when away from home were not uncommon at that time. And I wasn't Robinson Crusoe.

In July 1959 I was reposted to the School of Infantry at Seymour in Victoria as the Machine Gun Course Instructor, but the day I arrived the Vickers was replaced by the M60 light machine gun and I was made the 3-inch Mortar Course Instructor. One had to be flexible! Although similar principles for indirect fire applied, I did a mortar course before instructing. The (late) Captain Kevin 'Pip' Newman was the Senior Mortar Instructor. He was to later resign and enter politics in

Tasmania and then pass away prematurely. His son Campbell, former RMC graduate engineer officer, became Premier of Queensland, straight from a high profile stint as Brisbane's Lord Mayor. But he lost his Ashgrove seat and resigned in February 2015.

In March 1960 Kath and I moved into married quarters at Seymour, a similar old home to the one we'd had at Holsworthy, and our son Brett Ronald Carlton was born a year later on 20 June 1961. Years later I told him we gave him three Christian names in case he wanted to be an RMC officer. Obviously the month of September heightened my testosterone annually. Debbie was born on 19 June, Brett on the 20th and Sharon on the 23rd. An Army wife's lot is not an easy one and five days after Brett arrived the School moved north to Ingleburn in New South Wales where I continued to instruct on mortar courses until I was made Adjutant to the Commanding Officer, Colonel Gerry O'Day, whose nickname was obviously 'GOD'.

My family then moved up and into a similar old married quarters house as we had had at Holsworthy and Seymour. In my spare time, and mainly at night, most nights, I supervised and worked on the setting up of the Infantry Centre's military museum. I really enjoyed this task; it was very interesting researching weapon history to sort out display material such as the many types of .303 Lee Enfield rifles. I was able to trade duplicate weapons with the New South Wales Police museum and private collectors for types we did not have and thus improve the overall display. It was one of these private museums to which I gave the Garand rifle and M1 carbine brought home from Vietnam. I did all the printing on the cards for the description labels. Corporal 'Mac' McMahon, a quiet and loyal NCO, was the museum curator who, with me, spent endless hours sorting out the chronological display from the boxes of weapons brought up from Seymour. He had a never-ending task of cleaning and oiling all the guns. I recall spending several nights a week at the museum trying to improve the display and it kept me away from noisy children at home.

In free weekend time I drove my VW 'Beetle' with a mate 'Sailor' Mealing over to the coast and we spent leisure time fishing off the rocks. We also went down to Iluka and camped there for a week and caught the loveliest and tastiest big whiting I have ever seen.

In November 1962 a new posting to either the New Guinea Pacific Island Regiment or to 2 Commando Company Melbourne was offered. Being a parachutist, I chose 2 Commando, the posting as Adjutant, Quartermaster and Training Officer and moved down to Melbourne, leaving my family at Ingleburn for some months until we were allocated a high-rise Housing Commission fifth-floor flat in Prahran as a married quarters – no fun for my wife with three young children. By then we were on the brink of formerly separating. I may not have shown it as much as I should have at the time but in retrospect I feel sorry for what Kath had to go through. She was a good mother and while I wanted to put the family in a home of their own I did not have the financial resources. Sadly, this situation continued until I was able to buy them a home after my return from Vietnam where I had saved enough for a requisite house deposit, and had the assistance of a small War Service Home Loan plus a second mortgage.

Commando work involved courses in various Special Forces techniques. Additionally I had to qualify in all the tests for the coveted Green Beret, which was not that easy, especially with all the Reserve people breathing down your neck and betting you would not make it – but I did. I then qualified as a shallow water diver, then diving instructor/supervising officer, small craft handler, then small craft instructor, parachute stick commander (qualifying B, above average), and ultimately as a parachute jump instructor (PJI) after a six-week course at RAAF Williamtown near Newcastle.

There was an old 30-foot triple diagonal plywood UK Navy surf whaler boat used by the CSIRO in Antarctica in the commando base hangar at Ripponlea. The hangar was fitted with various parachuting training aids so that the soldiers could practise exits, canopy drills and landings. The surf whaler, a surf boat with sails, had a Gunter mast rig, centreboard and well-used canvas sails. It was on a big trailer and we had an ex-World War II US Army Dodge 3/4 ton truck to move it. I was told it had only been used as a rowing boat, so I organised a sailing trip, and to my surprise it went very well. As it was on ledger as a vehicle, I then persuaded the local civilian stores officer at Victoria Barracks to provide the money for a 'new engine' – actually new sails – and to arrange for it to be painted, anti-fouled and permanently moored at the Royal Brighton Yacht Club Marina. We were permitted to race the boat we named *Strike Swiftly* and the locals in their whites were bemused by us soldiers sailing in greens and wearing our Green Berets. Worse, we did well, and were upgraded from C to B Class and in 1964 we won the annual Williamtown to Geelong Yacht Race, beating the illustrious Jock Sturrock, later to skipper America's Cup yacht *Gretel*. In Vietnam I heard on Radio Australia that the whaler had sunk on the same race in 1967, but at a World War II Commando Memorial service at

Canungra on 26 March 2013 I met the skipper who took over from me. His version was that he sailed back from Geelong with insufficient crew and she just heeled over in a big gust and 'bottled' (filled up with water), and had to be towed home.

Sailing Strike Swiftly 1964.

With all the specialist courses I undertook on top of normal training, work was seven days a week and most nights, and this had a further detrimental effect on my married life, with noises being made about me leaving the Army and becoming a 'normal husband', which I rejected as I had no trade other than Army, and no money. I spent most nights instructing on courses, then living in the Ripponlea Commando barracks, behind Caulfield Grammar School. The barracks weren't luxurious but they were on the job and provided a bed, a shower and a kitchen. Then aged 30 I had a couple of illicit romances, one of which became serious and continued briefly in Brisbane and again in Sydney after Vietnam, but which ended in early 1968 as the lady quite rightly wanted more security than a married man, and although I was separated I was still not divorced.

What I learned from 2 Commando was that pushing men to their limit engenders guts, ability, pride, confidence and teamwork. In late July 1965 I was promoted to temporary major and posted as a company commander to 6RAR, Enoggera, Brisbane, a new battalion earmarked for Vietnam in 1966. Kath and family remained in

Melbourne but in February 1966, after seven months on the waiting list, moved up from Melbourne to a nice St John's Wood married quarter house outside Brisbane, although I lived in 6RAR barracks. I was still saddled with family having to be in married quarters.

I had brief visits from my Melbourne girlfriend while I lived in 6RAR but was mostly away working. I had to be away on all sorts of exercises, from Canungra Jungle Training School, now known as Canungra Land Warfare School, to Shoalwater Bay, to Townsville's Mount Spec. In hindsight, and sadly for my family, I was more interested and involved in Army training and my girlfriend than in being a husband and father, and this had led to permanent separation in Melbourne.

Now, with my officers, company sergeant major and non commissioned officers I had to train our men for our role in war to kill the enemy and I planned to get right along with it in absolute service to my country which I loved. I pushed my men to the limit and those who fell by the wayside were sent to other companies. I knew I had a good team.

All this was to take place before I was to personally taste the awful inhumanity of man to his fellow man in Vietnam. Many years later I read and had to agree with American essayist Henry Louis Mencken that war will never cease until babies begin to come into the world with larger cerebrums and smaller adrenal glands.

SIX

THESE BOOTS ARE MADE FOR WALKING

It was in late July 1965 when I arrived at the new 6th Battalion Royal Australian Regiment (6RAR), Enoggera in Brisbane. Enoggera Barracks, variously called Alamein Barracks and Gallipoli Barracks, was officially inaugurated in 1908 when the area was used for field training, although the land was employed by military units as far back as 1855. Having been previously rostered for a parachute continuation training course I went back south to RAAF Williamtown for three days 25–27 October. I don't think the Commanding officer was impressed but nobody is indispensable and I went jumping.

I hadn't arrived when the battalion was raised on 6 June under the command of the newly promoted Lieutenant Colonel Colin Townsend, who'd been in Japan and Korea from 1949–51. He'd also briefly instructed at

Canungra Jungle Training Centre. I had met him at Brighton Camp in 1954 when he visited from Launceston where he was with the local CMF unit as a captain, the adjutant. His lady, later his wife, was then a Women's Royal Australian Army Corps Officer at Brighton.

In September about 300 National Servicemen, referred to as 'Nashos', of the 1965 first two-year conscription intake started to arrive after three months' training at the Recruit Training Battalion at Kapooka on the outskirts of Wagga Wagga in New South Wales. The government had committed to supporting the war in Vietnam and had sent the 1RAR battalion group of regular soldiers to Bien Hoa near Saigon in June 1965 and had begun expanding the Army using conscription to provide the soldiers for several new battalions. By the time I got there in mid-July 6RAR had been formed into company groups: Alpha, Bravo, Charlie, Delta, Admin and Support, of which Delta Company was under my command.

Lieutenant Colonel Colin Townsend, 1966.

I finished up with 68 'Nashos' and also had a Regular Army cadre – total strength about 125. We organised the new arrivals to the company into three platoons and a HQ and they collected bedding, uniforms and equipment from the quartermaster's store. The Regular Army soldiers included the Company Sergeant Major Warrant Officer Class 2

Jack Kirby, Sergeant Bob Buick, Sergeant Neil Rankin, Sergeant James 'Paddy' Todd, Corporal 'Buddy' Lea, Corporal Laurie Drinkwater, the Quartermaster Staff Sergeant Ron Gildersleeve, the Chief Cook Sergeant Bill O'Donnell and two other cooks, a clerk, Corporal Green and a driver, 'Bluey' Williams. Officers at that time were the 2IC, ex-UK Captain Iain McLean-Williams and Second Lieutenant Geoff Kendall who had graduated from OCS in December 1964.

Iain McLean-Williams was an expat Pom who was given the rank of captain based on his English commission. When we met at Enoggera we didn't see eye to eye but he did what he was required to do as well as he could. Iain appeared not to take things seriously, whereas I wanted things done properly with attention to detail; it was for me a case of one singer one song.

Delta Company 6RAR Officers and Sergeants early 1967.

A year later and after Long Tan I was rostered for a liaison trip carrying a briefcase with secret documents from our Vietnam HQ and Embassy in Saigon. I then travelled on a C123 Provider USAF transport plane, a smaller version of the C130 Hercules, to Da Nang up north and spent two days at the nearby Army Training Team base delivering the papers and then brought similar papers back to Saigon. While I was away Iain took our company out on patrol and got lost on one day. His map-reading skills left a lot to be desired. Eventually the company got back to base after going around in a circle. He actually told me later he had 'followed the sun'.

'Blessed are they that run round in circles, for they shall be known as big wheels.'

I told Iain I was not happy with his overall performance as 2IC and I'd like him to go. In November I spoke to the Commanding Officer Colin Townsend and asked for him to be replaced. Townsend appointed him in charge of writing the 6RAR battalion history book at his HQ for the rest of his tour. Captain Mick Weaver replaced him until he was wounded by accidental NZ gunfire in February 1967, to be replaced by Captain Ian McQuire. The book suited Iain's talents and he did a good job, even though the Long Tan battle area on the map page is drawn 1500 m north of the correct area – a printing error. Ironically he was posted back to me at 1 Commando in 1969 as my adjutant to replace reposted Captain Bob Supple but he did not last long before I moved him out to HQ 2 Div at Moore Park. Iain went on to upset other senior officers and was sent packing on at least a couple of occasions. Our former 6RAR Intelligence Officer Bryan Wickens told me he sadly died some years ago from massive liver damage. Iain and Bryan were both expat UK officers but, unlike Iain, Bryan was an excellent officer.

Back at Enoggera, the 'Nashos' were all riflemen/privates except for Second Lieutenant Gordon Sharp and Second Lieutenant Dave Sabben, who had done six months at the Officer Training Unit at Scheyville, Singleton, and who didn't arrive at Enoggera until January 1966. Up until November 1965 the emphasis at Enoggera had been firmly on basic Infantry Corps training. The theory was that you then built on this by adding specialised tropical warfare training which would meld section and platoon drills so the skills became second nature.

At this early stage Vietnam was only a rumour among the troops even though Colonel Townsend had already told me in confidence we would be moving out in June 1966. But when the battalion returned from Christmas leave the men were told we were to be totally ready for Vietnam by 26 May 1966.

I set about getting my men up to fitness standard – actually well beyond fitness standard – which was going to get me into a heap of trouble with 'Mousey' Townsend, his RMC Duntroon 1948 class nickname because of his size and looks, and his rather neat little bristling moustache.

For the Commanding Officer Colin Townsend to demand on arrival at his Enoggera office that I remove my Green Beret and go get a standard-supply peaked cap and report back to him seemed typical of the RMC attitude to the six months' OCS 'wonders'. I was proud of my Green Beret. You don't get it easily. Even before you were accepted for Commando training you had to prove you were way ahead of the pack physically and mentally. I had already qualified for my wings in 1954, made the grade, obtained further qualifications and had about 80 jumps up by 1966. But I now admit I should have gone to the Q store and got the correct battalion-type UK-style peaked cap before I went to report to the CO. I put myself in a position to be put down. Thank goodness the officers of today do not have to wear those stupid English peaked caps.

I launched into my training regimen of 10-hour-plus days over six-day weeks. Sometimes they became seven-day weeks. Exercises, weapon handling, patrolling, tracking and navigation, map reading, bayonet fighting, mine drills – intensive battle induction made up much of the long days.

Each morning after the men rallied at 6am, the CSM Jack Kirby and I had them form up on the company parade ground in shorts, boots, socks and singlets and then I either personally led them or urged them from the side around Enoggera village, up and down hills, for a good 5–8km. Every day.

I didn't engage a lot in physical training; I wasn't greatly into aerobics. It was mainly jogging that I chose. You work every muscle in your body when you jog. I believe if a man can jog 5–6km in boots in an hour up hill and down dale he's got guts and he will also develop physical fitness along the route. It wasn't too long before I increased our runs to 8km – with packs on.

My method of training which flowed on from my experience with

2 Commando Company was to demand a very high standard of performance in anything and everything they did. I was criticised for doing everything 'my way' but I knew if my men could achieve this supreme standard of fitness then their lives might be spared once they went into battle in Vietnam – although I don't think I even once said that. The men instinctively knew it but some thought I was a very hard tutor – a hard bastard.

I wanted the soldiers to have the real feel of being jungle fighters so we took up a collection and bought camouflaged jungle hats from a disposal store and we wore them during exercises instead of the issue slouch hat worn in New Guinea 20 years earlier. I delegated the shopping duty to Iain McLean-Williams. Just like when we went to Malaya in 1957 there was a reluctance to update equipment by our UK-trained generals who had seen service in New Guinea in World War II – 'Bully Beef and Biscuits' was good enough for them, so it was good enough for us. Their traditional slouch hats and leather boots were also good enough for us. We still didn't have UK or US-type tropical patrol boots that had canvas sides and let the water from rice paddies and creeks drain out – so we squelched around in wet leather boots, higher than the old brown ones, which did away with traditional webbing gaiters.

The new-style boots had a steel plate underneath the rubber to prevent injury from nasty steel punji stakes used by guerillas around the world, including in South Vietnam, which we knew as we had had Army advisers there since 1962, working with Vietnamese Army units. On arrival in Vietnam I obtained a pair of excellent US Army patrol boots, thanks to Warrant Officer Clem Kealy who had been an instructor with me at 2 Commando and was serving with the Training Team in 1966. I also carried a Special Forces issue Bergen rucksack instead of the standard World War II type issue pack.

Colin Townsend had a plan that involved basic training at platoon and company levels and a number of exercises that were to prepare us for going to war and facing the enemy. The role of Infantry is to seek out and 'kill the enemy', operations known as 'search and destroy' missions.

In our fitness program, I drew consistently from my Special Forces training. Not once did CSM big Jack Kirby demur. Where Townsend specified 10-km marches, Delta marched 12km. Fifteen-kilogram packs became 20 kg. Where an exercise described 'sandshoes', I ordered boots. Townsend was mad as hell with me but I argued that each company commander had the right to use his own techniques.

Townsend had seen a year in Korea in cold open country with much time spent travelling on top of US Army tanks, while I'd spent two years in tropical terrain in Malaya, similar to Vietnam – 'true grit grunts' as the Americans called us. The slang word 'grunts' came from American Infantry looking skyward as US choppers flew over, often en route to comfortable bases and good food. It was said the foot soldiers would pound the air with fists and make suitable gorilla grunts at the choppers flying home to their comfortable home bases.

In April 1966 when my yearly confidential report was due, the Lieutenant Colonel claimed in it I was 'disloyal' because I didn't follow battalion protocol with regards to training and wearing jungle hats. I vehemently questioned his disloyalty claim. We had a heated discussion in which he finally agreed with me that, unlike battalion operations in Korea, Malaya had been a platoon commanders' war, and that Vietnam to date was a company commanders' war and that I could train my company the way I wanted. I did not regard being a renegade as being disloyal.

Delta Company grew into the fittest, the fastest and one of the best tactically adept companies in the battalion. It was typical of Townsend's nature that, whenever he got the opportunity while battalion exercises were on, he made us take the outside section of the range, forcing us to move further and faster than anyone else. But by then we loved the challenge. My Regular Army men knew pretty much what was going on while our gutsy 'Nashos' thought it was all part of normal training. By then I'd shifted maybe 10 men out and the rest of us were operating at Commando level.

I also demanded absolute and distinctive actions when the men were given orders. If a soldier was told to fire he did – no questions asked. While I was to enjoy parachuting I learnt in my repetitive pre-jump training that, despite the fear of the unknown, when they said 'GO', you went, and that was the sort of discipline we inserted into our infantry training – when you are told to fire you FIRED!

I decreed during giving Orders for a field exercise that when in the field my men must never cough or fart on awakening as such noise might be heard by the enemy. This was for obvious reasons – to save their lives at war – but there were, I suspect, a few rumbles of outrage among some of them. Anyway it seemed they all found other places and times to cough and fart and those who couldn't manage this and my other essential decrees, I shipped out.

When we were in Malaya I tried to get a platoon together of only small men because when a man's not got a lot of weight to carry he can more easily get under or over bamboo and the like, quickly and simply, whereas big men are usually a bloody nuisance because you have to stop to help them. Generally I have a high regard for nuggety little fellows in Infantry – they make less of a target, move easily, and can carry more weight of equipment and ammunition. But of course there is a difference between being tall and supple and tall and overweight.

At Enoggera each platoon soldier had to do individual training and develop expertise in whatever weapon he was assigned. But the men also learned to interchange weapons because if someone got killed they needed to be competent in handling that man's machine gun or alternative weapon. They learned combat drills – what needed to happen if enemy contact came from left, right and rear. They engaged in platoon drills for when they were fired on or came across the enemy. All this was carried out at section, platoon and company level.

We taught them flanking manoeuvres and the senior ranks also did training with artillery and mortar fire control. This was going to be a lifesaver at Long Tan when officers and senior NCOs had to send fire orders to the artillery forward observer officer. The drill entailed giving instructions to the artillery guns and mortars in the rear and, if attached, via trained artillery forward observers (FOs) and mortar fire controllers (MFCs). They then had to tell their own guns and mortars where to fire. You need to be a sharp map reader to determine grid references for where the shells must fall. These were the references we sent to NZ Artillery FO Morrie Stanley at Long Tan, which allowed him to turn the artillery fire into deadly accuracy. Sadly, we did not have the battalion's mortars in range during the battle. And, luckily, apart from a couple of light 60-mm mortars, all the enemy's larger 82-mm mortars were not sited to fire on us, but were disassembled ready to be carried forward to support their attack on Nui Dat.

Me and Morrie Stanley.

Field craft camouflage was another skill. Field craft is the art of moving through the open fields, through jungle rubber plantations, through whatever terrain you find yourself in and trying to be invisible to the enemy. The soldiers learned the various techniques required to keep distances between men – taking advantage of cover in shade, in sunlight and the arts of camouflage. Hand signals were memorised to take the place of noisy verbal communication.

Camouflage was adapted to suit different types of terrain. In long grass you attached it around your shoulders and in the band around your hat. In trees you changed your body foliage. To take the shine off your face you used mud, Nugget shoe polish or your issue of camouflage cream. I also demanded their sleeves should always be worn down, hats must always be worn and shirt collars done up so the sun wouldn't reflect on their skin. Hands were also camouflaged. Shiny metal dog tags had to be worn around the neck but hidden inside shirts.

Interspersed with major trips for exercises our time was well taken up with basic Infantry training. Normal routine was to silently Stand-To at dawn and dusk for an hour with all your weapons and webbing ready as if you were to be attacked. Dawn and dusk were favourite times for being attacked. You learned to wait for an enemy attack in silence, every one of your senses primed. It also served to get everyone kitted with weapons checked ready for the day or night.

After various exercises and firing practices at Greenbank Range, and field firing at Tin Can Bay Range, along came our trip to Canungra Jungle Training School. This was a very hectic period where we spent long days climbing up and down ropes, under walls, over walls, through swamps, through tyres – all to improve the soldier's ability to perform under pressure. We were isolated and only permitted shelter and supplies as we could expect in Vietnam. The men were trained to shoot to kill and at close range. Mock villages offered booby traps and tunnels and 'enemy'. My men ran 5km each morning and by the end of the course they were doing 8km. I enjoyed Canungra. I think the men did too. They excelled. Being of the first intake the National Service men were very proud and quick to show they could do what was asked of them.

We were then dispatched to Shoalwater Bay military training area near Rockhampton for Exercise 'Foxhole', the last major exercise before Vietnam. We travelled by train from Brisbane to Rocky, with a night in cattle pens at the showground with no local leave, although much of the night was somehow spent in local pubs. We then went by truck to Raspberry Station, an old farming area where we set up our HQ. Other units had sent up soldiers to be our 'enemy' and there were officer and warrant officer umpires travelling with both sides.

On our last major exercise we had to patrol almost at forced march pace 22km to take out the fictitious enemy objective before dark. My very fit company thrived on the challenge and much to the CO's displeasure we were on the objective, eating dinner with our hootchies up by dark, while the rest of the battalion was still thrashing around in the bush until midnight. At one point during the day (late) Major Noel Ford with Bravo Company was going in the opposite direction and he chastised my forward platoon commander Second Lieutenant Geoff Kendall for apparently going in the wrong direction – but we were spot on. Noel was the one going the wrong way.

Delta Company logo designed by Dave Sabben.

It was while we were at Shoalwater Bay in April that Nancy Sinatra's hit song 'These Boots Are Made for Walking' was released and the soldiers took it on board as our company theme song and at least one soldier was prophetically heard to comment that the words 'One of these days these boots will walk all over you' were a warning to any Viet Cong we were to encounter in South Vietnam. Dave Sabben designed a logo based on the Greek (Delta) triangle, with red border (our company colour), encompassing a pair of boots. My mobile phone ringtone today is Nancy's song.

When we returned to Enoggera on 21 April we were moved up to Mount Spec west of Townsville for a final exercise at battalion level and back to Enoggera on 3 May. We were ready. The battalion cleaned up and packed. We were vaccinated, briefed on the theatre of war and given pre-embarkation leave. The entire battalion was sent on leave. I recall I went to Surfers Paradise with a couple of officer mates. On 21 May we got to march through the Brisbane streets to say goodbye to the homeland. Some of the officers downed farewell drinks in Victoria Barracks. It was both a gung-ho and solemn few rounds. We knew some of us might never see Australia's shores again, but our role was to kill the enemy, not be killed. The words of General George Patton of World War II fame, probably one of the greatest generals of that war, rang in my ears: 'No bastard ever won a war by dying for his country – he won it by making the other poor dumb bastard die for his country.' And I hoped that would apply to us.

Ironically, years after Long Tan, one of my former soldiers claimed in Lex McAulay's 1986 Long Tan book that I took a pearl-handled Colt .45 off a dead VC officer. I recall saying he had the enemy's black steel Tokarev pistol mixed up with General Patton's famous World War II Colt .45 and that from then on he could call me 'General George the Ratcatcher'. As I came to learn over the years, soldiers, and others, often get the facts wrong. I recently read a similar claim in UK Colonel Stuart Tootal's book *Danger Close* about 3 Parachute Battalion in Afghanistan – that after encountering IEDs and contacts few soldiers could give an accurate account of what, how and why the event happened, and they had no idea what went on outside their own limited field of vision. I take many stories with a grain of salt.

On 8 June 1966 we boarded a chartered Boeing 707 at Eagle Farm, Brisbane, and headed for Vung Tau via Manila and Saigon. At that point I was confident that all the hard yards had paid off. I knew all my soldiers were very loyal and extremely fit and at the same time very conscious of their own ability to react under pressure. The National Servicemen were keen to prove they were as good as Regulars. I appreciated that Delta Company was more than ready for whatever was waiting for them in Phuoc Tuy Province.

Brisbane parade prior to embarkation in 1966.

I realised I had to count heavily on my platoon commanders. 10 Platoon had Geoff Kendall, Gordon Sharp was my 11 Platoon commander and Dave Sabben led 12 Platoon. Gordon and Dave were National Service officers. Dave had actually volunteered for National Service when his conscription marble didn't roll out. He was a computer expert, tall, good-looking, quiet, very intelligent, a capable man and always a good leader. He'd been born in Fiji. While he was training to be an officer at Scheyville in Singleton he topped most subjects and in map reading he scored an impressive 100 percent. But none of us are perfect and I chastised him one day when he turned up on parade in pointed, very shiny Italian shoes that were certainly not his issue. I ordered him to take them off and put on normal shoes. We are today still very good friends.

Sadly, Gordon Sharp, an unwilling conscript but with the intelligence and education that pushed him into officer school, was killed at Long Tan. With great respect to a man who sacrificed his life for his men, he tended to be more of a soldiers' friend than a good leader. Just before Long Tan I replaced his platoon sergeant Neil Rankin with South African-born Bob Buick to back up Gordon. Neil Rankin and Gordon Sharp were two quiet men who played cards in the tents with their soldiers and became the men's friends. I did not agree with this because a leader needs to be fair, firm and friendly but never overfriendly. When the chips are down your soldiers have got to act immediately and not let any feeling of friendship get in the way. Bob Buick has described how Gordon kept on playing cards the night of the enemy mortaring of Nui Dat, and had to be pushed to get the platoon on alert and ready for action.

Bob, although disliked by some for his typical South African bullish attitude, what some called arrogant, was a loyal and excellent soldier, and was to get half the remaining 11 Platoon men through the battle when Gordon was killed early on. They lost 13 out of 29 men, many in the first few minutes of encountering a NVA company that came forward from their jungle hide to investigate the earlier contact in which 11 Platoon had fired on a small patrol. Bob took over and controlled the guns and his platoon fire via the section commanders for well over an hour until they could withdraw when 12 Platoon eventually got up behind them. I cited Bob for the MM for his command and leadership and I regret not citing him for Distinguished Conduct Medal (DCM), but CSM Jack Kirby got a DCM and the protocol was such tha Bob was relegated to MM. 11 Platoon as a group deserves the lustre of a DCM.

Some observers say my personal command ability saved my company; I guess it played a major part. That was my job. That was what I had been trained for. That was what I had to do on the day – direct the platoons, move them around, and get all the support that was available. But I want to emphasise that had it not been for Bob Buick's ability to call in and direct close artillery fire, the whole of 11 Platoon could have been over-run, with the enemy rolling on to the rest of the company. 11 Platoon's gallant stand gave me the time and space to organise a defensive position, more artillery, an air strike, ammunition resupply, and reinforcements, all of which contributed to saving the lives of most of our men. The helicopters would not have been able to hover over us and drop ammunition if the enemy had been there, or close nearby.

Geoff Kendall, with a kind round face, was born in 1941 into a struggling working-class family, his father serving in the Middle East and New Guinea in World War II. Geoff worked in odd jobs in the electrical industry, starting with Chandlers, then selling TV sets in his elder brother's electrical business at Tara, in south-west Queensland. His main claim to fame was that he was a good rugby league player and played for Wynnum-Manly, Brisbane, and then Wynnum. He saw an advertisement for OCS Portsea and was selected and commissioned in December 1964. Geoff was inexperienced but in 1966 he was a good platoon commander, although he became a temporary liability after Long Tan. He went on to a good career in military intelligence and developed into an expert linguist, stationed with a UK Intelligence Unit in Hong Kong and then our 1st Division Intelligence Unit, retiring after 24 years to run a hardware store at The Gap, west of Brisbane city. Fully retired, he now lives on Bribie Island.

While I was not aware of it at the time, I am told that in July 1966 he apparently went to Vung Tau in an APC 'ration run' and left his Owen gun there, to be returned by the Military Police. After Long Tan he admits he went seriously out of control at times. He was involved in 'borrowing' jeeps, and in company with 11Platoon's Lieutenant Paul O'Sullivan and a couple of other young officers, they borrowed a Land Rover 'jeep' from HQ ATF Nui Dat and set off for Vung Tau. After getting bogged in a ditch they then swiped a Vietnamese vehicle and a young lady was seriously injured. At Vung Tau, after leaving the vehicle parked with their pistols under the seat, when they returned after a visit to a local bar, it had gone. Reporting to the Military Police who had the vehicle, they were then charged. Paul O'Sullivan and Geoff Kendall were held back and court martialled, both losing seniority. They didn't come back on the slow 16-day HMAS Sydney trip with us but were flown home, apparently arriving before us!

Meanwhile I had to move Geoff out of the company as I felt he was no longer part of my team. Geoff admits he was a silly young officer but he was getting a lot of Long Tan and Vietnam 'crap', he says, off his chest. And he had certainly earned the right to do that. Based on my own questionable earlier adventures, and as imparted to me by my commanding officer in Malaya, I had told Geoff, 'It's not what you do, but don't get caught doing it.' My warning sadly went unheeded. We still talk to each other, but I detect a lingering resentment at me having moved him on. I think he was most surprised that I pursued the upgrading of his MID to the Medal for Gallantry (MG) in 2008, the MC I recommended having been downgraded to MID by Major-General Mackay in the 1966 awards debacle.

I had two other sergeants in my company who were wonderful at their jobs. One was Sergeant Bill O'Donnell, our cook, who also came out on the odd patrol and somehow prepared food for 130 of us out of pretty ordinary 10-man tinned ration packs, helped by his two assistant cooks. He was adept at swapping slouch hats and Aussie beer for frozen US Army packs of chicken and steak to add to our diet.

Staff Sergeant Ron Gildersleeve, our quartermaster sergeant, looked after all the stores brilliantly. Ron had served in the Merchant Navy and came out of the Army with only two fewer medals than Victoria Cross winner Keith Payne – 21 versus 23! Ron had been in Korea and Malaya and his loyalty and efficiency was a boost for all of us.

My company sergeant major Jack Kirby was an intelligent ox of a man at about 110 kg. He had a wonderful sense of humour and the men liked him. On a parade at Enoggera just before we headed for Vietnam a lady brigadier came to farewell our battalion formed up in company groups. The brigadier on the dais was rather, well, cuddly. Jack was standing behind our company rear flank. He quietly muttered, 'Men, you're looking at the biggest cunt in the Army.' From out in front I could hear the men behind me having a quiet laugh.

Jack Kirby was total guts. He never gave up during our runs at Enoggera even though his weight and height made it tough for him. He moved around the lines and talked to all the soldiers in all the platoons, not limiting himself to Company HQ. But he could surely bellow orders and the men knew he meant business. I appreciated his advice from time to time. He had common sense. He was my right-hand man and, above all, always loyal. Sadly he was to be killed by a tragic NZ artillery friendly fire disaster in February 1967.

Once in Vietnam, our 1st Australian Task Force (1ATF) was made up of about 5000 troops – in former military times it would have been known as a brigade. 1ATF included a headquarters with a brigadier commander, Oliver David Jackson OBE; two Infantry battalions (5RAR and 6RAR); an artillery regiment of three batteries, each of six guns, with two Australian field batteries, 103 and 105, and the 161 NZ Battery; plus a US Army 155-mm battery of six guns mounted on tracks, like tanks; and a US 8-inch nuclear-capable battery of two guns used for long-range interdiction. 1ATF also carried engineers, signals and an SAS squadron.

Each battalion, with about 850 men and commanded by a lieutenant colonel (ours being Colin Townsend) had a HQ and four rifle companies, A, B, C and D, plus Administration and Support companies.

Each rifle company, like my Delta Company, had 125 men: a HQ, plus a support section with two machine guns, and three platoons each of 34 men made up by three sections of 10 men. Platoons also had a HQ, commanded by a second lieutenant or lieutenant, a sergeant, a signaller and a batman.

Companies had cooks, a clerk, storemen and attached medical orderlies. Also attached were two regimental signallers and a mortar fire control sergeant, plus an artillery Forward Observer team of an officer and two signallers.

It was usual for the 2IC and cooks and the like to stay on base, so on any given day, along with some sick, some on local leave, and some detached to Task Force HQ area duties, not all 125 members of any company would be out on patrol. One hundred and five went out to Long Tan.

Brigadier Oliver David Jackson.

When on the move, it was usual to travel in single file – or one-up or two-up with the HQ group behind the leading platoon, and 10 m between men. Within platoons there were the same formations. In defence it was customary to have two platoons up front with HQ centre rear and a reserve platoon in the rear, thus creating all-round defence, with machine gun arcs of fire linked to cover 360 degrees. On open ground a defensive layout could take up an area 400 m wide and similar in depth, but half that size in jungle.

Each platoon had a large and heavy PRC9 VHF radio transmitter, which was on the company frequency. Company HQ (CHQ) had a set tuned onto the platoon channel and also one to Battalion HQ, and we had one spare radio in Company HQ with which we could contact helicopters or fighter plane Forward Air Controllers if required. The three-man artillery party with CHQ had two radios on their artillery nets. The VHF radios could be quickly switched to cover any frequency and during the battle of Long Tan I think every unit in the Task Force was listening or switching between my two radio networks, one to HQ6RAR, the other to my platoons.

Each rifle section had an M60 machine gun, and there were two in CHQ Support Section for me to do whatever I wished with them. So in the company we had 11 M60s, about 65 SLR 7.62-mm rifles, about 20 Colt

Armalite AR15 and AR16 5.56-mm (USA) rifles, and about 10 9-mm F1 Owen guns, which were mostly useless over the longer ranges in the Long Tan rubber plantation.

My lines at Nui Dat.

The Armalites were mostly old hand-me-downs from 1RAR and had problems, some say they were worn out. And I don't think many came with cleaning rods to clear frequent separated bullet cases. Some of the reinforcements who came from 1RAR, like Bill Roche, had actually bought their own new Armalites from US Army stores at Bien Hoa for US$85. The SLR was the outstanding rifle, but perhaps not quite on a par with the smaller Russian AK47 Kalashnikov 7.62-mm assault rifle used by the NVA and Main Force enemy and pretty much worldwide these days. The AK47 designer passed away in 2014 and a media article said some 12 million had been made in various countries. The AK47 was rough compared with nicely machined weapons, but worked under most conditions when others often clogged with dirt.

The 7.62-mm SLR was a self-loading battle rifle produced by the Belgian armaments manufacturer Fabrique Nationale de Herstal. During the Cold War it was adopted by many North Atlantic Treaty Organization (NATO) countries, with the notable exception of the United States. It was one of the most widely used rifles in history, having been adopted by over 90 countries, but now replaced in most by the AK47, also 7.62 mm, but with a shorter round.

Our L1A1 SLRs were Australian-made after 1959, while in Malaya we'd used the UK issue of the original FN. SLRs were more reliable than the first Armalites and preferred by riflemen as the bullet stopped the enemy, full stop. But the lighter Armalites were preferred for use by commanders and others who were not 'up front' and they could be tucked under an arm while reading maps.

Every section rifleman carried about 110 rounds of ammo, and several also carried spare MG belts of 200 rounds. The SLRs in 1966 only had three issued magazines holding 20 rounds each – only 60 rounds loaded – and the other bullets were in cardboard boxes of 20, which got wet and soggy so all the ammo fell out into the mud when we were reloading. After Long Tan more magazines were issued and resupply ammo was pre-loaded in magazines.

There was no typical German Spandau magazine for the M60 (US version of the Spandau) belt ammo and we used to put plastic sleeping mattress tubes on them to try and keep the dirt off the bullets. I banned my soldiers from sleeping on issue plastic mattresses as the tubes had a habit of making squeaking noises which were not good news in quiet overnight patrol bases, so we cut them up for the M60 belts. Despite that, we had five of 11 M60s out of action by the end of the Long Tan battle. Like old Armalites, they did not like mud.

We had been issued with the man-carried 84-mm Karl Gustav anti-tank weapons in Australia but the Swedes would not provide ammunition for use in the Vietnam War, and so we were then issued with the lighter M79 grenade launchers and had at least two per section.

Our endeavours were always to get ourselves better equipment. Such is life in the Australian military, or it was then. I have been told that the soldiers still struggle to get top equipment for their tours of Afghanistan although they seem to have ample modern and good weapons even though boot soles often fall off. Last Anzac Day regular soldiers back from Afghanistan complained they were not permitted to wear their medals on their field dress and were unable to wear parade uniforms as their shoe soles were faulty. Surely an exception to usual protocol could have been made so they could march through Brisbane proudly wearing their medals in field dress?

We were supposed to spend two weeks in Vung Tau getting acclimatised but on 14 June we were called forward to the new Australian Task Force base at Nui Dat about 40km north of Vung Tau, a week ahead of time. There were rumours of a possible enemy attack on the base. And there is no doubt that while no attack eventuated, the VC had plans to eradicate the 'US Puppets' at some time.

The camp was in a mature rubber plantation and the ground was wet red mud. We slept in our basic poncho shelters or hootchies until 16 x 16 tents arrived, and we then set about improving our standard of living. It was my philosophy that we needed a comfortable base so that we could rest after patrols. I could see that the base area was similar to the bases in Malaya and I told my men that any fool could be uncomfortable, but with a little effort, we could be very comfortable.

We dug drains and developed pathways using the aggregate gravel dug from trenches and even lined the paths with small banana trees brought in from an old plantation outside the wire, not that we had much wire at that time, nor any mines, as the hierarchy head-in-the-sand mindset was that the enemy would never attack our base. Our comfortable company base area became the source of another conflict with the CO, especially when I put barbed wire across the rear boundary in case enemy got through another company area.

The workforce was supplemented by men who chose 'my punishment' for misdemeanours rather than being formally charged. The only men who had to be referred to the commanding officer were those few guilty of accidental discharge of weapons or absent without leave after rare R and R breaks to Vung Tau, known as 'Vungers'. One of the soldiers who had come to us from 1RAR when it went home was Terry Burstall. Terry was often 'on the mat' in my tent office and chose 'my punishment'. Things in my company were a lot different to the time he was in 1RAR attached to 173

US Airborne Brigade at Bien Hoa. After Vietnam he was to get a PhD and become an author of two books about Vietnam, *The Soldier's Story* and *A Soldier Returns.*

Our lines at Nui Dat.

Led by Jack Kirby, Sergeant Bob Buick, Quartermaster Senior Sergeant Ron Gildersleeve and Mortar Sergeant Don Thompson we purloined parts of alloy huts from US Army sources and built an Officers/Sergeants Mess and a large Canteen hut for the NCOs and soldiers. Our cook, Sergeant Bill O'Donnell, ensured we ate well.

As the grass is always greener over the other side of the fence, we swapped our beer and slouch hats for US Schlitz and Budweiser beer and building materials, plus the steak and chicken packs mentioned earlier. The US Special Services Unit gave us a TV set with which we watched the nightly TV news and comedy shows broadcast from planes circling around Saigon. The US Army 155-mm and 8-inch Artillery people attached to the Task Force seemed to have plenty of R-rated movies to show on a screen in our canteen, and we often had fun nights, laughing at all the antics on the screen.

We sure as hell needed those fun nights considering the disaster that was to engulf us in August.

SEVEN

VIETNAM: SUICIDE MISSION

HISTORICAL BACKGROUND

Political alliances and obligations aside, how any American or Australian military adviser to the US President or Australia's Prime Minister could have argued a case for starting or joining a war in Vietnam beggars belief.

A 12-year-old school kid with even a passing interest in Southeast Asian history would have clearly seen that taking on the North Vietnamese, let alone the firmly infiltrated Viet Cong in the south, was tantamount to a suicide mission.

Yet, courtesy of the Menzies Government and out unilateral obligations, we embarked on just that.

The Vietnamese history is among the longest continuous histories in the world. With extremely fine poetry and art, and a centuries-old fight for independence, the Vietnamese also are deep-rooted masters of guerilla warfare. Their unique style of demolishing the enemy was first recorded 600 years before the birth of Jesus Christ and it was imitated to the very effective letter by Communist leader-heroes. Among these leaders was the multi-reinvented Ho Chi Minh, who was raised in a Vietnamese village, French-educated, a sometime Harlem baker who turned himself finally into the 'Bringer of Light' and became a long oppressed people's latest god. But he was also an accomplished student and very smart.

In 1941, Ho had returned to Vietnam to lead the Viet Minh independence movement, also operating with his legendary 'men in black', a 10,000-member guerilla force. Ho had learned a great deal about communism during his 30-year absence in France, Russia and then China, to be exiled after Chiang Kai-shek's anti-communist purge in 1927.

The Cuban foco theorists and the anti-Soviet Mujahideen in Afghanistan are late runners in adopting ancient Chinese general, military strategist and philosopher Sun Tzu's *Art of War*, penned in the 6th century BC. His hit-and-run acts of scavenging and seizing booty in enemy territory were highly successful even back then.

The central principle was moulded around forefront actions by units of small, fast-moving paramilitary groups to provide a focus for popular discontent against a sitting regime, and thus lead to general insurrection.

Chairman Mao Tse-Tung adopted Sun Tzu's *Art of War* military science and in turn handed on his own guerilla warfare and propaganda guidelines to the likes of Ho Chi Minh. Ho also inherited an understanding and reverence for the tyrannical tactics set down by Karl Marx and faithfully, some say mindlessly, adopted by Lenin, Stalin and Mao. Pol Pot later rode the same ideological wave to the mantra of winning the hearts and minds of the populace who, if they resisted, would have their bodies desecrated and ripped apart in the most painful acts of unpardonable punishment – traditionally in front of their families and fellow villagers.

Vietnamese landowner and resistance leader Le Loi launched a hugely effective guerilla war over 10 years against the Chinese invaders in the 15th century. His strategy was to win – by torture, rape and terror – the hearts and minds of the country peasants. Chillingly, his close friend, Nguyen Trai, a poet, wrote in 1426, 'Better to conquer hearts than citadels.' How was that for pre-empting and nailing the coming Communist doctrine centuries later?

Conspicuously, 200 years earlier the Vietnamese had defeated Kublai Khan's great Mongol invaders – not just once but three times. The defeat began with concentrated guerilla tactics and only ended in western-style open charge warfare once the Mongol hordes were so muddled and worn down they couldn't distinguish which end of their mounts were where or what.

The Vietnamese were born and bred in an ocean of blood. It may even have been as far back as Vietnam's beginnings around 500,000 BC but certainly was recorded several hundred years before the first Anno Domini that these uniquely devoted and impervious people were fighting for their ideological independence and physical freedom. In between wars under their warlords, and yes, their warladies, they were indulging in fertility festivals of sexual abandonment, primitive animistic cults, haunting music and poetry, fishing, hunting, cultivating rice and happily chewing Betel nuts.

Left to live in peace they were a pleasant and happy humankind. Today, I hold dear my friendships with the Vietnamese people now living in Australia.

In our modern era, our military leaders, our politicians needed only to read this one quote to realise the enormity of joining a war against the

Communists: *'In the army the task of supporting the government and cherishing the people should be handled through the ideological education of every commander and fighter, so they all thoroughly understand its importance. As long as the army on its part does the job well, the local government and the people will also improve their relations with the army.'*

Born in 1893, Mao Zedong, or Mao Tse-tung, was the son of a peasant farmer. He became a Marxist while working at Peking University as a library assistant and served in the revolutionary army during the 1911 Chinese Revolution.

He was inspired by the Russian Revolution and adapted the ideas of Lenin. Hence Mao proclaimed that in Asia it was important to concentrate on the countryside rather than the towns to create a revolutionary elite.

Mao was the supreme strategist and became one of the most powerful men in the modern world. He was also responsible for millions of deaths, including those in Vietnam by his protégés who simply re-invented and then perpetrated the centuries-old bloody avalanche of the murders of the innocents.

In 1937 when Japanese imperialists were occupying China, Mao Tse-tung produced an instruction manual on guerilla warfare in which he discussed the differences between guerilla and 'orthodox' military forces, as well as how such forces can work together for a common goal.

His theory of a People's War divided warfare into three phases. In Phase One, the guerillas earn the population's support by distributing propaganda and attacking the organs of government. In Phase Two, escalating attacks are launched against the government's military forces and vital institutions. In Phase Three, conventional warfare and fighting are used to seize cities, overthrow the government, and assume control of the country.

This Maoist model was adapted by Ho Chi Minh and brilliant military strategist and soldier Vo Nguyen Giap; thus the Communists had a superb integrated political and military strategy, perfected and waiting for the arrival of the American and Australian forces – professional and brave soldiers, yes, but hardly programmed to the extent of their adversaries.

Mao proudly quotes his Marx-inspired hero, Vladimir Lenin, in his book:

Lenin, in *On Guerrilla Warfare* said: 'As regards the form of fighting, it is unconditionally requisite that history be investigated in order to discover the conditions of environment, the state of economic progress and the political ideas that obtained, the national characteristics, customs, and degree of civilization.' Again: 'It is necessary to be completely unsympathetic to abstract formulas and rules and to study with sympathy the conditions of the actual fighting, for these will change in accordance with the political and economic situations and the realisation of the people's aspirations. These progressive changes in conditions create new methods.'

One wonders how many American and Australian military advisers to their heads of state read Mao – or even Lenin – before they committed their thousands of men and women to the Vietnam War.

Yet, in spite of the World War II and Korea stratagems rooted in my superior officers, I used my Malaya experience and prevailed with what I knew would save my soldiers' lives against a formidable enemy. I managed to prepare my Delta Company soldiers for jungle warfare so perfectly, beyond their meagre four weeks at Canungra Jungle School, that just a few months later 105 of them plus three New Zealand Artillery soldiers, with wonderful artillery support, were able to win out over at least 2000 of Ho's indoctrinated soldiers, most of whom just happened to also be expert guerilla fighters.

China's ability to aid the Viet Minh against the 75 years of French colonialist domination of Vietnam had declined when Soviet aid to China was reduced after the end of the Korean War in 1953. Then a Vietnam divided by the 1954 Geneva Accord saw Viet Minh communists relegated to the north and French and Republic support to the south, and this posed less of a threat to China. So China provided hundreds of millions of dollars of material and technical support to the Vietnamese Communists to try and unite the country under communism. Chinese-supplied rice allowed North Vietnam to pull military-age men from the paddies and to impose a universal draft that began in 1960.

In the summer of 1962, however, Mao agreed to resource Hanoi with 90,000 free rifles and guns. From 1965, China sent anti-aircraft units and engineering battalions to North Vietnam to repair the damage caused by American bombing, rebuild roads and railroads, and to perform other engineering works. This freed North Vietnamese Army units for combat in the south.

The Vietnam War has been defined as the prolonged struggle between nationalist forces intent on unifying Vietnam under a Communist government – and the United States, with the aid of the South Vietnamese, and 'free world' allies fighting to prevent the spread of Communism.

After years of playing political dirty pool and often getting snookered, the first American ground troops went in during March 1965. US military involvement ended on 15 August 1973. With the northern half of the country under its control, the Hanoi politburo ordered the final offensive against Saigon. The plan for the Ho Chi Minh campaign called for the capture of Saigon before 1 May. Hanoi wanted to avoid the coming monsoon and prevent any redeployment of Army of the Republic of Vietnam forces defending the capital. The struggle ended ignobly for the already departed allies on 30 April 1975, with the fall of Saigon.

North and South Vietnam reunified the following year on 2 July. The war wrought a huge human cost in fatalities alone. Estimates of the number of Vietnamese soldiers and civilians killed vary from 800,000 to 1 million. Some 200,000 to 300,000 Cambodians, 20,000 to 200,000 Laotians and 58,220 US service members also died in the conflict. Approximately 60,000 Australians served in the war; 521 were killed and more than 3000 were wounded. But like the American veterans, these figures do not consider the horrendous mental illnesses such as PTSD that so many Aussie diggers suffered and are still suffering, not to mention the physical illnesses suffered by veterans and their children.

Viet Cong insurgents knew exactly how to capture the hearts and minds, let alone the free extra fighting force extracted from the locals. They reportedly sliced off the genitals of village chiefs and sewed them inside their bloody mouths, disembowelled civilians to drive home psychological warfare, cut off the tongues of helpless victims, rammed bamboo lances through one ear and out the other, slashed open the wombs of pregnant women, machine gunned children, hacked men and women to pieces with machetes, and cut off the fingers of small children who dared to get an education. Squads were assigned monthly assassination quotas and the Cong killed at least 37,000 civilians in South Vietnam.

North Vietnam was also known for its inhumane and abusive treatment of American POWs, most notably in Hoa Lo Prison, alias the Hanoi Hilton, where severe torture was used to extract 'confessions'.

But none of the above takes into consideration the atrocities perpetrated by the French who were involved in or ruled Vietnam from 1858 to 1954. Little wonder that the populace was so ripe for picking by the Communists.

Vietnam was complicated from the beginning. The main military organisations involved in the war were, on one side, the Army of the Republic of Vietnam (ARVN), the US military and America's allies and, on the other side, the Vietnam People's Army (VPA), also known as the North Vietnamese Army (NVA), and the Viet Cong, or National Front for the Liberation of South Vietnam (NLF), the South Vietnamese Communist guerilla force.

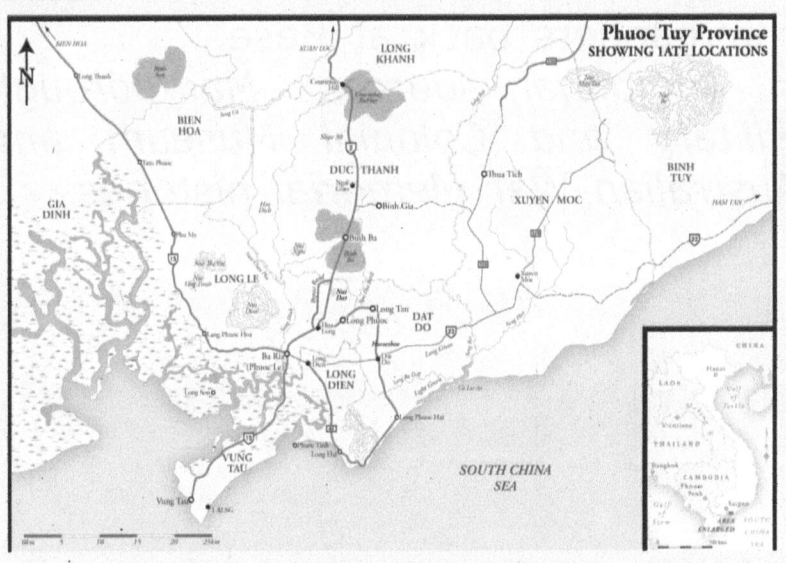

Australia's involvement in the war began with a commitment of just 30 men as Advisers in 1962, known as 'The Dirty Thirty'. By 1972 it would send almost 60,000 personnel to Vietnam, including ground troops, naval forces and air resources.

Some have said that Long Tan, in spite of its casualties, could well have gone the other way under a different commander. I accept that view as testament to my own training, experience and ability – how I trained my brave men, and how I commanded the battle against vastly superior enemy forces, using all the support I could muster from reluctant commanders back at Base.

Additional sources: Maryborough Military and Colonial Museum and Australian War Memorial histories.

EIGHT

BATTLE BEGINNINGS

The Battle of Long Tan was fought in frightful conditions against impossible odds on 18 August 1966. It is regarded and chosen by the Vietnam Veterans' Association as the most significant battle of Australia's involvement in the Vietnam War and has since taken on the well-worn handle 'iconic'. Although many claim Coral-Balmoral in 1968 to have been a much bigger battle, which it was, it was a Task Force operation fought by up to 2000 troops, with centurian tanks, ample artillery and air support including 'Puff the Magic Dragon' aircraft with revolving miniguns pouring out thousands of rounds per minute into the enemy, over a period of three weeks during which time 25 Australians were killed, with 276 enemy bodies located and no doubt more taken away.

Long Tan was the most significant sharp and savage defensive battle fought by just a single infantry company during Australia's participation in the

Vietnam War, losing 17 dead in four hours and accounting for almost 300 enemy, 293 bodies and four wounded taken prisoner, with many more taken away. More enemy were killed than by the battalions at Coral-Balmoral over three weeks. And I wish I had the tanks and air support that was available at Coral-Balmoral.

In the true spirit of the ANZACS, our small group of Australian soldiers, outnumbered by almost 20 to 1, fought this ferocious battle for near four hours against a superior regular Viet Cong regimental force bolstered by North Vietnam Army troops and efficient local D445 provincial soldiers – before the tide eventually turned in the unyielding Diggers' favour. It was and is a big story.

I almost did not get to Vietnam after a hearing test showed up high frequency deafness beyond the limit for Fit Everywhere Medicals. Very physically fit in other respects I had to argue with impregnable conviction that I was a company commander and not a forward scout and that, 'My men are my ears.' I got my bad hearing while a National

Service platoon commander conducting frequent range practices from a firing position under a tin roof for almost three years. The noise, the level of which can be equated to causing industrial deafness, was horrific and we had no regulated 'mickey mouse' ear protection.

I won out and was retained in the battalion and on 8 June 1966 we were flown to Vietnam in a chartered Boeing 707 via a refuelling stop in Manila. We were all intrigued by the very pretty young ladies around the terminal. Although I do not think my soldiers became involved, some men, not necessarily soldiers, found happiness with Filipina ladies and beautiful Thai women who were called the rather disparaging term 'Thai Takeaways'. Some who married and brought their brides to Australia found they were then 'taken to the cleaners' and lost houses and life savings. Others have been happy.

We were very pleased to go to South Vietnam and help in fighting the Communists. The plan was to stop the Communists moving further south, country by country – what was known as the domino effect theory. To me, as a young career officer it was a very worthwhile cause, and all my officers and soldiers were enthusiastic about going to help South Vietnam. It was also an adventure with the added benefits of an income tax-free salary plus a whole 75 cents a day combat pay and a way of getting better equipment, sadly always necessarily high on our priority list. And, as far as our Army was concerned, it was giving the race horses a run.

Of course, while we thought that maybe a few of us might be killed or wounded, we were given the impression that down south near the old French seaside resort town of Vung Tau, we would only be fighting local Viet Cong guerilla forces, as in Malaya, and we never imagined that 105 of us, plus a three-man New Zealand Artillery Team, would have to fight for our lives against about 2000 regular Viet Cong and North Vietnamese Army enemy at Long Tan, where my company regrettably lost 17 killed with 23 wounded, most of them young National Servicemen.

The news of Long Tan hit the headlines big time around Australia, in fact around the world. In Australia there was a public outcry at the loss of so many young National Service soldiers, particularly after the facts were flaunted in the US anti-war propaganda and moratoriums of 1970-71, which Australian protesters joined. Our Army was finally forced to withdraw in late 1973, just before the US forces pulled out.

After Long Tan I slated the allocation and standard of our equipment in contrast with the enemy's weapons and this gave rise to all our 9-mm Owen machine guns, which were great in New Guinea jungles, but useless in open country in Vietnam, being replaced. Commander Australian Force Vietnam the (late) Major-General Ken Mackay in Saigon HQ actually put his head on the chopping block because he ordered Colt Armalites without Canberra approval after I was called to Saigon to brief the world press about the battle and met up with the general. That was when I told him the Owen had been useless and the ammunition belts for the M60 did not have a magazine like the original German Spandau – the US did not produce similar magazines to keep the ammo clean. I have noticed in Afghanistan and Middle East media coverage that all light machine guns now have ammunition boxes attached.

Briefing the world press in Saigon.

At that time I thought General Mackay was an upfront officer but later I changed my mind when he downgraded Long Tan awards in favour of awards for senior officers far from the battle. He also apparently had a lot to do with rejecting the offer of Vietnamese awards and not forwarding Imperial award citation forms back to Canberra. Most of our award justice problems have been caused by those forms 'disappearing' in Vietnam rather than being filed for a normal post-war awards review.

For five years I had been with Army School Cadets in Hobart. I recall having great days on the range with the old belt-fed Vickers Medium Machine Gun. I wish I had had the Vickers in defence at Long Tan, as the M60s without the ammo magazines were easily stopped by the dirt on the belts. The Vickers MMGs were carried up the Kokoda trail, so we could have carried them too, or brought them in by choppers. But then we would have needed 7.62 mm versions to be compatible with our rifle ammunition.

Let me go back a bit. In Vietnam the US Air Force started bombing North Vietnam on 7 February 1965, and in March 1965 3500 US Marines went ashore at Da Nang. The Communist People's Army of Vietnam and National Liberation Front Forces increased their presence in South Vietnam in that anxious year of 1965.

To show support for the Government of the Republic of Vietnam and the USA, in August 1962 Australia had sent in the first 30 men of the Australian Army Training Team – the 'Dirty Thirty' – to give advice to South Vietnamese battalions. Then in June 1965 Australia sent the 1 RAR Battalion Group of about 1500 men to Bien Hoa, attached to US 173 Airborne Brigade, near Saigon, now Ho Chi Minh City.

The group included a NZ Artillery Battery, 161 Battery; the Australian 105 Artillery Battery; an APC troop; a Field Engineer Troop; 161 Recce Flight and a Logistics Company. This was an ANZAC Force. But working with the Americans was not that successful and it was decided to increase the Australian force to a Task Force of some 5000 men and take over responsibility of a separate area.

Australia wanted to establish its own force away from US influence. US Army-led operations were often flawed because they were prepared to take heavy casualties in their 'up the front' tactics, whereas we could not afford the casualties and sought other ways of attacking, often from the flank. Also, in New Guinea and Malaya we had learnt the value of sneaking quietly through the jungle. A former Army of the Republic of Vietnam officer Tien Nguyen told me that, in contrast, the Americans relied heavily on their superior fire power, and went on patrol in the jungle as if they were going on a picnic. The Viet Cong nicknamed them 'elephants' because of the noise they made and because the smell of their aftershave and Salem cigarettes could be detected miles away. Some, but not all, US troops also carried portable radios, dropped their rubbish, and generally moved around in close formations; to our way of training, totally unprofessional. But they also employed some excellent units, such as the Marines and green-beret Special Forces.

Planning for a Task Force base at Nui Dat in Phuoc Tuy province about 80km south of Saigon had begun in 1965 and was established when 1RAR went home in June 1966, with 23 men having been killed in action and 130 men wounded in action, many from mines, which were to cause most of the casualties in the following years of the long war.

Let me say here that in later years I came to realise that what the Australian people had been officially told about our entry into the war was similar to the story we were told about the Iraq War – not necessarily the truth. Very obviously our Vietnam commitment had been decided long before, as the introduction of National Service in 1965 paved the way for providing all the required troops to be seen to support the USA. Politically we had to support the US as no doubt we would want its help if we were invaded. We were known by the Viet Cong as 'US Puppets'.

The NLF regular enemy 5th Division had established its HQ in Phuoc Tuy/Ba Ria province in late 1965, based in the north-eastern May Tao mountains area, with 274 and 275 Regiments in the northwest and northeast respectively, and joined by the local provincial mobile battalion D445 in the south, which had been re-raised at Xa Long Tan village in 1965. In addition most villages had small guerilla units. Colloquially, all the National Front for the Liberation of South Vietnam (NLF) and local forces were referred to as VC (Viet Cong), with North Vietnamese Army units being NVA.

All up, there were seven enemy battalions and support units totalling close to 5000 troops. These did not include reinforcements from other provinces or any NVA units arriving in the Phuoc Tuy (Ba Ria) province. The 5000-strong 1ATF was to be inserted from May 1966. It would comprise Artillery units, an APC Squadron, a Special Air Service (SAS) Squadron, Engineers and other support troops, but with just two Infantry battalions with only four rifle companies of 120 men each. Taking out those on leave, sick or on base duties, left only about 800 Infantry fighting troops all up.

Government Army of the Republic of Vietnam (ARVN) battalions were in various regional government-controlled town centres like Hoa Long, Ba Ria and Xuan Moc. The 10th ARVN Division was based in Long Khanh province to the north, with a Sector HQ in nearby Ba Ria with an Australian Army Training Team Vietnam Liaison Officer Captain Mike Wells of 1 Commando Company on full-time duty. One of Mike's tasks was to attend regular Task Force briefings and pass on all the considerable intelligence information that was available from ARVN units and their agents spread throughout the province. Mike served with me in 1 Commando in Sydney after Vietnam. Years later he joined the Webb Dock wharfies' union fight. He now lives in Melbourne and we catch up from time to time. In recent years Mike has been able to add a great deal more information about the situation pre-Long Tan and after the battle, which had not been made publicly available.

It was usual for ARVN units to be based in most towns and outposts but they had a high rate of attrition from Viet Cong attacks, the enemy often killing families as well as soldiers. Most local people were on side with the Communist NLF forces by submission, rather than by will. Terrorism of villagers, especially village heads, or anyone who would not cooperate with the VC or who showed support for foreign troops was rampant. Public beheadings and other acts of savagery were common.

We were not well briefed by our military masters as to the enemy's organisation and the possible threat in the area which was to become the 1ATF area of operations in mid-1966. We were not made aware that in January 1965 NLF Forces of the 9th Division, which had come down from war zone D north of Saigon, virtually wiped out two ARVN battalions at Binh Gia just 30km north of Nui Dat where our base was to be established.

In April 1966, only a month before Nui Dat was occupied, the forward company of a US battalion was ambushed and isolated at Cam My, about 20km north of Nui Dat. The US battalion plan was to get the enemy to attack the leading company and then attack them but it was cut off by jungle and their inexperienced Artillery controllers were unable to give effective support fire.

The enemy, the northern provincial mobile battalion, D800, used well-proven tactics of getting inside the Artillery fire, 'holding them by the belt', then encircling the opposition and over-running it. Only 23 of the 134 US company soldiers were found alive, with most wounded discovered with their throats cut as the enemy moved in to retrieve their own casualties at night and stopped to leave their bloody messages en route.

The US Army's 'Big Red One', the 1st Infantry Division with three brigades and ARVN units attached, cleared Long Tan village (Xa Long Tan) on Operation 'Abilene' in April 1966 with little opposition. The ARVN troops then went in and resettled the villagers to other areas, such as Hoa Long and Xuan Moc. The local VC then mortared the US troops and in return they shelled and bombed the deserted village to virtual oblivion. Then there was the US Army operation 'Hardihood' in late May 1966. The American 173 Airborne Brigade cleared out the area around the proposed Australian base and Long Phuoc area in conjunction with ARVN units. The US Army force had attached the Australian APC troop from the 1RAR Group at Bien Hoa which included the future 3 Troop APC commander

Lieutenant Adrian Roberts. The American 1/503 Battalion sustained heavy casualties from D445, fighting mostly from tunnels just northwest of the Long Phuoc village area. They lost 19 killed and suffered 90 wounded.

On 24 May 5RAR moved up into Nui Dat from Vung Tau and started patrolling. That day the first National Service man, Private Errol Noak, was killed by friendly fire when Alpha Company fired on a Bravo Company listening post. It was reported by Task Force Commander Brigadier Oliver David Jackson to Army HQ as 'enemy action'! Thankfully that cover-up was later revised.

Although it was thought the two VC regiments of 5 Division, 274 and 275, were not in the local area, the October 1966 captured diary of Col Nguyen Nam Hung, deputy commander of 274 Regiment, indicated the regiment had intended to attack our new and undeveloped Nui Dat base on 10 June but then decided to set a major ambush on a light plane wreckage it had shot down just to the north. But 5RAR did not go out as expected, as the wreckage could not be pinpointed from the air, and the enemy withdrew.

Warnings from ARVN friendly sources about VC intentions to attack the base were such that 6RAR was called forward from Vung Tau to Nui Dat on 14 June, 10 days ahead of the original set date of 23 June. Now people are saying the enemy never contemplated attacking our Nui Dat base! They have short memories. I am aware the VC normally kept clear of well-defended allied bases but Nui Dat was poorly manned and defended, with no minefields and little barbed wire obstacles – a good target for a military and political victory.

In early June 5RAR had contact with small VC groups along the river 1500 m to the northwest of Nui Dat, explained as being nothing but mainly 'ineffective guerillas' – a quote from Second Lieutenant Dennis Rainer in the AWM Official History, who was awarded an MC for his platoon killing just three of eight enemy guerillas in a brief action, setting a standard for the gallantry MC similar to that which applied in Malaya and Borneo.

Both battalions were then heavily engaged in patrolling and 6RAR was sent out to Long Phuoc in late June on Operation Enoggera from the 21 June to 5 July to level the village and remove any VC using the deserted terrain. Tunnels, weapons and supplies were located but the only fire was from snipers, with probably one enemy killed and three wounded. The nearby Xa Long Tan village, 2km to the east, previously considered an aggressive village and 100 percent Communist – if not in spirit – had been deserted since the villagers were resettled in April and houses were badly damaged by bombing and artillery fire. I cannot recall my company ever patrolling into the deserted Long Tan village. In more recent years large tunnel complexes have been revealed by the former enemy, running 3km from Long Phuoc to Hoa Long and Long Tan, which were never located by our forces during the war.

Long Phuoc was razed and we unfortunately had to destroy many lovely old French-style homes with teak furniture. Sadly, we shot a suspicious figure dressed in black who suddenly appeared from the scrub, but it turned out to be an unarmed woman. We buried her and marked the grave with dignity. The soldier who shot her still feels regret, but she was dressed in black and out of bounds, so we automatically assumed she was the enemy. You don't have time to ask questions unless the suspect immediately holds their arms up, as if surrendering. Like in Malaya, it was kill or be killed.

On 19 July at 11.10am we had our first official VC 'kill' 4000 m southeast of the ATF area just off the road along the south of the rubber plantation on the same track 1km west of Xa Long Tan that led north 1500 m up into the rubber where 11 Platoon had its first contact on 18 August. A leading section of a half-strength 10 Platoon day patrol saw two enemy apparently having lunch, who fired at them. One was killed by then Private later Corporal Bill Roche with his M16 Armalite rifle. Bill was Regular Army and came to us from 1RAR Bien Hoa – he later went back with the 6RAR second tour and was one of the soldiers at the Cross dedication in the rubber in 1969. Later, Bill served in 1 Commando and then aided me in my campaign for awards justice. With a wonderful home library, he was able to provide the 2008 Long Tan Review panel with figures about awards given to battalions during the war, not known by the Prime Minister and Cabinet Office clerk at the inquiry.

Delta Company first official VC 'kill'. Photo courtesy Bill Roche.

Section Commander Corporal 'Black Mac' McDonald may have wounded the other VC, who fled east. The dead enemy soldier had black trousers and a light khaki shirt and could have been D445 or a local village guerilla from the supposedly deserted villages nearby. He was armed with an AK47 assault rifle, which he had fired at 10 Platoon, and held a fresh magazine which could be seen on his left side. He had a whistle in his gear which may have meant he was an non commissioned officer or officer. And apart from plastic sheeting for a tent, he had a small green bottle of Australian mosquito repellent, possibly purloined for their soldiers by locals working around our Vung Tau or Nui Dat bases.

This AK47 was significant because our critics were to later claim we should have recognised that an AK47 captured at the scene of a contact at the start of Long Tan was obviously a sign of Main Force regular troops as they were not on issue to D445. But D445 obviously had a number of AK47s in July. Thus the one captured at the first contact at Long Tan was *not* that significant. An always clairvoyant former Captain Charles Mollison, who had just been 'moved on' from Alpha Company 2IC by Officer Commanding Major Peter Smeaton to be a Liaison Officer at Hoa Long Village in early July, wrote in his 2005 book *Long Tan and beyond: Alpha Company 6RAR in Vietnam 1966–67*: '...that the enemy dress and AK47 should have alerted Smith to the fact that these were not local VC but Main Force Troops'. This was just one of his many unwarranted snipes at my company and me.

Two 6RAR companies, Bravo and Charlie, were involved with D445 in Operation 'Hobart' on 25 July after reports of enemy in the area to the north and northeast of Long Tan village. Delta and Alpha Companies were further east of the main action. 6RAR lost three killed and 17 wounded for seven VC killed. It was in this action that Maryborough's Corporal Jock Rutherford was awarded the MM and the enemy became aware of our accurate artillery support, calling it 'NZ artillery rain'. Jock was a delightful gentleman with a Scots sense of humour. Sadly I went to his funeral in 2012.

In late 1967 another MM was retrospectively awarded to Private Winterford for gallantry at Operation 'Hobart'. This award was due to the efforts of his Charlie Company Commander Major Brian McFarlane who requested an internal 6RAR review of awards in May 1967.

On 29 July intelligence reports from Mike Wells at 10 ARVN Division Sector HQ at Ba Ria, indicated increasing enemy activity northwest of Nui Dat and aircraft receiving ground fire. Mike also advised HQ ATF that information was received from ARVN agents that the 5000 enemy of the VC 5th Division were moving south to attack the Nui Dat base. We now know from enemy history that 275 Regiment had moved south from its home base near the northern May Tao mountains and was near Xuan Moc, 20km east of Long Tan, on 29 July.

6RAR was called back to base the same day. In subsequent days Signals Intelligence radio intercept of Morse code traffic along with US Air Force

Radio Direction Finding aircraft information indicated HQ 275 Regiment radio was approaching from the east. It would eventually lodge just northeast of the Long Tan rubber plantation on 14 August. This information was kept secret from all but a few officers in Brigadier Jackson's Task Force HQ. The report of the slow movement of just 1km a day shown in a map in the AWM Official History has to be treated with suspicion as the enemy could march 20km a day. To only move for about 20 minutes a day – a 1000 m walk – and perhaps be observed by locals does not make sense. There is an opinion the distance of 20km from Xuan Moc to Long Tan was arbitrarily divided by the days from 29 July to 14 August, so it became about 1km per day. But there is now no doubt 275 Regiment came into the jungle area east of the Long Tan rubber plantation about that time, perhaps fed and guided by the local D445 who may have been the meeters, greeters and feeders. There was a large rice cache just to the east. And we now know D445 soldiers guided the 275 Regiment heavy weapons units to the west of the Long Tan rubber from where they fired on Nui Dat early on 17 August.

275 Regiment history tells that the various 5 Division and D445 commanders met at the Suoi Lo O Nho River about 5km east of the Long Tan rubber plantation on 10 August to discuss their plans to destroy the Australians. When the battle started on the 18 August, the enemy HQ is stated as being at Ap Phuoc Hong, about 2km to the northeast of Xa Long Tan and 3km east of the battlefield. While it has been argued by 'X Spurts' that the VC would no longer attack fortified US Army Bases, the ATF base was poorly defended and a long way from the nearest US Army base, an ideal target for a pincer attack by 275 Regiment in the east and 274 Regiment in the north which would protect that flank and block any US Army reinforcements coming down the highway from the north, with D445 protecting the southern flank from reinforcements coming up from Vung Tau. I am happy to believe 5 Division was going to attack Nui Dat, which is what two NVA prisoners claimed.

Back in June, long before Long Tan, because of threats of enemy attack, Brigadier Jackson had asked for US Army reinforcements but that was met with ridicule by the Americans. He'd also tried to warn Australian Force Vietnam in Saigon the enemy was gathering. Chief of the General Staff Lieutenant General John Wilton had disregarded Jackson's advice. From then on Jackson seems to have adopted Wilton's mindset.

The crisis subsided. Reports of enemy were dismissed as being ARVN or our own troops, with our intelligence people suggesting that no more than one Main Force battalion and D445 could be expected in the area, certainly not two regiments of six battalions plus D445. SAS patrols supposedly saw nothing to indicate a large force was approaching the Long Tan rubber plantation. Author Terry Burstall in his *The Soldier's Story* claimed in 1986 that SAS patrols alerted the Task Force to a heavy enemy build-up to the east of Nui Dat, but this was to be denied by the (late) OC Major John Murphy MC. However, another book *In Action with the SAS* indicates that a SAS patrol led by Sergeant Urquhart saw heavy enemy movement 16km northeast of Nui Dat on 17 August but his radio was jammed by interference and the information only came to hand on 19 August when the patrol was extracted by helicopter – all too late for us.

Despite all the evidence the 547 Signals Troop OC and the ATF junior intelligence officer could not convince Brigadier Jackson there was an attack pending. Any attack on Nui Dat base was considered a preposterous suggestion by the brigadier. He is on record in the Official History as having said 'The enemy wouldn't dare attack my base.'

Even my Commanding Officer Lieutenant Colonel Colin Townsend, is quoted in the Official History as saying, 'I don't think they would have been so stupid.' More famous last words. I won't here begin to include the language so many of my men and observers have used in regard to these two men's extraordinarily inadequate verdicts on the deadly situation.

Mike Wells told me some years ago when we caught up in Canberra that his reports to HQ Australian Task Force's daily conferences were considered 'unreliable', coming from 'just a CMF (Reserve Forces) officer'. So continued the dangerous academic attitude of Royal Military College graduate command officers!

At Nui Dat normal and hectic base improvement routine and local patrolling continued, with everyone looking forward to the Col Joye and Little Pattie concert on 18 August. Very little effort was made to erect barbed wire around the base, let alone minefields out front. The base was poorly defended and an easy target for the enemy.

Apart from administrative and support troops, there were normally only two Infantry companies – about 200 fighting soldiers – left in the large base, thinly spread around the lengthy forward defensive line, with platoons securing large company areas. Had the enemy attacked in force, they would have easily rolled on through and decimated the task force. Staff officers' efforts to alert Brigadier Jackson to the perilous defence status fell on his increasingly deaf ears.

5RAR was ordered to clear to the north up to mid-August but little enemy activity was seen. Further patrols were sent out east to 5000 m on 31 July and my own Delta Company searched, between 13 and 15 August, east of the base including the Long Tan rubber plantation as far east as the bottom of Nui Dat 2. But we were not sent to patrol the jungle further southeast and the enemy left us alone. I am of the opinion the enemy was moving into and resting in that jungle and did not wish to reveal their presence before their planned attack on the night of the 18th – after the concert and with most of the soldiers left in the base mellowed by a few beers.

Alpha Company 6RAR was then sent out to continue patrols northeast of the base and north of Nui Dat 2 on the 16th and had a few contacts, including the killing of a VC mortar officer. They were called back to the northwest of Nui Dat 2 on the afternoon of 17 August to be closer to base. I do not recall being told the fine details of Alpha

Company's contacts and that the enemy troops were dressed in greens and had automatic weapons – one carrying a circular 82-mm mortar base plate – which would indicate they were most likely Main Force soldiers. The former Acting OC of Alpha Company Captain Charles Mollison was later rightly critical of the 6RAR and ATF HQs in not assessing the importance of the company's contacts. Of course, none of the patrolling companies were told of the 'rumours' of enemy forces moving in, nor of the Signals intelligence. Given the mortaring of the Base on the 17th it was amazing that the planned concert was still permitted to go ahead on the 18th by Brigadier Jackson.

On 16 August one of my forward listening posts reported seeing enemy just outside our company base area and we fired 6RAR mortars at the area. In hindsight, they may well have been measuring the distance for the mortars to shell the base that night. On the night of the 16th and into the morning of 17 August, I had two of my three platoons securing other subunit bases, one in Alpha Company and one in the

APC Squadron areas. That same night we had a few drinks in our canteen with two visiting US Air Force (USAF) Phantom pilots from Bien Hoa Air Force base just out of Saigon, and then we went to bed at about midnight. At 2.40am I recall that the dull sounds of the usual ARVN Artillery war in the distant east, perhaps near Xuan Moc, were shattered by a continuous *pop-pop-pop* of mortars from closer in the east. I waited and listened. Then, about 30 seconds later came heavy explosions in our central Task Force, Artillery, Engineer and SAS areas as the rounds landed and exploded. Shit! Our base was being shelled, normally a preliminary to an attack.

In my hurry to get from my tent 100 m to our underground command post, I put my boots on the wrong feet without realising it, without socks, and I badly chafed some skin. I reported to Battalion HQ via a telephone Situation Report at 2.50am what I thought sounded like an Artillery gun firing and this is recorded in the 6RAR Operations Log. More than 100 mortar and recoilless rifle rounds struck the central base area. The barrage continued for 22 minutes. Twenty-four soldiers were wounded; seven vehicles and 21 tents were hit.

The Task Force Artillery responded from 2.50 until 4.10am with counter bombardment gunfire on suspected enemy positions near the west of the Long Tan rubber plantation, plotted from compass bearings taken to the sound of the firing positions. While some say radar assisted, I now gather the radar at the Artillery Locating Battery was not working. We stood-to on alert until dawn but no attack eventuated. To this day no one has been able to properly explain why the enemy fired on the base on the night of the 16th to 17th but did not follow up. The enemy history claims it was 'to draw the tiger from the mountain' either into ambush or to weaken the base for an attack which would most likely be on the night of the concert. Former Captain Ian Darlington of ATF HQ claimed it was to disrupt the artillery and Task Force HQ. For what reason, as there was no attack? I was to say the enemy made a mistake and fired on the wrong night.

The enemy knows, but has still not yet revealed all, probably reluctant to describe and admit a major defeat. They continue to claim they set ambushes to the south and east of Long Tan, but that defies logic and fact and is more likely propaganda to cover their defeat.

At 4.50am Bravo Company 6RAR, the only complete rifle company in base, rostered to start their first R & C local leave break at Vung Tau on the 18th, was ordered by Jackson via Townsend to move out at first light to look for the enemy positions west of Long Tan – the enemy thought to have long gone.

Bravo Company took no sleeping gear or rations, expecting no action and to be back in base for a late breakfast ordered for 9.30am! However, while they saw no enemy, they did locate five vacated VC 82mm mortar positions west of the rubber plantation and were told to stay out overnight, to be relieved on the 18th. Next morning they moved east to the rubber and located three recoilless rifle positions, an artillery gun position, and blood trails from enemy hit by our counter bombardment fire.

There were also fresh tracks leading away to the northeast and southeast. Bravo Company, led by Major Noel Ford, also came across three female fruit pickers with legal ID Cards and sent them on their way back to their village.

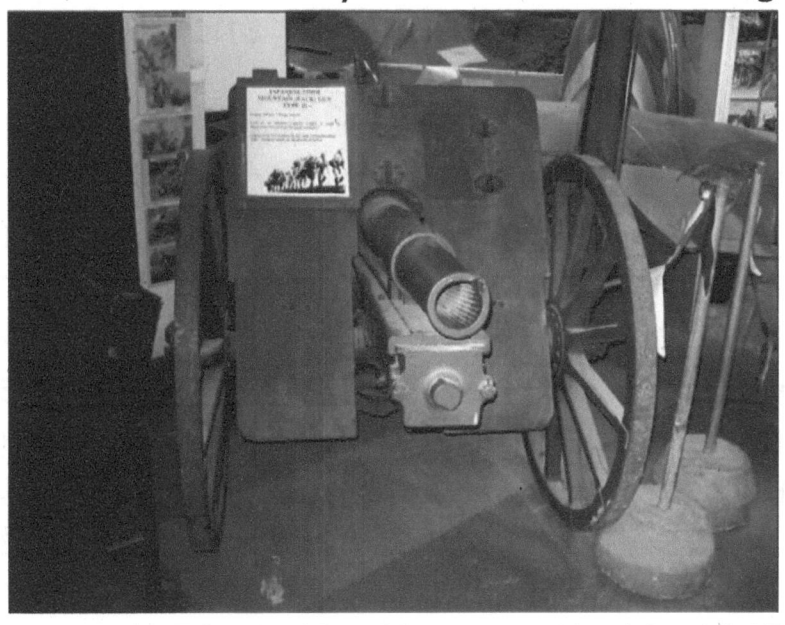

Japanese 70mm Howitzer captured in 1945. These were used by the Viet Cong.

Unknown to us, inspections by Task Force HQ staff on the 17th counted the craters of 67 82-mm mortar bombs, many 75-mm recoilless rifle rounds and at least five 70-mm artillery rounds, the latter coming from a World War II Japanese mountain gun, a Howitzer captured in 1945 and handed down over the years. Howitzers can have a high trajectory, which enables rounds to be fired over hills if needed – often very useful. They were used by the Japanese on the Kokoda track, and a World War II newsreel on Anzac Day 2014 showed our troops capturing one and turning it around onto the enemy.

Brigadier Jackson was personally shown enemy 82-mm mortar tail fins and evidence of 75-mm rockets, as well as an unexploded 70-mm round, clearly Main Force weapons, but he scoffed at the idea they were any more than weapons used by the local D445, yet they normally did not have heavy mortars and guns. His junior staff officers chose not to argue with the brigadier. The information was not passed on to battalions.

The penny did not drop about possible enemy Main Force attack. The secret 547 Signals Troop intelligence about 275 Regiment radio, which had been tracked moving in from the east was discarded by Brigadier Jackson as more likely to be just the HQ doing a reconnaissance. So after all the earlier warnings about enemy moving in on our base, I still wonder what the brigadier thought the bloody reconnaissance was for?

Unfortunately the junior ATF intelligence officer Captain Keep, who argued the 547 Signals Troop intelligence was indeed significant, had been flown to hospital in Malaya on 15 August and his superior, Major John Rowe, was also hospitalised at Vung Tau on the 16th with hepatitis. Thus, with the two intelligence officers in hospital, the pressure on Jackson about possible enemy attack had dissipated, and he could focus on the concert.

At 5.30pm on the evening of the 17th, Bravo Company was resupplied with rations by a porter party of 9 Platoon Charlie Company which had been redirected from an earlier task. This party then searched into the rubber south of Bravo Company, saw nothing of note and headed back to base at dusk. Next morning, the 18th, with no enemy threat perceived by either the Bravo Company Officer Commanding Major Noel Ford, Commanding Officer Lieutenant Colonel Colin Townsend or Commander 1ATF Brigadier Oliver

Jackson, at dawn Bravo Company was permitted to send 48 men back to base for a couple of days recreational leave at Vung Tau, leaving Company HQ and one platoon, just 32 men, to await relief before returning to base for leave.

I was told by phone at 8am to prepare to relieve Bravo Company but was not told of the larger enemy intelligence picture. Indeed, the battalion COs were not even told due to the supposed secrecy necessary to preserve the presence of the top secret Signals Intelligence Unit. Paul Ham states (on page 216) that Charles Mollison claimed in his own 2005 book:

> ...he was so convinced his company might strike a large enemy force on their patrol he had the Battalion Intelligence officer (IO) brief his company about the Sig Int on the 15th.

Paul Ham falls short of calling Mollison a liar but quotes 'a case of being wise after the event' as neither the Commanding Officer nor the Intelligence Officer were privy to the information. Indeed, circa 2006, when I asked our former intelligence officer why he had not given my company the same information, Bryan Wickens vehemently denied he so briefed Alpha Company.

Having then soon driven up to his HQ, I discussed the enemy with Lieutenant Colonel Townsend and we agreed that on the available information they were probably 40 to 50 of D445 60-mm mortar and RCL crews and they had long gone east the day before. Neither of us was told about the evidence of Main Force 82-mm mortars and other heavy weapons being fired into the base the previous morning and there was no mention to me of the Alpha Company contacts with a few, possibly Main Force, troops to the northwest of Nui Dat 2 on the 16th. The concert was the main item for that day, not a 'shoot and scoot' harassing attack by enemy mortars the night before. Lieutenant Colonel Townsend was almost apologetic in telling me to take Delta Company out to relieve Bravo because we would miss the music. As it turned out we would have our own – the music made by gunfire.

Indeed, given the attitude that we were only fighting guerillas, as in Malaya, and the heavy routine of patrolling and improving base conditions, little time was spent in educating ourselves as to the organisation and equipment of enemy forces, which were considerably more deadly than local guerillas. We had been issued in early June with a scenario that suggested the enemy could assemble a division in the Province, but as there were no reports of regular enemy nearby, that was filed. We assumed that if there were to be regular enemy forces approaching our area of operations we would have been warned by SAS Patrols and ARVN intelligence. HQ ATF knew, but did not pass it on to battalions.

In hindsight, Brigadier Jackson and others could have worked out that D445 60-mm mortars had a normal maximum range of only about 1500 m and that the 82-mm mortars were thus used over the longer range to hit the base. The fact that Bravo Company had located five vacated 82-mm mortar positions on the 17th did not hit a nerve at HQ ATF. I was not told. Nor was anything said to us about the 70-mm artillery rounds hitting the base, which would have confirmed my report of an enemy gun firing at about 2.50am on the 17th.

So, the mindset throughout the Task Force was still that all enemy in the area were merely local D445 or ineffective village guerillas. Jackson inexplicably decided that the planned concert for the 18th should go ahead, despite the mortar attack and intelligence of probable enemy forces approaching the base. The best attack time was obviously the night of a concert, which was well known by the enemy's agents who were, or worked with local Vietnamese around the central base area as labourers and grass cutters.

In hindsight, a large ambush could have been set to trap the enemy force as it attacked the base. What a lost opportunity! Again, the intelligence of the enemy situation was not acted upon, being kept secret among just four officers in ATF and not passed down to battalions or patrolling companies.

Author Paul Ham quotes in his book: 'Jackson's cavalier attitude and conduct of his command amounted to grave neglect and possibly a dereliction of duty', as was suggested to Paul in 2005 by former ATF staff officers.

But back to the morning of the 18th. Browned off at not being there for the big concert and tired after a sleepless night from the 2.40am mortaring until dawn, then another night of sentry duty, and a long hot forced march through 2-m-high grass with the amplified music from the concert in the background, our Delta Company led by Dave Sabben's 12 Platoon arrived at Bravo Company's position at about 1pm. We were glad to reach the relative cool at the edge of the rubber plantation. A few comments were made about how we should have been the ones going on the first R & C leave, rather than Bravo Company.

We had 105 men plus the three-man NZ Artillery Forward Observer party of Captain Morrie Stanley, Bombardier Willie Walker and Gunner Murray Broomhall in our ANZAC group.

OC Bravo Company Major Noel Ford and Lt Bill Kingston during Operation Hobart.

Because of soldiers detached to ATF HQ for work duties, there being no ATF Defence and Employment Platoon (D and E Platoon) at that time, and some men sick, and a couple at a Vietnamese language course at Vung Tau, our three platoons were under-strength at about 29 men instead of 34.

OC Bravo Company Major Noel Ford, my OCS Portsea roommate, showed me the various signs of the enemy positions and various fresh tracks, including a blood trail. After sharing some of our lunch rations, his HQ and platoon group left to return to Nui Dat at about 2pm.

Noel didn't need to say anything but I knew he was glad to be out of there even though he had seen no enemy, but he was to later suggest we were led into an ambush. He did not suggest that possibility to me at the time, perhaps it was another case of being wise after the event. Nevertheless I instinctively felt we needed to be on guard. But we were not led into an ambush. We could have gone north, east or south but I chose east to get through the rubber into the jungle to the east for a more secure night base, with less mosquitoes. Unfortunately for us that is where the enemy regiment was resting up.

Having had a welcome hour resting over lunch while I looked at the evidence found by Bravo, we moved out as soon as I gave orders. Operation 'Vendetta' (revenge for the mortaring) as I'd named it, was properly under way.

NINE

INTO BATTLE: A 'RORKE'S DRIFT' IN THE RUBBER

Moving in from the western edge of the Long Tan rubber plantation and having decided to head east, I moved my company with caution. My gut feeling was that we had to be ready for action, despite Brigadier Jackson and Colonel Townsend's lack of concern about what was out there, having approved the 48 men of Bravo Company going back for leave at dawn. After the mortar attack early the previous morning this casual attitude was somewhat disturbing – but at this level of Army hierarchy you certainly did not tell your commander to go jump, as much as you may have been inclined to on numerous occasions.

I had briefed my platoon commanders and other members of my Orders Group and at 2.45pm we set off east, through the symmetrical rubber tree lanes running up a slight slope. We moved carefully and quietly as we had trained – well-dispersed, one platoon up, one left rear and one right rear – in an arrowhead formation, coincidentally the shape of our Greek Delta Triangle company logo. Geoff Kendall's 10 Platoon led in front of my HQ, Dave Sabben's 12 Platoon was left rear and Gordon Sharp's 11 Platoon on the right rear.

I calculated from what I knew and had been told that after the mortaring of the base, the enemy, assumed to be 60-mm mortar crews from the 350 to 450-strong local D445 battalion, would have gone east-southeast to tunnels around their deserted Xa Long Tan village base, near 4km away. I also wanted to get into the jungle on the other side of the rubber for a more secure night base. It was very quiet, in hindsight 'deathly quiet'.

But in fact a maelstrom awaited us with the VC's 5th Division, some 1400 troops of the 275 Regiment, 400 NVA troops and the local VC D445 Provincial Battalion of about 350 troops, plus support units, sitting pretty to the east and south of the plantation. The enemy's 274 Regiment of the 5th Division, another 1400 men, were to the north somewhere, maybe some 5 to 10km away. So more than 4000 enemy troops were in the terrain to the east and north, mostly battle-tried and well-armed regular forces, able to move 20km a day if needed. 10 ARVN Division had earlier warned HQ ATF that 5 Division had up to 5000 local and reinforcement troops at its disposal.

  We had been given a written brief in June that the VC 5th Division was capable of moving into our area, but the threats advised in June failed to materialise, and to date there had been no signs of Main Force units. I must admit most of us had in our mind that we were only up against local village guerillas or platoons of D445, especially as we had not been told of the latest intelligence known at Task Force HQ that suggested 275 Regiment was just east of the rubber plantation. Bravo Company had been near our present position the day before and much further east into the area just that morning, with a platoon of Charlie Company in the rubber further south the previous afternoon, and they saw nothing of the enemy. And we had been in there on the 15th to the base of Nui Dat 2, not far northwest of where the enemy was hiding. We saw nothing of note and the enemy obviously did not want to give their presence away before their proposed attack on our Nui Da base on the 18th. In hindsight, they could probably have taken us out that day if they wished.

Then about 200 m in we came across a track junction and signs of bloodstained enemy web equipment, clothing and Ho Chi Minh sandals made from tyres, dropped in a hurry. Our artillery CB fire had obviously hit some of the heavy weapon crews. In 2012 the enemy history stated that they had lost two killed and buried them. Obviously several more were wounded. I could have changed direction and gone north on well-used fresh tracks but I knew Alpha Company had been up that way for two days and had only just started to return to Nui Dat, so I opted to continue east towards the jungle, aware that Bravo Company patrols had been into the rubber well past here just a few hours previously.

But just in case of any enemy having moved in ahead since then, I decided to change formation to 'two up', well-dispersed, 10 m between men, covering a wide area some 400 m across and 400 m deep, with Geoff Kendall's 10 Platoon on the left, Gordon Sharp's 11 Platoon on the right and Dave Sabben's 12 Platoon in rear to protect our central Company HQ, which included me and the three-man New Zealand Forward Observer artillery team, plus my batman, two signallers, two medics and the Support Section.

I radioed the Commanding Officer using our Sunray code. We were both Sunrays (commanders). Townsend was Niner and I was Four, so I called 'Niner, this is Four, fetch Sunray.' I told him all was quiet and we were heading east. My platoon commanders kept in radio contact with me and there were occasional messages on the radio handsets. In 1966 we did not have headsets but the volume was turned way down and the signallers muffled any loud messages on their shirts.

We moved ahead slowly, searching for signs of enemy in the dirty rubber plantation; dirty in that there was a lot of low scrub and big weeds amongst the now untended relatively young trees, which were maybe 8 m tall and about 300 mm across the trunks and in symmetrical staggered rows. They were tall enough, but not wide enough to hide behind, or hard enough to protect a man from bullets. And apart from the enemy the forward sections had to watch out for camouflaged 'punji pits' containing poisoned metal or sharpened bamboo stakes, and hidden tunnel entrances which could house snipers.

It was about 3.40pm. A little further on there was a wide track running south to north and while 11 Platoon was covering each section as they crossed, a squad of six to eight Viet Cong walked up from the south, almost right into the Platoon HQ area. They were nonchalantly chatting to each other, heads down, obviously unaware of our presence, which suggests they may have been from another unit from down south en route to the north or that the main enemy in the east had not been aware of Bravo Company and our company being at the western edge of the rubber. Being smart cookies, that was probably most unlikely.

11 Platoon HQ fired, with Sergeant Bob Buick knocking one VC over with his Armalite, the others dragging him away through the trees to the east. They left an AK47 rifle which platoon commander Second Lieutenant Gordon Sharp later picked up and carried. He reported the contact to me by radio and asked my concurrence to follow up. I agreed to 11 Platoon following up; normal procedure with small contacts. Why not? I held the company in place, and then reported the contact to Battalion HQ, logged in 6RAR Operations Log at 3.40pm: 'Contact with 6 to 8 enemy dressed in greens at YS478873 possibly wounding one. Enemy fled east.' I waited for further advice from 11 Platoon. I then reported the AK47 find, logged at 3.55pm: 'Recovered one AK47 carbine at scene of contact.'

This photo shows what the battlefield looked like on the day of the battle. A typical rubber plantation near Long Tan.

This small patrol certainly did not act like a 'clearing patrol' to look out for (their) enemy, or seem aware of us being there and, as it turned out, they gave the game away and 275 Regiment then came out of hiding.

In hindsight it seems that the 275 Regiment did not want to reveal the presence of a large force about to attack Nui Dat as they could have easily ambushed and taken out Bravo Company the day before – about 80 men – or their remaining group of 32 men along with our company of 108 (total 140) when we arrived at the rubber edge on the 18th, which would have been a huge victory for the enemy. And we had been in the same place just three days ago, with no sign of the enemy who, as we now know, had arrived four days previously. But then they could mostly move around at will and apparently had been resting in the jungle to the east of the rubber since the 14th, having been met, guided in, and fed by the local D445 from a large rice cache later located to the east. Indeed, apart from being the meeters and greeters and guiding the 275 Regiment mortar and heavy weapons crews to firing positions for the shelling of Nui Dat in the very early morning of the 17th, some of the D445 could have assisted in digging the many weapon pits that we were to find two days later in the jungle area east of the rubber plantation.

Gordon then reported that he thought the enemy may have taken refuge in a rubber tapper's hut ahead and he started to clear the hut area. He then reported finding nothing except some bloodstains and a grenade. He moved on again, about 300 m ahead of Company HQ and the other platoons.

With local D445 in our mindset, aided by our Task Force Commander Brigadier Jackson's insistence that that was all that was 'out there', few people, including me, twigged that enemy in greens with an AK47 probably meant Main Force. The AK47 wasn't that conclusive as we had captured an AK47 from the D445 VC soldier we killed on 19 July. And the significance of the green uniforms did not register either with me, or with Townsend when I radioed him. I gather Second Lieutenant David Harris, Task Force HQ Liaison Officer and Brigadier Jackson's Aide, alerted Jackson to the possible contact with Main Force troops, but David had no idea of the Signals Intelligence about 275 Regiment possibly being just to the east of the rubber plantation. Even though he was Jackson's Personal Assistant he was kept in the dark, as were the unit commanding officers.

D445 being in the mindset, ignoring the green uniforms with the AK47 was perhaps a mistake I made but I have never tried to cover it up. I wish I could say the same about a raft of cover-ups by some among the big brass. But, even if I had thought they could be Main Force, what would I have done? Turned around and headed home after a contact with just six to eight enemy? No – our job was to locate and kill the enemy. 11 Platoon could handle six to eight enemy, and I had absolutely no idea that there was a reinforced regiment resting further east waiting to attack Nui Dat that night. As briefed by Townsend, we were looking for about 40 to 50 of the local D445 battalion.

Again in hindsight, one wonders why the brigadier, after being told about the contact, and alerted by his aide Second Lieutenant David Harris, did not then tell us via CO 6RAR's radio that there could be troops of the 275 Regiment to the east as had been suggested by all the previous intelligence which he had been given. He could then have warned me and perhaps suggested we hold and await reinforcements or return to base (perhaps to take part in a large Task Force ambush to entrap the approaching enemy). But he remained tight-lipped. Why?

We continued slowly into the rubber with Gordon Sharp's men travelling faster to try to pin down the fleeing VC. About 300 m soon separated 11 Platoon from the rest of Delta. The Company HQ area was then mortared from the south, probably ranged onto the area of the first contact. We heard the *pop-poppop* from one or two enemy light 60-mm mortars and several bombs, maybe 10, landed harmlessly about 30 to 50 m to our right where 11 Platoon had been earlier. When you hear the *pop-pop-pop* you gauge you have about 30 seconds before the bombs drop somewhere and you know they will travel up to at least 1500, maybe 2000 metres. Then unaware of 275 Regiment and their larger 82-mm mortars, I recall thinking the VC who had mortared the base were probably now down south towards Xa Long Tan village and that I could move down that way tomorrow as we had little daylight time left today.

I immediately moved the other two platoons and Company HQ about 300 m to the northeast to get away from the impact area and we silenced the mortars with artillery CB fire from the six US Army 155mm guns at Nui Dat, pinpointed by compass bearings taken by Sergeant Don (Jack) Thompson my Mortar Fire Controller, and the NZ Artillery Forward Observer Captain Morrie Stanley, along with sound-ranging estimations. Morrie radioed the estimated positions back to the guns at base. To the best of my knowledge we were not mortared again and some reports of enemy mortar fire during the battle could have been as a result of Rocket Propelled Grenades (RPGs) or even our own artillery fire landing very close.

It was lucky that when we halted soon after we were behind and west of a slight rise in the ground, the area which was to later become our company defensive position and protected most of us from the majority of the direct enemy fire, which went just over our heads. It was only the enemy who closely approached or who went up trees who could fire down into us. And to our advantage, they were to be silhouetted in the gunfire smoke, making easy targets for my machine gunners and riflemen.

11 Platoon was still moving ahead when very heavy firing broke out. At about 4pm Lance Corporal Barry Magnussen who was in Sharp's leading section spotted a mass of enemy up front. It seemed that at least one enemy company had moved forward into the rubber to investigate the earlier contact and incursion into their area. Seconds later a streaming tracer avalanche flashed out of the rubber like a swarm of enraged fireflies. RPGs and machine-gun fire followed, tearing into Sharp's platoon. Men fell instantly. 11 Platoon was horribly pinned down.

Gordon Sharp radioed to me that he was taking casualties and that the enemy had several machine guns and appeared to be about to attack him. The tone of his voice suggested the enemy had the audacity to attack him which was not what he expected, and definitely not in the book. He called for artillery fire through the forward observer.

It was 4.20pm. Rain vomited from the sky. I had never seen such monsoonal rain either in Vietnam or Malaya, never breathed in such volumes of water as it turned the ground into a relentless churning machine that sprayed a mist of red mud onto our greens and into our faces, reducing visibility even further in the encroaching darkness rolling in under the heavy cloud cover. Morrie Stanley and I, lying side by side, were trying to clear the mud off our maps so that we could accurately spot the platoon position and get the artillery firing right on the enemy.

Gordon Sharp reported the enemy was probably of company size – well-armed regulars rather than local D445, and that he had already lost a third of his 29 men killed or wounded. I told him to withdraw, but apart from the problems of trying to withdraw under heavy enemy fire and risking more casualties, he did not want to leave his casualties to the mercy of the enemy. He asked for more artillery fire. Morrie Stanley responded. The six NZ 105s fired again.

I had to try and get another platoon through to them and assist them to withdraw. There was little point in attacking with the whole company and risk being swallowed up – best to retain a secure base and develop from that. I knew I had to send a platoon around to a flank to take the pressure off 11 Platoon. 10 Platoon, the front left platoon, was 200 m further forward than our HQ and northwest of 11, so it was best placed to help 11 Platoon. I spoke to 10 Platoon commander Lieutenant Geoff Kendall by radio and he told me he was not in contact and was able to move forward and assist Gordon. I told him to go further out around the left flank to try and get through to 11 Platoon from the north to aid a withdrawal. They dropped their packs and moved ahead but then saw more enemy moving in onto 11 Platoon from the area to the northeast, from near the base of Nui Dat 2 hill, so they set an immediate ambush and killed many. At the same time 10 Platoon took several casualties who were wounded in the ensuing fire fight with more enemy, and could not gain more ground.

Then 10's radio went dead, shot out, the bullet also wounding the signaller, one of my four Indigenous soldiers, Private Brian Hornung, passing through his shoulder into the radio. Bleeding and in pain, he bravely made his own way in the rain and enemy fire back about 300 m to Company HQ. 11 Platoon radio also went off air about the same time and, given the amount of firing up front, I thought the two platoons may have been overrun, but after a while the 11 Platoon radio came back on air. The aerial had been shot off and then replaced. Now they were in shit trouble and I pretty well knew we had at least a couple of enemy companies out in front of us, maybe more, maybe all 350 to 400 VC soldiers of the local D445 Provincial Mobile Battalion with Main Force reinforcements, given Gordon Sharp had suggested regular troops.

In the middle of all this, and just before 4pm, I called Major Noel Ford Officer Commanding Bravo Company by radio, who was by that time halfway back to base. I told Noel it looked like we had bitten off more than we could handle and asked his platoon group to return. He agreed. I did not know at the time but he was ordered not to move by 'Mousey' Townsend, as logged in the 6RAR Ops Log at 4pm, thank you, an order that may have come down from Brigadier Jackson, as with the aim of holding the APC Reaction Force back to help protect his base from an attack by the other regiment, 274, suggested as being to the north of Nui Dat base.

With 10 Platoon's wrecked radio back with us, my senior signaller, Corporal Graham Smith, tasked one of my Support Section soldiers to take the spare radio forward. Very busy on two radios and with Morrie Stanley, I do not recall the details but the soldier started off then collapsed in the mud, apparently wounded by an odd shot or piece of shrapnel. He was carried to the Company Aid Post (CAP). Private Bill 'Yank' Akell, later a Regular Army major, my second regimental signaller, grabbed the spare radio and bravely ran forward alone through the rubber to 10 Platoon, maybe 300 m, killing two enemy in behind 10 Platoon on the way with his Owen Gun, and restoring communications. My lucky day – and his for surviving. I then had good radio communications with both forward platoons and it is worth saying that our VHF radios, unlike the AM radios in Malaya, were free of interference from the electrical storm raging at this time.

I assessed we had the significant problem in that the enemy had the superiority of force. One of the principles of war is that a clear superiority of at least five-to-one (or an atomic bomb) is the winning combination. The enemy obviously had superiority, not us, but they had not yet mortared or shelled us with any effect. I recall thinking the rubber trees could impede them firing their many mortars and observing their effect even if they had them set up to fire. But we now know all their many 82-mm mortars, 75-mm Recoilless anti-tank guns (RCLs) and any artillery 70-mm mountain guns were ready to be carried forward to fire in support of the Nui Dat attack, and not set up to fire on us, luckily for us. And they were then moved to the rear out of harm's way after our artillery fire and air strike threatened them. More luck in that regard. And the enemy history tells that the telephone lines they had laid on the ground as they moved forward were mostly destroyed by our gunfire shrapnel, causing command problems as their commanders were unable to properly communicate between their HQ and units. They were using bugle calls to signal assembly and assaults, but could not receive information and give orders other than by runners who would have had problems in the heavy rain, smoke and gunfire in locating their units, even if they survived our fire. Luck was again on our side.

At 4.25pm I called CO6RAR requesting reinforcements be helicoptered in to our west into the clearing on the rubber's edge near where we met up with Bravo Company, but this was refused by Townsend on the grounds of an insecure LZ (Landing Zone – typically used for choppers). I thought it would have been eminently suitable for an insertion supported by armed choppers, but I was not then aware there was no reinforcement force or choppers readily available. The other battalion, 5RAR, was mostly out to the north of Nui Dat, albeit not in action, and 6RAR had no unencumbered companies. Alpha was just returning to base; Bravo was split, some halfway back to base, others going on leave; Charlie had platoons securing Nui Dat base lines, and we were in trouble.

Unlike in Malaya our 6RAR Support Company was not organised as a Rifle Company, but after Long Tan the Anti-tank Platoon was put under my command. However, because there were no enemy tanks to shoot at with their big 106 mm RCLs, it became a fourth rifle platoon to fill a gaping hole in the southern Nui Dat base defence perimeter alongside our company position and I also used it on patrols. If in a Fire Support Base role we took the RCLs and I recall later in December we had a competition with APC crews firing at suspected enemy hillside caves. It replaced 12 Platoon on a company patrol on 6 February 1967, to be among those hit by our own Kiwi artillery fire.

I believe Brigadier Jackson was reluctant to call for US Army helicopter and troop support, the US Army having earlier in June laughed off his requests for assistance. US choppers were 20 minutes away at Bien Hoa or Vung Tau. I was not aware our few RAAF helicopters of 9 Squadron were not then permitted to fly into 'dangerous areas'.

As though we were all at a ladies' tea party in downtown Toorak, Colonel Townsend instead proposed an Alpha Company reinforcement force would come out in armoured carriers 'later that afternoon'! It is logged in 6RAR Ops Log that Alpha Company was then 'warned for movement' at 4.30pm.

I was not fully aware that Alpha Company had just arrived back in Nui Dat and the men were still having showers, a barbecue meal and a beer prior to going to the concert. Neither was I aware there was no normal Ready Reaction Company in reserve at Nui Dat as required by Task Force Standard Operating Procedures (SOPs) which could have been flown out in US Army choppers from Vung Tau, maybe within 30 minutes or so, certainly within an hour, so with us by 5pm. Most of the APC crews were at the concert. Indeed, the Col Joye and Little Pattie concert, not a big battle – which was seen as just a nuisance – was the main item on the agenda of the day for most people back at Nui Dat.

At 4.40pm Gordon Sharp reported to me that at least two companies, maybe three, were attacking him on three sides and he gave more grid references for artillery targets. Morrie Stanley transmitted Sharp's updated target grid references to the guns, which answered with shattering accuracy, shredding the enemy's forward troops.

A short time later Sergeant Bob Buick told me by radio that Gordon Sharp had been shot and killed. That rocked me. Not only had others already been killed, now the normally happy young National Service platoon commander was dead – it was so sad. That wasn't in the game plan and I feared the worst for the rest of the platoon and that the enemy would roll on and the whole company might come under attack. But I couldn't dwell on that and pushed it out of my mind. I had other things to do to aid our survival, like getting an air strike onto the enemy after working out the map coordinates for the strike zone across the front of 11 Platoon, getting all the artillery fire I could muster, discussing the best target areas with Morrie Stanley, and getting 11 Platoon survivors out of trouble and back into the fold to be part of a company defensive position to better fight off the attacking enemy.

Sadly, Gordon was fatally shot through the neck when, despite advice from Bob Buick to keep his head down, he bravely raised up on his knees to better see and direct the artillery fire for his platoon. Bob Buick then took over command of the platoon and very effectively directed the artillery fire for over an hour until the platoon could withdraw when 12 Platoon got up behind them. His section commanders, Corporals Bluey Moore, Jeff Duroux and John Robbins gallantly controlled the machine gun and rifle fire of their sections against the attacking enemy, who some described as just walking forward into our fire, as though drugged. 11 Platoon men bravely slugged it out with the enemy. Corporal Bluey Moore's section shredded an enemy flanking attack which could have overrun the platoon.

In 1986 the *Melbourne Age* published a story 'A Horror Relived' in which several of the 11 Platoon soldiers recall that tragic afternoon. Former NS soldier 21-year-old Private Alan May tells:

> The enemy weren't diving for cover from tree to tree, but just continued to walk in like zombies. It was like shooting ducks in a bloody shooting gallery and for every one shot there were two to take his place. I would have killed at least forty Vietcong myself. I remember one bloke I hit in the chest with a tracer round. He did a backflip then stood up screaming and pulling at his chest trying to put the tracer fire out.

At 4.50pm, having had only the six 105-mm guns of the NZ Direct Support Battery to that point, I called for the whole regiment of artillery in support, which with the US 155s was another 18 guns. I was told by my NZ FO Morrie Stanley that Artillery HQ at Nui Dat said I could not have them, as one battery was facing north for 5RAR, although not firing, and another battery was in general support, also not firing, and the US 155s could not be used for close support. This was in spite of my asking Morrie Stanley to tell his HQ that we had probably the best part of a battalion attacking 11 Platoon on three sides and I wanted all of the guns in support.

I got onto the radio, to Sunray Niner, and yelled at Townsend, 'I want all the guns in support – the whole regiment. Give me all the guns they've got!'

Townsend, probably in his comfortable HQ CP with his 1948 RMC classmate and direct support NZ artillery battery commander, Major Harry Honner, curtly responded with a cryptic, 'Leave the guns to the gunners!' I thought the guns were supposed to support the infantry and put fire where we wanted it!

Very angry by now, I again demanded all the guns, 'I want the whole regiment, now.'

Soon after Morrie Stanley told me we finally had the guns of the whole regiment – 18 NZ and Australian 105s plus the six US Army 155s firing in depth, 24 guns in total – the first regimental gunfire since Korea. In hindsight I can imagine the brass at Nui Dat saying, 'That young OCS major wants the whole regiment – who does he think he is?'

Morrie and his signallers worked off grid references relayed by my platoon commanders or indicated by me. I've long said that it was the artillery fire that saved us from annihilation that day, even though my gallant men also created a heavy toll on the enemy and held their ground. At one time the artillery radio net went off the air and Morrie used my command net radio to relay messages until communication was restored. Former Captain Charles Mollison wrote to the CO in late December 1966 after the Long Tan awards were announced, with none for Alpha Company, requesting recognition. He was to complain about Adrian Roberts being reluctant to move his APCs forward and that I was disorientated and didn't know where I was and where north was because I was trying to direct the guns myself. But as the artillery net was down for a while it was Morrie using our radio net to pass fire orders, not me! I had no need to take over from Morrie! He and his signallers did an outstanding job that day. And Morrie and I knew exactly where we were and where north was.

Ironically our Artillery HQ, to the disgust of the US Battery Commander, Captain Glenn Eure, would not allow the six US 155s to be used in close support so they fired in depth and from what we have now been told by our former enemy, their big shells decimated parts of 275 Regiment's HQ and rear areas.

The brass reckoned then that the big 155s with a 90-kg explosive shell were not accurate enough to use in close support, yet they are now the main and most accurate artillery close support gun in most armies, including ours. After arguing and finally getting the regimental gunfire I wanted it was about 5pm and I then requested an air strike with rockets, bombs and napalm across the front of 11 Platoon, giving the appropriate grid references off my map. I also requested helicopter ammunition resupply, thinking the fight might go into the night and we would need much more ammunition. I was aware that we might not get the choppers in if the enemy closed up on our HQ area before they arrived.

But I was not aware it would take almost an hour for the choppers to get there, the delay in the main being caused by arguments between Brigadier Jackson and Group Captain Raw over the RAAF policy not to fly into danger areas. In the end (late) Flight Lieutenant Frank Riley DFC, the lead pilot of the two 9 Squadron Iroquois at Nui Dat with the concert party, stepped in and said, 'To hell with orders; Harry Smith wants ammunition; I am the captain in charge of my aircraft and I am going out.' Cliff Dohle, the second pilot, said he would also go along, as did their co-pilots Bob Grandin and Bruce Lane. Bob tells he said to Frank it was a suicide mission, and Frank replied I will go alone, but Bob went along. They cranked up the choppers and flew over to 6RAR Landing Zone to load.

With radio communication back, Geoff Kendall told me he had several wounded, and could not get further forward. I told him to withdraw so I could send 12 Platoon out around the other flank, the southern side. The FO party, my signallers and I prepared to move with 12 Platoon out around the right flank. But while we started to move off, I realised it would be impossible for the FO and myself to control the battle while on the move, trying to read maps in the sheeting rain and mud and talking on our radios to Battalion HQ and the platoons, plus Morrie relaying fire control directions to the guns at Nui Dat. I recall thinking that if the FO got hit then the artillery support might wane. Although we had been trained in elementary fire control, it would have been less effective if we were doing it. So I told 12 Platoon Commander Dave Sabben to leave a section to help secure the Company Aid Post (CAP) and Company Headquarters (CHQ) area from attack from the west and to take his reduced platoon, only 20 men, out around the right flank to take the pressure off 11 Platoon so they might be able to withdraw. Although 10 Platoon was not yet back at our HQ area, I took a punt that it would be back soon. So Morrie and I stayed put and got on with the job.

A couple more wounded men from 10 Platoon were coming back to join wounded soldier Brian Hornung in the CAP I had organised in a hollow to my rear. Normally members of the 6RAR band, attached Medical Corporal 'Doc' Dobson and his offsider Private 'Geordie' Richardson tended to the wounded, who numbered 22 in the CAP by the time the enemy withdrew just before 7pm. Doc Dobson did a wonderful job and no doubt saved many lives. The CO's Battalion HQ party omitted to bring the medical officer out in the APCs which arrived later, just after 7pm, so Doc and Geordie with support from platoon medics, cared for the wounded until they were evacuated by APC, then by 'Dustoff' choppers around midnight.

12 Platoon moved off but ran into enemy about 75 m from the rear of 11 Platoon and had their own fight. They killed many enemy, but took wounded, including Sergeant Paddy Todd. He

covered the later platoon withdrawal with rifle fire but when he decided to leave he found himself unable to walk, shot through both ankles. This brave man told others to leave him then crawled all the way back to Company HQ, killing several VC who threatened him on the way.

When 10 Platoon arrived back at CHQ area I sited it on the right, the southeast, the main front. Some enemy followed them back in but they were eliminated by the platoon, and the HQ area remained secure, not under direct fire but still in the path of enemy overshoots from the 11 and 12 Platoon areas, most of which were high – we could see the many colourful but deadly tracer rounds going past, above.

The USAF Phantom fighter jets which were on Combat Air Patrol above Saigon soon arrived, guided by an Airborne Forward Air Controller (FAC) in a light plane, but despite us throwing coloured smoke grenades in each platoon area, the FAC told me on the radio he could not identify us because of the heavy rain, cloud and gunfire smoke. Artillery HQ stopped the guns for them but I then told 6RAR to take the planes away so I could get the guns back. On the advice of 6RAR Ops the planes then dropped their load to the east on the enemy's rear areas, causing damage and confusion.

Just before 6pm the two RAAF Iroquois helicopters, flying in atrocious weather, arrived overhead of CHQ. The first helicopter flown by Frank Riley had flown past in the rain cloud then came back and located us by our coloured smoke grenades. Frank then called Cliff Dohle's chopper forward from a hover near Nui Dat. There was an initial delay as pilot Cliff reported seeing a different coloured smoke, perhaps thrown by the enemy listening to our radio net. Although they did not have many radios and laid telephone lines as they moved, we now know the enemy had a few Chinese HF and VHF radios plus a couple captured from US or ARVN troops.

But we then threw more smoke grenades which were acknowledged correctly and we talked the choppers in over us. Graham Smith, my senior signaller, handled the chopper radio traffic for me very well. Frank's A1020 chopper is in the RAAF Museum at Point Cook. Cliff's A1022 is now at the Caloundra RSL. It had been recovered from Nyngan NSW where it had been badly vandalised and was refurbished by volunteers at Caloundra aerodrome so that it now looks like new.

Luckily the choppers were never under fire as all the action was about 400 m east where 11 and 12 Platoon were and the enemy could not see or hear the choppers for trees, heavy rain and machine gun and rifle fire noise. The choppers dropped the ammunition, which was still in metal-strap-banded boxes wrapped in blankets for the wounded, 'right into our lap' – spot on. CSM Jack Kirby, Sergeant Neil Rankin and others had to cut the metal straps with machetes and prise the large boxes open and then open all the smaller ones inside to get to the cartons of bullets and belts for the M60s! After Long Tan all resupply ammo was pre-loaded into magazines, which was good for those in future battles. 1ATF was not really geared up for a battle of this nature in August 1966, but no one expected more than some of D445 battalion being in the area.

Cliff's Iroquois A1022 now located at Caloundra RSL. Photo courtesy Felicia Smith.

The choppers then flew back west to Nui Dat and I got the guns back firing immediately. During this ammo drop 11 Platoon had had no gunfire support but was thankfully able to hold the enemy off with small arms fire. Not dug in, with almost half already killed and vastly outnumbered, the gallant performance of that decimated platoon cannot be underestimated. Although they were not aware of the bigger picture, they gave us the time to get better organised, get the ammo resupply, and thus they saved the whole company from being overrun.

Our masters were all very inexperienced and careful in 1966, but now I see choppers being used in Afghanistan while artillery fire continues, simply by flying under or alongside the barrages. Of course they have GPS navigators to assist. The pilots of our RAAF choppers were restricted by RAAF Canberra policy of avoiding losses. It is recorded in the Official History that in the heated discussion between Raw and Jackson, when he eventually returned to the Command Post from his tent, to his credit Jackson remarked: 'What if we lose a couple of pilots – what about losing a whole company of Infantry?'

Corporal Graham Smith, my senior regimental signaller, was way ahead of my orders to get the radios onto the 'Albatross' helicopter VHF radio net and controlled the radio messages to and from the pilots. He did a great job on the radio that day. Morrie Stanley was able to get his signaller Willy Walker's good work recognised with an award of a NZ MID, but sadly, and although well deserved, our medals' ration deprived my senior signaller of the same award. Two of the three-man NZ team were given awards, along with both RAAF pilots. More on the awards debacle later. Jack Kirby and Graham Smith relieved me of menial tasks and I was able to devote my thoughts and time to controlling the overall battle. People often ask me if I was frightened, but I can honestly say I was too dammed busy to be frightened and it never once entered my mind we would not survive. It was only after the withdrawal at midnight I said to myself, shit, I am still alive. I was confident my gallant soldiers who had trained and worked together for over a year would win out with all the artillery fire we had at our disposal. Some said it was the artillery fire that caused most enemy dead, but 10,300 small arms rounds fired at close range must have taken a toll. And given many of the bodies were dissected and torn apart by shrapnel, they may have already been shot by my soldiers. There were no autopsies to decide.

At about this time, some 17 survivors of the original 29 of 11 Platoon, several of those wounded, and most virtually out of ammunition, having gallantly held the enemy at bay for well over an hour, made a break. Sergeant Bob Buick called in close artillery fire and then gave an order to move out and regroup further to the rear, near where 12 Platoon was. It was not an organised withdrawal, more a case of just getting out. The order to move was along the lines 'When I say go, run back – go.' Vic Grice was killed as he got up, then Barry Meller was wounded in a leg. He was dragged along by Lance Corporal Barry Magnussen but told him to leave him. Ron Carne lost a large piece of his backside from enemy machinegun fire.

Bob Buick is said by some to have yelled 'every man for himself' and left. But in fact he went over to a flank and helped Private John Beere tend to a mortally wounded soldier, Private McCormack, who died and then they ran back, covering each other. They saw coloured smoke from 12 Platoon and joined them. 49 years on, a couple of his former soldiers still claim Bob left the men despite John Beere, later an ARA major, testifying the facts to the Long Tan Veterans Association some years back. They said they would not publish John's letter as it could upset Private McCormack's next of kin, while I suggested they did not want to air the truth. Bob rose to be a Warrant Officer and retired on the Sunshine Coast. We are still good friends.

Dave Sabben radioed to tell me that 11 Platoon were with him and I told him to withdraw to CHQ area. Both platoons came back to my HQ area, but with 15 of 11 Platoon men missing, presumed dead, along with 12's Sergeant Paddy Todd. After the wounded went to the CAP, Bob Buick had only seven soldiers left and I placed them on the northwest side of our position. A wounded Paddy Todd was to crawl in later and was almost shot by 10 Platoon until, in the gloom, he was told by Second Lieutenant Geoff Kendall to 'take off his hat' to indicate he understood the order and was not enemy. Corporal Buddy Lea went out and aided by Neil Rankin and Bill Roche, dragged him in.

Earlier, at about 5.30pm I had asked 6RAR where the Armoured Personnel Carrier force was, and said, 'If it is not on the way now they might as well not come out as they will not be here by dark!' I was not aware that the APCs waiting to embark Alpha Company at Nui Dat, as well as the Bravo Company HQ with Second Lieutenant John O'Halloran's 5 Platoon group which was halfway back to Nui Dat, were still there and had all been held back over an hour on orders from the brigadier.

Although my main critic has since said I was in panic, those who know me better agree I was just frustrated that people back at base were trying to run the show. If I called for reinforcements and regimental gunfire then that is what I expected to get. I was in command at Long Tan from start to finish – end of story. And if the APCs had not left they might not arrive before dark, and then be unable to locate us, with the consequence we might take many more casualties or be overrun during the night. I was not then fully aware the enemy was being cut to pieces by the artillery gunfire and our own machine guns and rifles, and, unable to overrun us, would start to withdraw at dusk, just as the APCs arrived at the rubber edge well to our south.

That radio message, heard over all radio nets tuned in to our frequencies back at Nui Dat, apparently prompted Brigadier Jackson to tell Townsend to release the APC Force, logged at 5.30pm. But by the time Alpha Company loaded into the waiting APCs at their company base in the northern area, they did not leave there until 5.45pm. This was more than two hours after the battle had begun and one and half hours after I had requested reinforcements be provided. Despite their barbecue and beer, one has to ask why Alpha Company was not already loaded in the APCs or resting alongside allocated carriers, awaiting the executive order to move so as to prevent them taking another 15 minutes to embark. The waiting APC crews were very critical that the soldiers seemed more interested in their barbecue. But I think few people back at base realised the full force of the predicament we were in, even though the noise of all the artillery firing had interfered with the concert. When the realisation of the action at Long Tan hit home, the concert was disbanded. Col Joye was kidnapped by soldiers of 5RAR and Little Pattie was flown back to Vung Tau.

Later I was to find out that Brigadier Jackson had delayed the APC force for well over an hour when he realised he had failed to recognise the warnings he had received in recent days, fearing his base could be attacked by the other enemy regiment, 274, reported in the north. He came to realise the SIGINT and ARVN intelligence was right and that now the shit had hit the fan. It is recorded in the Official History that he handed over control to CO6RAR.

Although hearsay, it is said he told one of his staff he might have to pack his bags.

Colonel Bob Hagerty AM (Retd), former Major, 1APC Squadron Commander in 1966, tells me he went to look for Jackson, his CO, to request he send more than just 10 APCs out to Long Tan in case the first troop was ambushed. Jackson was not in the HQ CP so he went to his sleeping tent to find it closed up. After calling out and getting no reply, he opened the flap to see Jackson sitting in the corner. He asked him for approval to send more APCs in case of ambush. The gruff reply was 'Just send one troop'!

Jackson was obviously originally prepared to hold back the reinforcements I requested for well over an hour and thus perhaps sacrifice my company for his base. I have been advised he also told CO6RAR to stop Bravo Company from returning to us, although there is another view that they had simply been forgotten by HQ6RAR until they later asked if there was some valid reason why they could not return to reinforce us as I had earlier requested of Major Noel Ford. Whatever, I did not get the extra platoon I called for and could have used. By the time they returned the enemy had started to withdraw.

In the rubber I sited my three platoons, or more correctly, two and half understrength platoons – about 50 effective men in up-front sections – in a defensive layout facing the southeast. I went around each of them, spoke to their commanders and aligned their machine gun arcs and fields of fire and then waited for the enemy onslaught. The enemy had temporarily lost contact with us when 11 and 12 Platoons withdrew, disappearing into the heavy rain and clouds of smoke from the exploding artillery shells.

Jack Kirby distributed more ammunition. He had earlier taken spare ammo off the gunners and the reserve sections to bolster the front-line weapons. We only had three SLR magazines issued at that time, so only 60 rounds loaded, but everyone had more ammo, at least another 40 to 60 rounds, in what became useless soggy cardboard boxes, spilling the bullets into the mud, and making it bloody hard to clean them and reload magazines.

I carried over 100 rounds for my Armalite rifle in magazines. I was the only company commander in 6RAR who carried a useful rifle and used it, as I did in Malaya, rather than the issue 9-mm Browning pistol which could at best be uselessly thrown at the enemy. The Australian 9-mm round had little punch, would often not even re-cock a German Luger pistol and we found 9-mm bullets lodged in enemy webbing, even at close range. My After Action report and interview with General Ken Mackay in Saigon saw all 9-mm F1 Owen guns given to drivers and alike, replaced with Armalites for signallers, section and platoon commanders. The Owens might have been good on jungle tracks in New Guinea in 1944–45, but they were of little use over the longer ranges of rice paddies and rubber plantations in Vietnam, although Yank Akell killed two VC with his Owen gun – but they had bobbed up just 3 m in front of him.

While I had some time to organise our company defensive position the enemy arrived soon after and launched successive suicidal battalion-sized attacks. The withering enemy AK47, SKS rifle and RPD machine gun fire had a large tracer content and they filled the oncoming darkness like a million fireflies coming at us. My Mortar Fire Controller Sergeant Don Thompson was lying behind a rubber tree about 5 m in front of me, with tracers ripping though the tree just above his head, and the white latex running down the bark. I recall we joked the wasted latex wouldn't be used to make condoms. Anyone who rose up in these onslaughts had their head shot off.

Some say it was like Rorke's Drift 1879 where about 170 British soldiers in a fortified stockade and buildings held off 3000 Zulus armed with spears and a few old muzzle loaders. With 15 men missing and some in the Aid Post, we had about 80 soldiers in the open holding off up to 2000 suicidal 'Zulus' in green uniforms armed with modern AK47s and SKS rifles. Rorke's Drift suffered 17 killed and 16 wounded and killed 350 enemy. We were to lose 17 killed and 23 wounded and kill 500.

Rorke's Drift attracted 11 Victoria Crosses, 5 DCMs and several Mentions. We were to get four medals headed by one DCM and a Military Cross, normally a platoon level award, and five Mentions. Other awards I recommended were scrubbed. More on that later.

    Just after dragging Paddy Todd in, Indigenous South Pacific Islander Corporal Buddy Lea, a section commander in 10 Platoon was hit in the left chest by a burst of three AK47 rounds and badly wounded. His 2IC Lance Corporal Jack Jewry crawled over and knelt over him to dress his wounds, but then fell heavily onto him, shot dead. Others dragged Buddy to the CAP.

Buddy Lea and me in Hervey Bay 2010. Photo courtesy Sensis.

Patched up by our medic 'Doc' Dobson, Buddy then spent five weeks in hospital at Vung Tau before returning to Australia for further recuperation. He then served on for 30 years to 1995. He lived near me in Hervey Bay and was well known at the RSL and in the local community. Buddy was a very loyal man. Separated from his wife after Vietnam, the plight of so many veterans, his lovely daughter Miesha and her two children lived nearby. A stroke affected a leg and left him unable to drive and his main carer became a former soldier, Sergeant Reg (Gillie) Gillian. We saw each other often and I tried to take him with me when I spoke to schools as he was always a hit with the kids with his jovial and humble manner. Sadly, in July 2014 he was diagnosed with terminal lung cancer and died on 12 September. The VC did not get him, but the big C did, and he was farewelled by over 1000 people at his huge funeral. Gillie and I miss him.

Back to the battle. Looking ahead, we could see the horrendous damage caused by the artillery bursts, enemy bodies being flung up in the air by the exploding shells, yet the enemy came on again and again in waves like robots. They were obviously psyched by their political commissars and one of my forward soldiers claimed to have seen a Caucasian in the rear giving directions – maybe a Russian adviser? In Lex McAulay's book (page 89) Private Harry (Horse) Esler, who died in May 2015, tells of a large man:

> There was a big fellow in a white dustcoat. He seemed taller than the rest and was shouting orders. I had a few shots at him.

I don't know if he had a bulletproof vest or I am a lousy shot, but I could not get him. But someone else got him, the big bastard, but he was not found among the dead next day.

It is recorded Alpha Company reported finding the body of a big person, definitely not Vietnamese, along with other bodies further to the east the next day.

It is well known that Russian pilots flew MIGs for North Vietnam and it is a fair bet they had advisers with the VC, same as we had AATTV advisers with ARVN units. 1968 ATF battalions claim to have seen Russian and Chinese advisers or political commissars with the VC in the Long Green. It is believed 4000 Russian soldiers served in Vietnam, with seven killed. And in 2015, Hanoi admitted 320,000 Chinese troops served in Vietnam.

Enemy who managed to get though the artillery gunfire, crawling over their dead comrades, were mown down by my front-line soldiers, bodies piling up on top of each other. Enemy snipers were shot out of trees or killed by artillery rounds exploding in trees, known as tree bursts. To my knowledge, not one enemy who got through the gunfire penetrated 11 Platoon or our subsequent company defensive front line, which says a lot for the training, gallantry, teamwork and dedication of my officers, NCOs and men. One VC started to crawl in between 10 Platoon sections but was quickly dispatched by Yank Akell. Our role was to 'kill the enemy' and we certainly did that. Sadly, the enemy killed 17 of my men, but we were exposed on top of the mud and it was impossible to dig trenches as they just filled with mud and water from the monsoonal rain. Apart from Jack Jewry, Privates Rick Aldersea, Max Wales and Paul Large were also killed in the final defensive position by enemy fire and we had another 21 soldiers wounded, plus the 13 dead and two wounded in the forward 11 Platoon area recovered the next morning.

At times the enemy assault waves, signalled by the spine-chilling sound of bugles, when repelled by the guns and my forward men would fall back to reorganise or be replaced by fresh troops and those brief breaks gave me time to walk around to check on my platoons and the wounded in the company aid post. I recall one soldier, I think Shorty Brown, who was to win an MM on the second tour and later become an Army chaplain, looked up and said to me, 'Do you think we will get out of this boss?'

I just winked at him with a grin of confidence, then returned quickly to my own spot next to Morrie Stanley and my signallers when the next assault commenced. 'Big Jack' Kirby just defied the enemy fire to move around and hand out ammunition and we all wondered why the big man was not hit. In lulls he would move around further and hand out more ammunition and give affable advice to soldiers like, 'If you don't know him, shoot him son.' That was Jack at his best with the men. Jack was to carry a couple of wounded back to the company aid post under fire, as portrayed in the painting by Bruce Fletcher now at the Australian War Memorial, and at one time he went forward under fire and killed the crew of a heavy enemy machine gun being set up out front to give us an even harder time. Jack Kirby is often quoted as being the 'unsung hero of Long Tan' and I'm trying to get him the posthumous Victoria Cross he deserves, which I recommended to the Commanding Officer in 1966. My request was denied, Townsend told me he would only sign a DCM.

Painting by Bruce Fletcher, held at the Australian War Memorial.

A 12 Platoon soldier, Lance Corporal Peter Slacksmith wrote:

I don't know anyone who won a Victoria Cross. But I go to my grave perfectly satisfied that I saw a man win one. I witnessed, first hand and close, Jack Kirby, a soldier's soldier if ever there was one, perform feats more than up to the standard required.

Mrs Harley Webb wrote:

Not only did Jack Kirby save Harley's life in the heat of the battle, carrying him back to a safer position when he was wounded, but Harley said on more than one occasion he came to resupply him with ammunition and verbal support during the battle. A very brave and caring man.

In the face of larger enemy assaults, I asked my forward observer Morrie Stanley to order 'drop 50' (metres) to stop the enemy closing up to us inside the gunfire, as was their tactic 'of getting inside the gunfire and holding them by the belt' while they overran their enemy. Unbelievably, that order was refused by Artillery HQ at Nui Dat because it was considered back at base to be 'unsafe'. 'Unsafe'? It was incredible that they would tell me it was unsafe. I often think I had more trouble with those back at base than I did with the enemy. I believe they thought this young major was reckless and too inexperienced to be playing with the fire of 24 of 'their' guns. They still could not comprehend that I, young OCS Major Harry Smith, not them, was running the show on the battlefield and their role was to support us.

I grabbed the radio mike from Signaller Graham Smith and told my HQ to tell the gunners to; 'Fire the bloody guns where we want them to fire, otherwise you will lose the lot of us.' Soon after, Morrie said they approved the 'drop 50' and the guns fired in closer. The 3500 rounds from our Nui Dat base back to the west always went over our heads, so the blast and shrapnel, even from close tree bursts, went forward into the enemy with great effect, causing them horrendous casualties.

I have to say the gunners fired with deadly accuracy despite the conditions on the gun line, where internal communications were shattered by lightning. I am not aware of any accidental 'drop shorts' as they are known, like the ones that sadly hit Alpha Company HQ and wounded Peter Smeaton in July and my Company HQ area in February 1967, or the 6RAR mortar bomb that landed next to my tent at Nui Dat, sending shrapnel over the sandbags and my bed into my hanging clothes locker, putting neat holes in my clothes including my leave civvies which were bought with a $40 clothing allowance. As an aside, I claimed for the cost of buying replacements and two years later the reluctant finance system paid up $40. And why not?

The defensive battle, the deafening noise and the incessant tracer fireflies continued until about 6.50pm when it was almost dark. The rain was easing and I was planning on using all the USAF air support on call, like Puff the Magic Dragon or Snoopy (heavily armed Dakotas with mini-guns); flare ships; armed helicopters and the like. They were all on call, either in the air or ready to take off from Bien Hoa, 20 minutes away.

At one time near the end, the attacks having waned, I was walking around behind CHQ and happened to see a number of enemy camouflaged with tree branches moving through the rubber trees on our right rear flank, maybe 75 m away. I dropped to a more stable kneeling position and with some of my CHQ soldiers opened fire. They all withdrew just before the Bravo Company group of 32 men arrived back from the southwest at about 6.55pm. I fired two magazines from my Armalite rifle but did not see any result other than the tree branches turning around and heading back east. Awareness of the Bravo Company platoon group returning may also have hastened their retreat.

I placed the Bravo Company platoon group in position in reserve to cover the southwest sector. Luckily, there was impenetrable thick bamboo to our northwest side. Noel Ford was holding up his pistol and one of my soldiers said, 'Sir, you do not have a magazine in your Browning!'

Noel, an academic, retorted, 'Oh, my batman must have forgotten it.' Some of his soldiers later reported Noel leading them, pistol at the ready, as they hurried back at a jog to join us after being halted for near an hour and a half. He was to suggest in his After Action Report that I had been deliberately led into a VC ambush by following discarded enemy gear.

That theory did not hold water. Apart from the discarded bloodstained gear only being near the edge of the rubber and not set as in a long 'follow-me' trail, Bravo Company also went way in to the rubber tappers' hut that morning, and I could have gone north, south or east and I just happened to choose east. A case of him being wise after the event, but it has been picked up and reiterated in yet another large book, *Vietnam – The Complete Story of the Australian War,* 2012, by author Bruce Davies, who never interviewed any participants, but claimed we were led into an ambush and that the body count was exaggerated. My personal opinion is that his book might be a complete story, but that part which relates to Long Tan, such as the ambush theory and less enemy casualties, is *complete jargon.* After all, I was there and I can say we were not ambushed, otherwise I would not be writing this. I can assure readers that the body count was accurate and consistent with my men firing over

10,000 rounds into the enemy at short range and the horrendous casualties caused by the 3500 artillery rounds we directed. I didn't order a small bulldozer just to bury a few bodies. And some ill-informed media coverage for 2014 Long Tan day was still claiming we were ambushed. Maybe it sounds better? Noel Ford was very lucky that his company group was not ambushed on arrival on the 17th or during his patrol's excursions into the rubber to the hut that morning of the battle.

Just before 7pm and not under direct fire, Major Noel Ford and I walked around and discussed the situation. He explained to me he had been held back by HQ 6RAR until he had eventually asked why his group could not return. They had seen enemy waving to them on their way into the rubber to our southwest, believing Noel's men, in wet greens, to be other enemy, and they had earlier been mortared by a few ineffective 60-mm rounds fired from up north somewhere. As well, one or two Alpha Company men atop one APC that had got ahead had accidentally fired on them, thinking them enemy, causing one soldier, Private Carey Johnson, to be wounded in his mouth and shoulder. He had the guts to continue to carry his M60 machine gun until they reached us soon after and was later evacuated to hospital with our casualties. His section commander Corporal 'Spike' Jones, to get an MM in Operation 'Bribie' in February 1967, took over his M60 while he was treated in the CAP.

Enemy action continued to wane and by 7pm Noel Ford and I were still openly walking around under very high enemy tracer fire, checking the platoons and wounded in the CAP, and discussing what the enemy might be going to do next. Reorganising for another big attack? From where? I did not know then that the enemy had taken terrible casualties; their plan to attack Nui Dat thwarted, and they were unable to overrun us. Having seen reinforcements arriving from the west and probably aware of the APCs coming up from the south, their regimental commander had given the order to start withdrawing, probably about 6.45pm. They started leaving in echelons – on their way home.

Author Terry Burstall in his second book *A Soldier Returns* writes about a 1987 interview with former VC HQ 5 Division Staff Officer Colonel Nguyen Thanh Hong (nicknamed 'Hai'), located at the VC HQ at Ap Phuoc Hung, just east of Long Tan rubber. He told Burstall:

> When we could not destroy your troops in the required time frame we decided to withdraw. The artillery was hitting us hard and we knew reinforcements would be arriving and we did not have the strength to stop them. We were disappointed we could not overrun your troops but the weather was a factor which created problems with our communications. We were hoping you would follow us out to Ap Suoi Cat, out of gun range, but this did not happen. Much of the cleaning up, weapons and badly wounded were removed during the battle, and were carried to the Nui May Tao mountains.

This is similarly reflected in recently published 275 Regiment history. Terry later interviewed 'Ut Thoi', Colonel Nguyen Thoi Bung, who was Commander of 275 Regiment at Long Tan and supposedly on Nui Dat 2 during the battle and he said he had three regular battalions, with D445 in the south. His story was essentially the same – perhaps it was a party line. He died early in 2014 at age 88, just after this photograph was taken in late 2013, having been a Major-General and commander of VC 9 Division circa 1973. Historian retired Brigadier Ernie Chamberlain sent me his obituary, pointing out there was no mention of Long Tan – perhaps it was a rare defeat best left out.

Colonel Nguyen Thoi Bung, who was Commander of 275 Regiment at Long Tan.

In the rubber, just after the Bravo Company platoon arrived, we became aware of APC engine noise, and then two or three APCs arrived, unopposed, 100 m south of Geoff Kendall's 10 Platoon, then turned around and went back south! What the f ... k went on?

The few remaining enemy to the front of 10 Platoon then got up and withdrew as part of a total regimental withdrawal which had started earlier. You don't move a badly mauled regiment carrying casualties in one minute. At about this time the enemy attacks seemed to cease, although there were tracers still coming over, but mainly high, and we thought they were going to attack again. In my After Action Report I said the enemy were still firing at us when the APCs arrived near us. However, as I later learned, the enemy had left and gone east and were firing back west at the APCs, which had turned east when 300 m south of us, having just been joined by the 6RAR HQ Group, and were chasing them, with the enemy overshoots at the APCs coming back west over us.

The APC troop commander, Adrian Roberts, who had been with 1RAR Bien Hoa and on US Army Operation 'Hardihood' in May in this area fortunately knew the best place to cross the flooded Suoi Da Bang River. The acting infantry Alpha Company commander, Charles Mollison, had suggested going directly east out of his northeast Nui Dat area which meant the APCs would never have got over the river and arrived that night. Roberts got his way, thankfully. Adrian, nicknamed 'Humphrey Bear', was later vilified by Mollison who did not understand Adrian was in command of his own APCs when on the move to an objective. I always use the analogy of a McCafferty's bus where the driver is in charge, irrespective of the status of passengers. In 2012 a former Chief of General Staff General John Coates AO MBE wrote a paper about *Armour in Vietnam* and made it clear that 'the dispute between Charles Mollison and Adrian Roberts was due to the inexperience of the infantry officer who did not understand that irrespective of rank, the Armoured Commander is in command while on the move'.

Townsend unfortunately backed Mollison in his After Action Report and was later required by Jackson to issue an amendment, dated 2 November, in essence an apology, giving credit to the APCs. Charles Mollison claimed Adrian Roberts was an inexperienced young officer. But his time in the ARA and experience with APCs at Bien Hoa and on local Operation 'Hardihood' in May surpassed the 14 years of CMF night parades, weekends and camps attended by his accuser who thought he was 'God's gift to company commanders' despite others having served in action in Korea and Malaya. Sadly all this soured relationships between 6RAR and the APC Squadron but did not interfere with cooperation at our level on future operations. As with the 9 Squadron helicopters that attracted flack because they were based in luxury at Vung Tau, we all got on very well at company level.

Having got through the Nui Dat base, although delayed by an unknown change in a perimeter wire gate which had to be opened lest the barbed wire got entangled in and disabled the APCs' tracks' running gear, Adrian Roberts went well southeast out of Nui Dat and disregarded two orders to stop and wait for Colin Townsend but sent two of his 10 APCs back for the HQ 6RAR party. Adrian rightly assessed it was more important to get to Long Tan before dark than to wait for Townsend. Given the delay in releasing the APCs which sat at Alpha Company base for the best part of an hour and a quarter, it has never been explained why the CO and his signallers were unable to link up with the APCs before they left. One opinion is that he told Adrian via the Ops Officer he would fly out later (in monsoonal rain?) but was then told to get out by Jackson as he would have three companies on the ground. Adrian's eight remaining APCs then swam over the river some 2500 m well to the south of us, leaving another to guard the crossing and await the other two sent back for the 6RAR HQ group.

So just seven APCs moved north into the rubber and then contacted enemy, company-size D445, at 1100 m south of Delta Company at about 6.30pm. Alpha Company's Sergeant Frank Alcorta said, in Lex McAulay's 1986 book *Battle of Long Tan* and in emails to me in 1998, that when the enemy fired, he quickly rolled off the top of his APC, followed by his M60 gunner (late) Private Ron Brett:

I was surprised to see the VC panicked and broke ranks, fleeing to the east, throwing weapons, equipment, everything – I just could not believe my eyes. Had they pressed an attack I don't see how we could have stopped them. Yet they broke and ran.

No doubt this retreat was caused by the fearful noise and sight of the APCs and the impromptu dismounted assault by 11 men of Lieutenant Peter Dinham's 2 Platoon Alpha Company on the far right, supported by APC .50cal fire. While it took some time to get the ramp down, the other nine men dismounted to support Alcorta and his gunner Ron Brett. Why two men were on top of the APC in enemy territory when there was room for 12 passengers inside defies logic.

On the left flank the enemy fired a 57-mm RCL round at the APCs, but missed. Then the enemy crew was killed by the APC Crew Commander with his Owen gun when he found his .50 cal machine gun failed to fire because no firing pin had been installed in the hurry to move out. His driver passed up fresh magazines. He was recommended for an MID, but this was upgraded by Brigadier Jackson to the DCM. This DCM failed to compare with Jack Kirby's gallantry and the embarrassed recipient has become a recluse.

The enemy, D445, left behind eight bodies, one wounded, and several US Army type weapons probably captured from ARVN units which were picked up the next day when some of the APCs and 2 Platoon returned to the site. Claims by Alpha Company of 40 enemy killed may well have been an estimate but were unsubstantiated by just eight bodies and one wounded being found there the next day. The evidence suggests that D445 did not return to the battle site that night as they would not have left a wounded man, bodies and weapons behind, including the prized 57-mm RCL. Given they normally go out of their way to remove evidence I feel confident in saying the enemy did not return to that area at night, just as they did not return to our Delta Company battlefield area in the north that night. They left at dusk, carrying and dragging away as many dead and wounded and weapons as they could, many having already been removed during the battle by their evacuation and transportation units as now stated by the former enemy.

The seven APCs moved on, contacting another enemy company group at 800 m south of us who were already withdrawing, going home, and moving west to east – perhaps another company of D445, as is reported in the Official History and in one version of the enemy history. One of many different versions is that D445 were to move west to close the ambush. What ambush? Another version is that D445 set a 3km long ambush along the road from Long Phuoc to Xa Long Tan to entrap the Australians that 'came down out of the mountain' after three days of mortaring their Nui Dat base.

Adrian Roberts stated the enemy fired at the APCs and then their .50 cals took a heavy toll. The enemy were seen to drag away bodies with pre-fitted ankle straps. No bodies were found there the next day. These troops may have been the lot to our south that my CHQ had fired on. Or they may have been some of 275 Regiment trying to outflank us, or, at about 800 m south, part of the supposed 3km long D445 ambush along the Long Tan road, and being told to withdraw as part of the overall regimental withdrawal which apparently started about this time, 6.45pm.

One APC crew commander, Corporal Peter Clements, was shot in the chest and seriously wounded and that APC was sent back to base by Adrian Roberts. This was to cause bitter criticism by the Infantry commander, Captain Mollison, as it had Alpha Company 1 Platoon HQ and men on board, but no helicopter Dustoff casualty evacuation was possible because of the incessant rain and cloud. Adrian has admitted this error was due to compassion. But as happened, most of Alpha Company, other than 11 men of 2 Platoon, did not get engaged in dismounted combat. So the absence of 1 Platoon HQ did not really matter and a senior section commander could have taken over, but the criticism of the APCs went on, and still goes on! There is no love lost between the Alpha

Company and APC men. Part of the angst initiated and continued by Mollison was due to the troop commander Adrian Roberts receiving an MID award and a crew commander getting a DCM, while Alpha Company missed out on any Imperial awards. Our late commanding officer had told me in 1999 when I queried awards that he did not consider that Alpha Company – protected inside APCs, firing only 523 rounds as recorded in their After Action Report, less than a minute of M60 fire, with nil battle casualties – warranted any awards other than two of the 15 Vietnamese medals offered to 6RAR, with Delta Company getting 13.

Sadly, Corporal Clements died in Vung Tau hospital nine days later. There were no others killed or wounded in the APC/Infantry force, although Alpha Company was to claim in its 2005 book that three soldiers were wounded, rather than injured: one had concussion by an ammo box falling on his head inside an APC; one had a slight injury caused by an almost spent ricochet off the APC turret shield, and another was slightly injured by a piece of a tree branch. If

I had counted all my men with small injuries or wounds who remained on duty our wounded toll would have been nearer 40 than the official 23.

The APC force was described by many as being a 'relief' force but I asked to be reinforced, not to be 'relieved to go home', the Oxford definition. The correct title was the APC Reaction Force: the Field Force Victor 2 description as defined in Australian Task Force Standing Operating Procedures and Vietnamese award citations. Field Force Victor 2 was the combined US Army and ARVN HQ in Saigon which worked to the US Military Assistance Command Vietnam.

The remaining six APCs moved on, unopposed by enemy, to be finally joined about 300 m south of our position at about 6.55pm by the two APCs with the CO's Battalion HQ party and the other APC left at the river which had caught up. This latter group of three was commanded by Troop 2IC Second Lieutenant Ian Savage. Colin Townsend was of course in that HQ party. At this stage the enemy had already started to withdraw and most had gone east. It is recorded Townsend passed a message through his APC commander Ian Savage in the rear to tell Adrian Roberts, up front, to turn right and attack the last enemy who could be seen moving away in the gloom to the east.

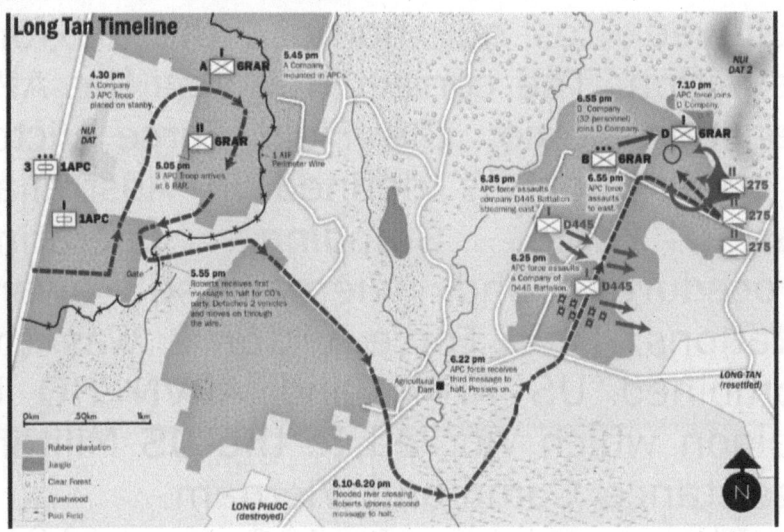

Adrian Roberts's carriers turned east to chase the withdrawing enemy. They chased them for about 500 m. The enemy returned very heavy fire but then disappeared into the trees and darkness. Alpha Company later claimed they had run through a gauntlet of a US 155-mm artillery barrage after the contacts to the south, yet an examination of the artillery fire mission log in the War Memorial Archives in

1999 showed no targets to the south and no doubt the cautious Artillery HQ would not have approved fire on the APC route. Put down to an accidental salvo or perhaps enemy mortars, it was revealed by former 2 Platoon commander Lieutenant Peter Dinham in 2006, then a retired colonel and awarded the AM (Member of the Order of Australia Medal), that the artillery fire was encountered after they turned and went east, which sounds logical because that is where the guns were targeted – out to the east of us, on the original enemy assembly and regimental HQ areas.

The enemy having disappeared into the gloom, the APC troop then moved back northwest to Delta Company area, arriving at 7.10pm, dismounting Alpha Company on our southeast flank, not 'on our west and then assaulted through Delta Company towards the enemy in extended line, fearing the worst' as recorded by author Mollison in his Alpha Company book. Despite media hype that 'CO6RAR led the APCs and broke up the enemy surrounding Delta Company', we were never surrounded – far from it.

And Colin Townsend arrived after the battle was over – the enemy having earlier withdrawn from Delta Company's position.

I moved over and met Captain Charles Mollison when his company dismounted at the 10 Platoon area on our southeast. He was brandishing a pistol, waving it around. Platoon Commander Geoff Kendall, carrying an SLR from one of his dead soldiers after his Armalite failed, said in Terry Burstall's first book, 'I can remember smirking to myself and being bemused by the fact that he was carrying this pistol.' One of his men in rear and still with a sense of humour said, 'He looks like Roy Rogers without his horse.' Some of my men cheered, patted and kissed the APCs. If the enemy were to counter-attack, we now had nine APCs, all with .50 or .30 cal machine guns, to support us. While some were to claim Delta Company was a spent force, we still had 70 fit soldiers and the platoon of 31 of Bravo Company, thus almost a full company, plenty of ammunition, and a regiment of artillery placing a wall of steel between us and the enemy. But we weren't aware the defeated enemy had already left the area for their home base.

The dismounted Alpha Company was soon followed by Colonel Townsend and his signallers who came forward and discussed the scenario with me. He naturally took command and then ordered Alpha Company to move across our front in a screen. There was no enemy in sight but it had to be considered they might counter-attack. By then the only noise was the loud crackling sounds of the hot APC diesel engines cooling down. But not an angry shot was fired then, that night, or over the next three days, except for a couple of rounds to kill two mortally wounded enemy the next day. These were acts of compassion, one by Bob Buick, the other by Private Dave Harwood of Alpha Company, both narrated in the 2005 Mollison book. The author criticises Bob Buick, but not Dave Harwood, but of course Buick was in Harry Smith's company!

And when I use the words mortally wounded, I am talking about poor bastards with their innards and brains spilling out of their ragged bodies – and barely alive in their awful agony. I add here that in 1986 *The Age* published a tale by author Terry Burstall, a 12 Platoon soldier in 1966, which claimed we shot and murdered 17 wounded enemy that day. The suggestion was that it was a reprisal for killing our 17 in action. Sadly, the article by Stuart Rintoul in which this tale appeared was never retracted. In 2014–15 some of our detractors are still claiming that Bob Buick 'murdered the enemy soldier and that I condoned the killing'. I believe Bob's decision was correct, borne of sympathy, not hate, despite all the 13 dead soldiers he lost from 11 Platoon the day before. I would have done the same to put the poor bastard out of misery. I have earlier described how I shot an unarmed wounded terrorist in Malaya because I thought he was about to throw a grenade at us. And we had shot an unarmed girl dressed in black at Long Phuoc in July because we thought she was enemy. That was war.

The night wore on, with the artillery firing defensive fire tasks to the east. There was no counterattack. And given the 293 bodies, four wounded and some 90 weapons left behind, including a wheeled machine and 60-mm mortar, RPGs and lots of 82-mm mortar bombs and other ammunition, there is no evidence the enemy returned to clear their remaining casualties as was their normal tactic. The recently published history of 275 Regiment clearly indicates they were badly mauled by the 'artillery rain', were unable to overrun us, and were given the order to start withdrawing, probably about 6.45pm. It also states Mrs Phoung's medical evacuation unit which was comprised of about 80 mostly female nurses, and a transportation unit which usually relayed messages and laid telephone lines, braved the artillery fire to carry out dead and wounded. And shallow mass graves were located further east on the 20th, with another 48 bodies and weapons never added to the 245 body count published on the 19th, making 293. Charlie Company 6RAR found another wounded VC. And Mike Wells tells that ARVN units found more mass graves further east towards the May Tao mountains where others died in their massive underground jungle hospital complex located by 6RAR on Operation 'Marsden' in 1969, with documents listing 878 enemy soldiers who had been killed, later dying from their wounds, or who were missing, presumed dead.

Some Alpha Company men thought they heard moans from 11 Platoon wounded, although more likely it was wounded enemy, and a couple of their men, Corporal Ross Smith and Private Peter Bennett, twice bravely went forward in the dark to seek them out. Later, CSM Jack Roughley also went forward alone, and found nothing. Had they asked they would have been told the 11 Platoon missing were at least 350 m out and they were wasting their time and venturing into possible danger.

Near 11.30pm, the CO decided to withdraw everyone back to the west of the rubber to evacuate the casualties. With respect, what an illogical and dangerous manoeuvre that was. If the enemy had still been around we might have been ambushed and that would have caused havoc and probably many more casualties, if not annihilation, moving through the experienced regular enemy's territory. At that time we really did not know the terrible damage we had inflicted and that the enemy was not really capable of ambushing any withdrawal, and had all left the area on the way back to their Nui May Tao jungle base.

All three company commanders, Noel Ford, Charles Mollison and myself, argued with the CO that a landing zone could have been made at the secure site now defended by Alpha, Delta and part of Bravo Company, plus 9 APCs, ringed by Artillery Defensive Fire tasks simply by the APCs pushing the rubber trees down, aided by the axes they carried, and the casualties taken out from there by Dustoff choppers. But we were overruled by Townsend. Further, there were only six hours to dawn and none of the 23 casualties in the company aid post appeared critical and so could have survived the wait. Maybe the CO was told by Jackson to get out, although it defied a crucial principle of war not to leave a secure base ringed with artillery Defensive Fire tasks for the unknown.

The APCs, with Delta Company and the casualties on board, led the way out to the west and when we got to the rubber edge Troop Commander Adrian Roberts formed a hollow square and we called in the casualty evacuation Dustoff choppers. Avoiding use of any torches, other companies' soldiers held on to each other's backpacks and tracked back through the pitch-black rubber. The USAF Dustoff choppers from Vung Tau soon came straight in with lights blazing in contrast to our own RAAF Hueys which came in cautiously and then went back to their comfortable Vung Tau barracks for a midnight steak and a beer. The RAAF always did things well, claiming they had to have good accommodation with air-conditioning to avoid pilot fatigue. It was still the same in 1975 when I ran free-fall course jumps near Dubbo. The Hercules C130 crew stayed in an air-conditioned four-star motel while we soldiers who had to jump out of the plane at 12,000ft, near 4km up, were relegated to the cheapest pub in town. Nevertheless, the RAAF always supported us and we got on well.

During the long night the Australian Task Force got into the act and named the operation 'Smithfield' (I'd called mine 'Vendetta') and opted for a 6RAR/5RAR battlefield clearance (clearing casualties and weapons) at dawn. But that did not eventuate until almost 9am when other companies of 5RAR and 6RAR arrived with more APCs in case the enemy was still there. Generally, Australian military operations were given a city or town name for battalion and above actions. When Long Tan was underway the Americans in Saigon apparently asked HQATF, who then asked the 6RAR battalion operations duty officer at Nui Dat, Captain Max Turrell, what the name of his operation was. He said, 'We haven't given it one but as Smith is having a field day out there we'll call it Smithfield.' That was announced about 11pm on the 18th and I recall sitting in the back of the APC with Mousey Townsend when the word came down of the name and that it would be a Task Force operation next morning. Mousey turned to me and said, 'The bloody Task Force Commander is getting in on the act.' He was referring to Jackson undermining his battalion by taking over the stage, which is what the CO did to my company.

It was suggested to me by the CO that my company go back to Nui Dat at dawn and on to Vung Tau for leave but I refused, wanting to get back to my 15 missing men and aware of the reports of US soldiers' bodies and wounded being monstrously mutilated by enemy up north – some while they were still alive – testicles cut off and placed in mouths, or throats cut. And I thought it essential for our own morale and peace of mind that my courageous men be first back in to recover our missing soldiers and first to see what we had done to the enemy, despite some enemy perhaps still being there.

There were some objections, with Geoff Kendall suggesting there were 'other companies that could lead the push', but I successfully overrode them and we led the advance back into the battlefield in Adrian Robert's APCs in the morning.

TEN

AFTER THE BATTLE: UNCOVERING THE TRUTH

The battlefield looked as though it had been hit by Godzilla or a tornado – trees shredded and bleeding white rubber sap and blood from bullet holes, and bodies, body parts and weapons scattered in the mayhem. Some bodies were hanging from rubber trees, snipers shot by my men or blown up there by the artillery. Whether the over 200 enemy dead had been shot or killed by artillery, many were torn apart by the thousands of large pieces of sharp and irregular steel artillery shrapnel flying through the air like razors. Private 'Sting' Hornett, who now lives in Bowen and gave his 'Ratcatcher' Flag to the Maryborough Museum in 2011, indicated one he shot, still hanging in a tree, recalling the enemy soldier must have been a 'medic', given all the bandages he had dropped into the mud.

Giving an Orders Group to my company staff on the morning of 19th August before our battlefield clearance.

It seemed as though a gargantuan mincer had been at work, dissecting, shredding, mashing, spitting out monstrous shapes that had once been limbs of men – lives torn apart. What carnage. Feral pigs gorged on the pieces. I have never since believed there is anything after death for us; death is just the end.

Astonishingly two of our 11 Platoon wounded had survived overnight: Privates Jim Richmond and Barry ('Custard') Meller. Jim was prostrate, bleeding from back wounds, and it was said he had not moved for an hour after being shot. In the hasty withdrawal under heavy enemy fire, with no opportunity to check pulses, he had been left as he was thought to be dead. Barry Meller, already wounded in the mouth, started back in the withdrawal but was then shot in the leg and had to be dragged along. He pleaded with his rescuer Lance Corporal Barry Magnussen to get himself out and leave him and he would hide. Barry Meller was to give a story to the Australasian Post magazine how he then sat quietly against a tree all night and a VC came up, removed his boots and took a cigarette he offered, but was to later retract that untruthful version. The VC had long gone.

Lieutenant Dave Sabben the morning after the battle.

Thirteen of the 11 Platoon missing lay dead. And they were still holding their rifles pointing east towards the enemy in front, as though they had read Lawrence Binyon's 'For the Fallen': *'They fell with their faces to the foe'.* The captured AK47 rifle was alongside Gordon Sharp's body. What a terribly sad sight that was, all these young soldiers dead, 13 of them from one platoon of 29, soldiers I had known, trained and led over the past year, and in in a war we should not have been involved in but, worse, killed by enemy the Task Force Commander Brigadier Jackson could have told us might have been out there! The saving grace, if that, was that we had killed at least 20 times the number we had lost.

11 Platoon area the morning after the battle.

Thankfully, the enemy had not entered the 11 Platoon area or touched any of our weapons nor mutilated anyone. It is likely that when they withdrew at dusk, dragging many of their own casualties away, they were kept fully occupied. There were a lot of dead and wounded to move out; their normal tactic was to not leave any evidence of their casualties. They took just one of all the 10 Platoon packs dropped when they went forward around the left flank. And it was recovered from a VC killed in a later operation 'Portsea'. They ratted some of the other packs and Sergeant Neil Rankin lost his camera. One of the 10 Platoon soldiers told me they could see the enemy going through their packs and fired at them, and in a short time there were more enemy dead there than packs.

Just some of the enemy weapons recovered.

The day was spent burying enemy bodies, counted at 245 as individual 6RAR platoons and others from 5RAR buried the dead in their allotted areas of responsibility on the battlefield and advised numbers to HQ. I saw a dead

VC officer with a Russian-Chicom Tokarev pistol in a nice holster on a belt with a red-star buckle and claimed that as a trophy of war. There were other pistols and small items like binoculars and compasses souvenired by others. There were three wounded prisoners, two from the North Vietnamese Army 806 Battalion of 45 NVA Regiment and one local D445. He was found with eight D445 bodies at the APC encounter area 1km to the south. All the weapons left behind, about 80, mostly AK47 carbines, plus SKS rifles and RPD light machine guns, a 60-mm mortar and the wheeled machine gun (a wheeled Soviet Guryunov heavy-barrelled MMG of the type which took a toll on the Germans at Stalingrad) were piled up, with all the mortar bombs, RPGs, grenades and ammunition found on or around the dead. Some of 2 Platoon Alpha Company in a section of APCs went back 1km south to their initial encounter area and recovered the eight D445 bodies, one wounded and various US Army type weapons like Garand rifles, a Thompson SMG, and a 57-mm RCL.

Later, Alpha Company went in APCs to the village of Xa Long Tan, and it is noted in the 6RAR Log that they were placed 'Under Command' of the APCs, which is what the CO should have ordered the day before. This would have prevented the command problems between Adrian Roberts and Charles Mollison.

Resting during battlefield clearance.

I was there when the three prisoners guarded by Private David Collins with his rifle at the ready were interrogated by the 6RAR intelligence officer, Captain Bryan Wickens. The two NVA 806 Battalion soldiers told us through an interpreter that they were on their way to attack our base. Some 'X Spurts' were to claim we had walked 'heads down arse up' into a set-piece ambush. Rubbish. They had just listened to the propaganda from Hanoi Hannah who claimed the VC had ambushed and destroyed an enemy battalion, tanks and planes. I am of the opinion that VC tales of an ambush were fabricated for propaganda to cover up the failure of their proposed attack on Nui Dat and all the casualties they suffered in the rubber at Long Tan.

Hannah was the silver-tongued Trịnh Thị Ngọ, who was born in 1931 and made English-language broadcasts directed at US troops for North Vietnam. She came from a rich factory owner's family and was eager to learn English because she wanted to watch her favourite films like Gone with the Wind without subtitles. Her family arranged private lessons in English. When she was 25 she began reading the English language newscast for Vietnam's national radio station that was aimed at listeners in Asia's English-speaking countries.

Private David Collins guarding a prisoner.

Ngo made three broadcasts a day, reading the list of the newly killed or imprisoned Americans, attempting to persuade US GIs that the US involvement in the Vietnam War was unjust and immoral. She played popular US anti-war songs in an attempt to incite feelings of nostalgia and homesickness among the troops. Although she used the alias Thu Huong (in Vietnamese it means 'the fragrance of autumn') the GIs usually referred to her as Hanoi Hannah or the Dragon Lady.

Few, if any, desertions are believed to have resulted from her propaganda efforts but the soldiers were often impressed by her military intelligence, especially when she mentioned the location of their own unit! Then it was customary to lift a can or bottle to toast her and throw beer cans at the radio. She also managed to list specific American casualties. Most of her information came from publications such as the US military newspaper Stars and Stripes.

On 20 August all rifle companies of 6RAR and one of 5RAR followed up on the blood-spattered enemy withdrawal route out to the limit of artillery support gun range. Shallow graves, probably dug during the battle were located with another 48 bodies mentioned earlier, another wounded, and a number of weapons, but these bodies were not officially added to the 245 total previously advised up the line to HQ Field Force Victor 2 on the 19th. There were also a large number of trenches in the jungle area east of the rubber, and this may well have been the lying-up area for 275 Regiment after their arrival on the 14th, while preparing to move on Nui Dat.

Some say the initial body count total was premature but it was used anyway for the widely transmitted US Body Count media release – before all the bodies were buried and before the search covered a wider area on the enemy withdrawal route. The dead were mostly brainwashed young soldiers willing to die blindly for the Communist cause and many perished with photographs of loved ones in their uniforms. It took two days to bury the poor bastards. I had requested 6RAR Ops Officer to try and get a small bulldozer flown in by a USAF Chinook, but that did not eventuate, so all the graves, albeit shallow, were dug by hand. The droning flies provided the mourning wail.

By the time we had left the battlefield area on 21 August the enemy body count was 293 plus four wounded prisoners, almost 300. Years later official enemy records finally told the truth – that despite their original reports of only 30 killed, some 1000 were killed or wounded and later died from those wounds. That was out of what we by then estimated had been a total of some 2000 enemy that we actually faced. Forty-seven years later the history of the local enemy Provincial Battalion, D445, along with some of the 275 Regiment History published in 2011 made interesting and somewhat humorous reading.

Enemy records were researched by retired Brigadier Ernie Chamberlain CSC, a former Intelligence Corps officer who served in Vietnam and who is fluent in the language. He translated the histories and the D445 History is now available on the Internet. He has also worked on translating the 274 and 275 Histories. It appears the captured enemy soldiers identified as being from the NVA 806 Battalion of 45 NVA Regiment had joined 275 Regiment as its third battalion, and we only faced three battalions with support troops, plus

D445 in the south. Brigadier Chamberlain told me the NVA Battalion was originally D605 and had trekked 2000km south over 112 days to infiltrate South Vietnam and join 275 Regiment in May 1966. Given the inaccuracy and confusion with unit designators, and enemy records containing all sorts of propaganda and hyperbole, that may or may not have been fact. Ernie told me he simply 'translated the enemy story'. As I said to the retired brigadier last year, there was still a fucking awful lot of them out there! Even just four battalions plus support troops was still around 2000 of mostly well-tried and well-equipped enemy soldiers trying to take our 100 out.

I think it is worthwhile looking at what little the D445 Battalion History says about the Long Tan battle:

> In the 1996 Wet Season, the headquarters of the 5th Division coordinated with the military headquarters of Baria – Long Khanh Province to direct a major destructive strike against the Australian forces on the Ba Ria

battleground. Comrades Nam Truyen (Commander, 5th Division), Na Tam (Deputy Commander), Ba Ut (Commander, Ba Ria Provincial Unit), Ut Dang (Deputy Commander, Long Khanh Provincial Unit), together with staff elements of the two units, held many meetings to carefully consider and assess the situation, while delegating Comrade Nguyen Huu Nghia, second-in-command of the reconnaissance company of 5th Division and the 445 Battalion's reconnaissance element to go and examine the battlefield in the Long Tan and Long Phuoc region of Ba Ria. After three days they had completed their study. In the Lo O stream base the Province's military command section and headquarters of the Division convened a conference of the 445 Battalion and the 275th Regiment of the 5th Division to thoroughly study the outline of the ambush battle to destroy the Australians at Long Tan. The forces to participate in the fighting comprised:

The 2nd Company of 445 Battalion being the forward blocking force at Hamlet 1 of Long Tan village; 1st and 3rd companies as the rear blocking group, and the 3rd Battalion of 275 Regiment with the responsibility of the flanking thrust (the decisive point). We reinforced the area of the killing ground with 12DH5 and DH110 mines (like claymores) and 42 American Mk1 mines; the 80-strong Vo Thi Sau civil labour company – comprised mainly of females and led by Chin Phuong as company commander to support the battle; a surgery element led by Dr Phong and Dr Kinh; a forward element was established two kilometres north of Long Tan (Nui Dat 2 and Ap Phuoc Hung) to directly command the battle. The ambush configuration for the battle was almost three kilometres long (on the Long Tan–Long Phuoc road).

At 10.15am on 18th August 1966 two Australian battalions and an armoured vehicle squadron advanced in three columns that moved in parallel into our battle zone. The main column advanced along the road to Long Tan with four tanks in the vanguard, followed by two infantry companies supported by two armoured vehicles. The two subsidiary columns advanced as pincers – parallel with the main column and at a distance of 300 metres from it. Each of the pincers comprised a battalion with two tanks in support. All three enemy columns fell into our encircling ambush. Ut Dang ordered secrecy and to wait until the enemy is truly close and only open fire when the order is given by headquarters.

Everything went without a hitch until the last minute. When an enemy tank was 50 metres from the forward blocking position the trigger was pulled on a recoilless rifle but the round misfired! The enemy then discovered our battle position. They fired thick and fast while withdrawing and redeploying their formations. Comrade Le Tanh Trung, a 5th Division reinforcement to D445 armed with a B40 (RPG), had just got up to fire on a tank when he was shot through the chest by an enemy heavy machine gun. The hero had fallen. Nguyen Huu Nghai came forward and grabbed the B40 and hit the leading armoured vehicle, setting it on fire. Comrade Vinh, number two on a 57-mm RCL, followed up by loading a second round for Comrade Tan to hit and set fire to the second armoured vehicle. The third armoured vehicle was destroyed by two B41 (large RPG) rounds fired by the reconnaissance unit from 5th Division. The engagement of the forward blocking force became increasingly fierce. The situation was like a 'Battle Royal' as the enemy massed quite close to our positions. The battle became close combat, fought in groups and by areas – it was difficult for our infantry and artillery to support one another. Rain began to come down in buckets. Our 57-mm RCL was nullified and many of our comrades in the crew were killed and the crew commander captured.

After the first few minutes of confusion our forward position was still able to force the enemy into the killing zone. They fell into our minefield and were killed in large numbers. Our rear element also began to storm into the enemy in the killing zone – while at the same time, our flanking attacking group advanced. The enemy was in a miserable situation and surrounded, but the tanks and infantry in their subsidiary columns continued to press into our area that lacked anti-tank firepower and counter-attacked us. Following this the enemy regrouped and used coloured smoke to mark their positions and called in directed artillery fire. We were unable to move even a half-metre to finish off a number of the enemy because of their 'rain of artillery' fire from the New Zealand orchestra. Almost all our attacking elements suffered casualties to the enemy artillery. Comrade Sau Chien was seriously wounded by an AR15 round that passed through one ear lobe to the other. Comrade Sau Chien, commander of 1st Company was killed.

After about an hour of fighting, the headquarters ordered our elements to withdraw. Mrs Chin Phuong and her comrades – unafraid of death, ran fearlessly though the enemy's falling artillery and – together with the troops, carried the wounded to safety. In this large battle with Australian forces, we wiped out an entire company and inflicted heavy casualties on one of their battalions. COSVN Headquarters awarded the Liberation Combat Exploits Medal Third Class for the battle. However it was also a battle in which we suffered heavy casualties. In 445 Battalion 2nd Company alone there were 23 casualties, of whom three died. The 5th Division lost 30 comrades killed and over 60 wounded. Our casualties were mainly inflicted by the enemy's artillery. Once more, 445 Battalion's cadre and soldiers again discovered a dangerous trick; the use by the Australians of direct and counter-assault artillery fire.

This very brief D445 version is absolute codswallop and grossly exaggerated, probably to impress the highly controlled local population in Phuoc Tuy and was based on a supposed 3-km long ambush set along the road from Long Phuoc to Long Tan village, well south of where the main battle was fought. We, one rifle company, did not venture south along that road and the main battle was fought in the rubber 2km north of the road. The enemy also claims to 'have lured the tiger from the mountain' by three days of continual mortaring on our Nui Dat base and then decimated one of two Australian battalions and many of the tanks which then came out astride the road, some running into a minefield, with 'our panic-stricken survivors fleeing 6km south to Dat Do'. They claimed the mortaring of Nui Dat was carried out by 275 Regiment heavy weapons teams guided by local D445 soldiers. D445 did not have heavy weapons in 1966, just a few 57-mm RCLs and 60-mm mortars. D445 history completely disregards the main battle between Delta Company and 275 Regiment in the north as though it alone fought a successful battle with a large Australian force in the south. This is far from the truth. The only glimmer of truth is the 57-mm RCL crew killed by Adrian Roberts's APCs as they entered the rubber in the south. No APCs were hit or set on fire as claimed.

In the 275 Regiment History, it is said that the regimental commander gave the order to withdraw at dusk after being unable to over-run us and suffering heavy casualties from what was described as New Zealand 'artillery rain'. The time allowed for the battle had run out, and no doubt they were also aware of the returning Bravo Company platoon group and seven APCs approaching. The enemy's inability to take out these two relatively small groups indicates how badly they had been mauled. If, as some say, they had planned an ambush then the only available APC route in the south would have been well and truly blocked and ambushed by anti-tank guns and ample troops with heavy weapons. And the enemy seen by Bravo Company as they neared our position would surely have taken them on instead of waving at them. There is little doubt the mythical ambush was poorly planned and commanded, adding weight to the original concept that the VC 5th Division plan was to attack the poorly defended Nui Dat base, not to set an unlikely ambush in or east of the rubber plantation. 275 History does not mention D445 being in the south.

The truth is my company of 105, more than half young National Servicemen, bolstered expertly by the NZ Artillery party, was sent out to relieve Bravo Company and continue the search through the Long Tan rubber for an estimated 40 to 50 enemy who had mortared the Nui Dat base for only 22 minutes at 2.40am the previous morning – not three days! We just happened to get in the way of the enemy regiment about to advance on Nui Dat.

For my men it was a painful and long wait to hear the real truth of our victory at Long Tan. When it finally came we were a bit surprised but not shocked. We knew we had, in crude Aussie slang, rooted the enemy.

Later, in October 1966 when our forces captured the diary of Colonel Nguyen Nam Hung, the Deputy Commander of 274 Regiment, he indicated 275 Regiment had lost 500 killed in action and 800 wounded in action. Given the 293 bodies they left behind that was quite realistic. In 1969, 6RAR on Operation 'Marsden' captured hospital records in the May Tao Mountain 5 Division base area listing the names of those who had died. It said that KIA, Missing, and Died of Wounds numbered some 878. I add that although the enemy diary was said to have been seen by Brigadier Stuart Graham who took over from Brigadier Jackson in January 1967, that diary, and the alleged official list of enemy killed found in the May Tao hospital in 1969, seen by journalist and photographer the (late) Denis Gibbons AM who was at 'Marsden', are not in AWM or National Archives, and may well have been souvenired as trophies of war.

While some dispute the figures, for another 500 to have been dragged away and to have died from wounds en route to or in jungle hospitals by 1969 is not unreasonable as the normal ratio is three wounded to one dead, and they left behind near 300 bodies. This illustrates their large number of casualties, and they normally tried to remove all dead and wounded to hide the facts of their losses from their enemies.

Chinese Army records, shown by a Chinese General to former Australian Army Officer Geoff Jones working in Beijing on Army Landing Craft electronics in 2006, gave the eventual final figure to be 1500 who eventually died or were disabled from wounds. He relayed the information by email to Bob Buick. I have spoken to Geoff, and while others dispute his story, I tend to believe what he says, as the information fits with what we already knew or have ascertained from enemy history published in more recent years. Critics are quick to point out that D445 recovered to fight at 'Bribie' in February so they could not have been too battered. But they do not understand D445 was not in the main battle nor hit by our artillery fire and only two companies were involved with the APC Reaction Force in the south, the rest being near Xa Long Tan with some perhaps guarding the enemy heavy weapons sent to the rear.

Only eight D445 bodies were left behind at the site of the APC encounters, indicating that most of D445 Battalion probably survived and were to fight effectively against 6RAR in Operation 'Bribie' of February 1967, although it now appears some 275 Regiment units were also involved. Enemy history indicates the Main Force Regiments had the same attitude to D445 as that of the early ARA to the CMF – part-time warriors, so keep them out of the way on a flank, or similar. Consequently, 275 Regiment and D445 Battalion enemy history about Long Tan makes little mention of other units in the battle area, mainly just themselves.

In a 2006 *60 Minutes* TV interview in South Vietnam with Dave Sabben and

Bob Buick the former D445 enemy also changed their old tune of their ambushing and destroying a battalion, tanks and aircraft, to one of yes, 'you (the Australians) won the battle at Long Tan' but they 'won the war'. Well, I can't dispute all that! But without doubt our chance encounter thwarted a VC 5th Division attack on our poorly defended Nui Dat base.

Contrary to the opinion of commentators far from the action there was no ambush – the enemy came forward from the jungle to the east of the rubber plantation to investigate the first contact. They obviously did not wish to be located, as they left us alone on the 15th when we were near the base of Nui Dat 2 and the hut in the rubber; did not worry Alpha Company near Nui Dat 2; and left Bravo Company alone on the 17th when they could have wiped out a company if they had wished, or the best part of two companies on the 18th when we arrived to relieve Bravo.

All this happens to have been confirmed by ARVN intelligence facts advised to HQ ATF by Australian Army

Training Team Vietnam Ba Ria Liaison Officer Captain Mike Wells in the weeks and months after the battle. But, like his warnings before the battle, because he was just a CMF officer, another commando with a green beret, he was not believed by those in command at Nui Dat HQ ATF.

Mike Wells speaks of ARVN battalions locating mass grave sites out to the northeast in the weeks after the battle. I gather that after the war all body remains were dug up and reburied in local cemeteries, marked with a simple plaque dated 18.8.66. It is claimed by Australians now living in Vung Tau that about 1000 of these plaques for those lost in 1966 or who subsequently died in later years have been counted or advised as being in main town centres around Phuoc Tuy Province.

Surprisingly there was no dedicated action to immediately cut off the enemy retreat. ATF was fully committed and reluctant to move Artillery out to a fire support base and permit Infantry to venture further afield. US Army and ARVN units launched Operation 'Toledo' in northern Phuoc Tuy province several days later, from 23 to 31 August and again 2 to 8 September, to trap the enemy 5 Division units, especially 275 Regiment after their defeat at Long Tan, but the operation was apparently badly conceived, too late, and caught no one.

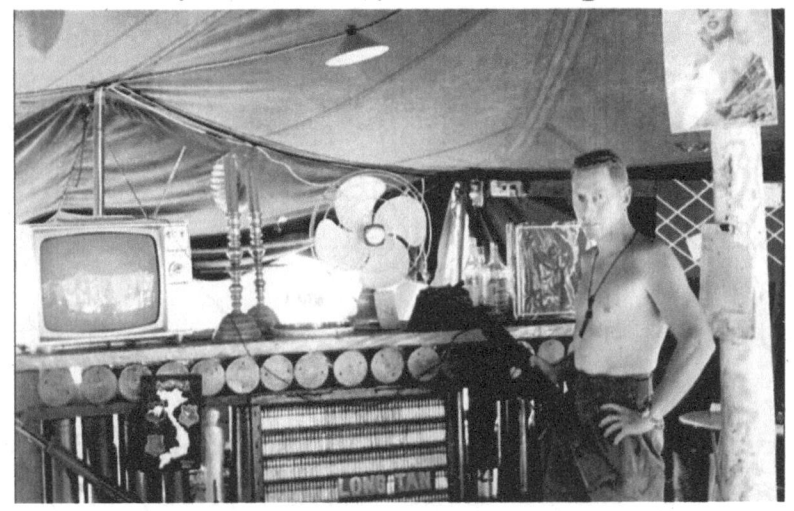

Long Tan Souvenirs in the officers/NCOs canteen Nui Dat.

Certainly, and sadly, Long Tan saw our largest loss of young National Servicemen in the Vietnam War and they fought with great courage and determination. But there was quite naturally a public outcry about the casualties, particularly the National Servicemen, which caused immediate instructions to be given to avoid further heavy conflict. I am aware that Australian Force Vietnam HQ in Saigon was then ordered to ensure that each platoon comprised equal numbers of National Service and Australian Regular Army men and to use Artillery fire before Infantry attacks. Of course there was no way the platoons could be reorganised along those lines, but it was likely fed to the public to counter claims of National Servicemen being used up front and more susceptible to being killed.

In our defence, we only had 108 men up against 2000 enemy, not that I am suggesting they all attacked at once. I think that when they finally located our company defensive position, after being confused as to who, what and where we were, they attacked with successive suicidal battalion attacks, which we were able to repulse with wonderful artillery support and our own machine guns and rifles, causing them horrendous casualties. Not one enemy got inside our front line. And thankfully, all the enemy's 82-mm mortars and other heavy weapons were not set up to fire on us, as in a normal ambush killing ground, otherwise the outcome may have been a lot different.

Me wearing the captured Tokarev pistol, dressed to fly to Saigon to meet Dad.

Let me recap on the serious errors made at ATF HQ. For these errors to have happened within the Australian military is extraordinary.

We were not told the Australian Army Training Team Liaison Officer at nearby Ba Ria had advised the Task Force HQ the enemy 5th Division was moving south towards our Nui Dat base and that mercenary ARVN commando troops had deserted from Binh Ba, just to our north, because they were frightened of the approaching enemy forces moving on Nui Dat.

Neither the two Battalion COs nor commanders of patrolling companies like mine were told that Radio and RDF Intercept had tracked the NVA-reinforced 275 Regiment moving in to just east of the Long Tan rubber on 14 August. We had patrolled the rubber on the 15th and seen nothing. Bravo Company was in there that morning, with Alpha Company further north. All the evidence suggests the enemy was secretly lying in wait to attack the base on the night of the Col Joye and Little Pattie concert. Many dispute that, but I clearly recall the two NVA prisoners saying they were on the way to attack our base, confirmed by 10 ARVN Division agents. Good enough for me.

Others believe that the well-rehearsed enemy stories of an ambush in the dense rubber plantation was simply propaganda to cover up failure, as no-one normally sets an ambush without a clear killing ground. Author Terry Burstall tells of a 1987 interview with a former enemy regimental commander who claimed they were to have ambushed our 'battalion' when it got though the rubber into the clear area southeast of the Nui Dat 2 hill. How would they have known any troops would have gone out that far, or why? The D445 story is that a 3km long ambush was set along the Long Tan–Long Phuoc road well south of the battle area. Whose ambush story should be believed? I suggest neither.

We were not ambushed, nor led into a trap. We could have gone north along fresh tracks, probably made by enemy who went north and passed by Alpha Company, but I elected to go east to get through the rubber into jungle for a more secure night base free from mosquitoes. Underneath all the propaganda, there is an element of truth in that the 5 Division plan was to lure troops out from Nui Dat with the mortaring of the base on the 17th to weaken the defences for an attack on the night of the concert. But it all went wrong for the enemy. Only a company was lured out, Bravo Company, and it was not molested, and then my Delta Company with artillery support just happened to get in the way the next day.

The three-and-a-half-hour battle started at 3.40pm with 11 Platoon firing on a small enemy patrol moving up from the south, which fled east. The platoon followed up and ran into many more enemy who had come forward to investigate the noisy intrusion. The platoon took heavy casualties, with 13 men killed, including the platoon commander. The action then developed into a violent company defensive battle, while the main activity back at base was the concert. And, looking back, the new Task Force and senior commanders were not really geared up for a battle of the nature of Long Tan. I confess I never envisaged a regimental attack on our base with the attackers lying in wait east of the Long Tan rubber until the night of the concert.

At 4.20pm I called for reinforcements by helicopter, but the request was denied as no ATF ready reaction company was on line. I was told Alpha Company in APCs would be sent out 'soon', but they were then held back for well over an hour. I asked Bravo Company to come back. They were told not to move back. Initially we had just six guns of 161 NZ Battery. I requested every gun – the whole regiment in support – but this request was also denied.

I think they thought that young upstart Smith was joking, and I had to argue to get the 18 105-mm guns plus the six US 155s. When I told the forward observer to 'drop 50' onto a big assault, he said Artillery HQ denied it because it was considered 'unsafe'. Unsafe! I grabbed the radio and said those few very choice and heated words to those protected in their command posts back at Nui Dat, as outlined earlier. They then fired where we wanted it.

Brigadier Jackson and others had refused to think the enemy might attack Nui Dat. 274 Regiment was located to the north of Nui Dat, and when the shit hit the fan at Long Tan, Jackson then thought 274 might come down and attack his base and that is why he was reluctant to release the APCs with Alpha Company after I had called for reinforcements, which were ready to move.

We now believe all the enemy's many 82-mm mortars and a similar number of RCLs and heavy machine guns and at least one 70-mm artillery gun were ready to be carried forward to support the attack on Nui Dat. They were not set up to fire on us at Long Tan, as you would expect in the ambush scenario many have postulated. The enemy was expert in setting ambushes, and they did not set an ambush for us in a rubber plantation with no clear view of the killing zone. If they had set a proper ambush for us I would not be writing this now. I add that Kiem, supposed CO of D445 at the battle in 1966 and who was interviewed by various historians, including those from the AWM, was discovered by Brigadier Ernie Chamberlain in recent times to have not even been with D445 in 1966 and thus most of what he told was far from the truth and mostly propaganda.

When the US 155s and Phantom airstrike caused havoc in rear echelons, the heavy weapons were apparently all moved well to the east out of harm's way, back to a rice cache base area protected by local VC forces, perhaps D445, half of them not being involved with the APC encounters in the south and none with us.

Prior to Long Tan the mindset was local units, the black/khaki pyjama'd local D445 battalion of about four-hundred soldiers with a variety of US-type weapons captured over the years. We were told the well-armed Main Force (regular) units of two Regiments, 274 and 275 of the VC 5th Division, 5000 men, were well to the north.

Before Long Tan there were small contacts, such as a 5RAR platoon in June killing three local VC said to be 'ineffective guerillas', near the Suoi Da

Bang River. In July we took sniper fire when destroying the local village of Long Phuoc just 2km south of our Nui Dat base and shot a woman dressed in black. My 10 Platoon had shot a D445 VC armed with an AK47 earlier in July. Bravo and Charlie Companies 6RAR saw some heavy action with local D445 in July on Operation Hobart, losing three killed and 19 wounded, the enemy repelled with artillery fire they called 'NZ artillery rain'.

We now know the enemy 5 Division/275 Regiment HQ was initially at Ap Phuoc Hung, 2km east of the rubber, the commanders having earlier met on 10 August to the east on the Suoi Lo O Nho river base 4000m east of the battle site to make plans. Their forward operational HQ might have then moved west to the slopes of Nui Dat 2 during the battle. D445 might have been the meeters, greeters and trench diggers for 275 Regiment but during the battle they were always to the south and, despite their unit history claims, were not in a 3-km ambush position along the Long Phuoc–Long Tan road. As recorded in the Official History, only two companies were in the area north of the road and, according to the former commanders who spoke frankly to Dave Sabben and Bob Buick in 2006, the rest of the battalion was near their home base of Xa Long Tan village.

When the APCs had not arrived by 5.30pm and were obviously unlikely to arrive before dark, I said a few more words in growing frustration and they, and Bravo Company, were finally released, leaving at 5.45pm. Then the helicopter ammunition resupply arrived at 6pm, delayed at least half an hour by deep and meaningful discussions about the 1966 RAAF policy of not flying into dangerous areas.

But we repelled successive suicidal enemy assaults with the artillery fire we directed through NZ Captain Morrie Stanley. That tremendous weight of gunfire, along with over 10,000 rounds fired by my forward soldiers at close range, inflicted massive casualties on the enemy. There are those who still dispute the numbers we killed. A 2014 website, 'Axis', claims the Battle of Long Tan was 'Another Anzac Myth'. One statement is that Lieutenant Andrews's

9 Platoon buried only 50 bodies in the whole Delta Company area, and that Terry Burstall claims to have seen only 50 bodies. Neither of these two reports relate to the whole area of the battlefield, just their own platoon areas. I did not go around and count them, being far too busy with my own casualties, but I can assure you there were bodies everywhere. Bob Buick tells he and a soldier, M60 gunner Peter Dettman, marked bodies with tree branches to avoid a double count and marked 130 just near the 11 Platoon area. The total of reports collated by HQ6RAR from various platoon areas was 245 buried, with 48 more found in a shallow mass grave to the east on 20 August. The 275 Regt enemy history states only 60 or so were killed but a former VC officer adds that he knows over 200 were lost on the battlefield. On the other side of the 'Axis' website coin, another article by Long Tan documentary producer and former commando Martin Walsh suggests the first 'Axis' author does not comprehend the damage done by over 10,000 small

arms rounds fired at close range and 3500 artillery shells.

The 6RAR Bravo Company platoon group arrived back just before 7pm. The APCs with Alpha Company gallantly broke through two D445 enemy company groups about 1km to the south, the second one already withdrawing east, and then, joined by Battalion HQ, they chased the badly-mauled enemy out east, returning to us at 7.10pm, the battle well and truly over.

There has been a great deal of angst among those who supported us at Long Tan because we have been given three Unit Citations. Yet the US, ARVN and now Australian authorities, not us, decided it was Delta Company which fought the main battle and suffered all but one of those killed (the APC corporal who later died of wounds).

I often think perhaps a better way to describe Long Tan is that there were two battles – the one fought by Delta Company and the Artillery, the other by the APC Reaction Force – maybe 30 minutes all up in the two actions with D445 on the way in. The APCs have not been properly recognised for their gallant approach from Nui Dat, swimming over the river, and assaulting the enemy in the southern area of the Long Tan rubber plantation and in their final withdrawal to the east.

I was debriefed by the US Army and GRVN Army at HQ FFV2, Saigon, in late August and I became aware of the respect they had for Long Tan and us Australians. That respect had also been evident in Korea. It was at that debrief I was told by a US Army colonel we were to be recommended for a Unit Citation by their Honours and Awards units, which investigates actions, as opposed to our system that relies too much on the personal opinion of senior officers who are often nowhere near the action. I was also told by an Army of the Republic of Vietnam colonel that they would match that unit award. I explore that in a later chapter.

Meanwhile we owe our lives to my gallant men and the Artillery units who caused enormous enemy casualties. Apart from the blood and gore on the battlefield I recall all the blood trails on the enemy withdrawal route just east of the 11 Platoon area. Forty-nine years on I can still see all the bushes stained red from the blood of all the wounded as they were carried or assisted to walk in their withdrawal to the east.

The ammo resupply by the RAAF helicopters also contributed to our success because after the helicopter resupply forward section weapons were then able to fire at will, not conserve ammo.

We returned to Nui Dat on the afternoon of the 21st. At midnight, the CO rang me to request I submit urgent recommendations for awards as Canberra wanted to placate the public who were protesting the loss of so many young soldiers, mostly National Servicemen. A week later I was requested to submit citations for Vietnamese awards to be presented on 2 September.

While I have always been deeply saddened by the loss of the 18 young men in a battle that should not have happened, in a war we could not win, and, as well, the 521 men who gave their lives during the Vietnam War, I must say I now feel too for the families and loved ones of those young enemy soldiers we killed. Many of these soldiers were just teenagers.

But, both sides did what each side was required to do – kill the enemy – a wretched task that has always plagued the human race and is still going on today. But that is war and that is what we were trained and paid for, to do our duty to the death, if that happened.

The rest of the yearlong tour passed slowly after Long Tan and those who had been involved were different people seeing the war through very new eyes. We trained reinforcements whom we received after Long Tan and the 2 December 1966 IED mine disaster where we had one killed and 10 wounded and the 6 February 1967 NZ Artillery disaster which rained 105mm shells on us, causing four killed and another 13 wounded, and conducted more patrols and ambushes. In January 1967 we were presented with the ribbons for our Imperial awards, about half those recommended in late August.

Delta Company was a flanking cut-off force on the possible enemy withdrawal track at Operation 'Bribie' in February 1967, which saw Bravo Company unnecessarily lose men when ordered into a frontal attack rather than to outflank enemy bunkers. We went into the battleground next morning with Charlie Company and found five dead and Private Vic Otway of Bravo Company, left behind, wounded but alive. Vic had been in the platoon group that came back into Long Tan. The toll from 'Bribie' was seven killed and 26 wounded for eight enemy bodies left behind.

A rather nice interlude happened after the battle when my father flew into Saigon in late 1966 on his way to Japan. Dad was by then an executive with Cadbury-Fry Pascall in Tasmania. Our ration packs contained the normal hard tack but also a little bar of Cadbury's chocolate – the trouble was it was white instead of that traditional lovely rich brown. Colonel Townsend asked Brigadier Jackson on my behalf if I could go up to Saigon to meet with Dad who had written to me asking if he could visit the Nui Dat base. I flew to Saigon on one of our Caribous that made that journey daily – the 'Vung Tau Express'. Dad and I met at the Continental Hotel and I stayed overnight. It was a nice bonding session for a father and son who had never been very close.

Me and Jim Campbell. Photo courtesy Ron Smith.

Next day we flew down to Nui Dat and Lieutenant Jim Campbell DFC, one of our Army aviation chopper pilots, later to fly in the original Sunshine Coast rescue helicopter crew, flew Dad in a Sioux helicopter out over the Long Tan battlefield. I showed him around our company base with captured heavy weapons at our flagpole. Dad was very moved.

I tackled him about the white chocolate in our packs and showed him where our ration packs were stored outside the Battalion QM store. He quickly saw it wasn't sun-sheltered and on returning to Tasmania he wrote to the Army explaining the problem and how it could be remedied. Not long after, Army rations suddenly included 'proper' chocolate, rich brown in colour, because a storage shelter system had been put in place, thanks to my father.

Father and son at Nui Dat, with captured 60mm mortar and machine gun..

After Long Tan, we were often visited by Jean Debelle, an Aussie Red Cross nurse who wrote letters home for our many wounded in hospital, and who was to author a 2006 book *Write Home for Me.* Rumours abounded about Jean and me, and when I spent the last night in Vietnam at Vung Tau the soldiers claimed I was with Jean. Not so – Jean looked up to Delta Company but she was very much involved with a US doctor whom she later married. I spent that last night with 9 Squadron RAAF helicopter pilots who flew me down to Vung Tau in a 'private taxi' Huey chopper, with the Red Cross girls on board. Next morning, they flew me out onto the deck of HMAS *Sydney* just before she sailed, much to the disgust of the CO. We had a great rapport with 9 Squadron and most pilots were happy to deliver rations and stores to our patrols from our own company LZ, and give me a lift to Vung Tau when required. After Vietnam, with 1 Commando and the Parachute School I often used 9 Squadron helicopters for parachuting and rappelling.

Me and Jean Debelle (first on my left) at Nui Dat canteen.

Jean Debelle was Red Cross and what a superb organisation that was and is. There were 43 dedicated members of the Royal Australian Army Nursing Corps in Vietnam. Australian women civilians also went to Vietnam as journalists, entertainers, Red Cross support and in civilian medical teams. It saddens me that as a result of exposure to various elements of the war, too many nurses are now ill or failing and the civilian nurses are getting no compensation for their disabilities. When will we ever learn to stop man's inhumanity to man – and to women?

ELEVEN

COMMANDO ACTION, SAILING AND DIVORCE

With more blood on my hands than a man deserves in 20 lifetimes Delta Company and I sailed home from Vung Tau on the aircraft carrier-cum-troopship HMAS *Sydney* on 30 May 1967 and docked at Brisbane on 14 June. It was a slow trip and we were not told she was to escort a former UK destroyer, the HMS *Duchess,* which had been plugged up with concrete in Singapore after its hull rusted out en route to Australia. I note in the media Defence is still buying worn-out ships 46 years on. About two days out of Vung Tau we seemed to be going around in large circles, as an island was going past to the left one day, then to the right the next day. The ship's crew were tight-lipped but eventually we were told we had detoured via offshore Singapore to escort *Duchess* back to Darwin, so the trip was to take a week longer than usual, 16 days, just what we needed, and although anxious to see loved ones and families for the first time in a year, the delay and relaxation probably helped what is now termed the 'healing process'.

Delta Company and I were glad to see the end of Vietnam; what we had thought would be an adventure turned into a disaster with 23 young soldiers killed and 47 wounded; 70 casualties out of a nominal strength of 125 men over the year tour. The original company had been badly knocked around at Long Tan; then by the mine incident in November, and the NZ artillery accident on 6 February 1967. That day I was in hospital at Vung Tau after a rare but bad asthma attack and my company was patrolling southeast of Long Tan under the acting commander, new 2IC Captain 'Mick' Weaver. On 6 February 'Mick' told Artillery FO Lieutenant Barrie Winsor to call in an artillery strike on a suspected Viet Cong position some distance away. Most of the two 105-mm salvos, 12 rounds, accidentally fell on the company HQ area and Jack Kirby was mortally wounded. Another three soldiers, two Anti-tank Platoon under command and one gunner signaller were also killed and 13 others wounded, including 2IC Mick Weaver and FO Barrie Winsor. Bob Buick nursed Jack until he died in his arms. The regimental medical officer, Captain John Taske, arrived in a Sioux helicopter and was to officially pronounce Jack as dead. The dead and wounded were evacuated to Vung Tau by Dustoff choppers. What a disaster. What a loss of such a brave and wonderful man like Jack Kirby. I miss Jack to this day.

Ironically it was Dr John Taske, on loan or locum from 5RAR, who sent me to hospital on the 5th and so, as fate would have it, I was not there that sad day otherwise I might have been hit – a lucky day for me. John Taske at age 56 was to climb Mount Everest in 1996 when a storm resulted in the death of another nine climbers. In hospital on an 'air machine' recovering from the severe asthma attack, I was shocked by the tragedy and when I saw the bodies and wounded come into the hospital at Vung Tau I immediately hitched a ride on a chopper back to Nui Dat to rejoin my company and the asthma just disappeared, not to return until 1974 when commanding the Parachute School, although it has come back again in recent times, albeit not when sailing offshore and away from grasses and wattles that cause the problem.

With all the new reinforcements to replace our many casualties, it was never going to be the same in the last few months before we went home in early June, celebrating the battalion's second birthday at sea. On arrival in Brisbane we marched through the city and were welcomed home by crowds as heroes, and the next day our 1965 first-intake National Servicemen were discharged after their two years' service.

In hindsight it was 'hand in your pay book and goodbye' and then sent back to what was once home. But in many cases things had changed after two years away in the Army with a year in Vietnam.

Then came the problems of settling back into family and work life with all the sorrowful memories of the year in Vietnam. In some cases previous employment positions had evaporated and girlfriends had found other men. And in the years after 1967, Vietnam Veterans were to become a blight on the community and even some RSL clubs would not welcome them as 'returned from active service' men. They were not considered as 'proper soldiers', perhaps because of the 19,000 conscripts who served in the unpopular war in Vietnam? It is no wonder many Vets 'went over the hill' into places such as the 'Hippie' areas west of Ballina, away from society, but most of my former soldiers appeared to take it in their stride.

I was surely a changed man, troubled by the loss of so many of my men over the 1966–67 year, although very proud of having been the commander of these gallant men at Long Tan. I was saddened by the lack of gallantry awards for my men – half the 16 we had recommended and only one front-line soldier recognised.

Further, 10 and 12 platoons which had killed many enemy were only given MIDs for their platoon commanders, nothing for their soldiers.

As described in the AWM Official History Volume 1, 'To Long Tan', (page 564), the awards were 'insulting for the heroism displayed', especially with two senior officers getting high DSOs with Long Tan mentioned in their citations. The battle was to be put up on a pedestal after the end of the war when chosen by the Vietnam Veterans Association in 1987 as their iconic battle and they, not us, chose 18 August as Vietnam Veterans Day. In 2015, with few World War II soldiers still alive, the previously shunned, but now accepted, Veterans of an unpopular war make up the majority of the RSL membership. There is considerable discussion about removing Vietnam Veterans' Day and reverting to Anzac Day as the day to remember all wars. I concur. By all means let various units and battles be remembered by those who fought on their special day, but the 10-year war should be remembered at the same time as all other wars in which we participated, going right back to the 1860–61 Maori Wars.

But, with advice of a posting back to Commandos, this time as commanding officer of the would-be CMF Commando 'Battalion' I RNSWR (Cdo) at Georges Heights in Sydney, I was looking forward to forgetting all the distressing events of Vietnam and getting on with life with the Green Beret men again, along with parachuting, diving and amphibious work. Indeed I blotted out Vietnam. Coral–Balmoral 1968 did not even register. The first volume of the Vietnam Official History titled To Long Tan was not published until 1993; the second On the Offensive in 2003, and the last one Fighting to the Finish only came out in 2012, with AWM Historian Ashley Ekins kindly presenting me with a copy at the Long Tan Cross ceremony in August 2012. So apart from odd media snippets there were no official references as to what took place, and I really did not want to know the gory details lest it brought back memories of Long Tan. It was not until recent years that I became fully aware of what went on during the rest of the war. Paul Ham's excellent 2007 book *Vietnam: The Australian War* was the incentive to learn more. Paul kindly gave me a copy as a thank you for my earlier interview and I could not put it down.

After three weeks' leave during which time I visited estranged wife Kath and the kids and went to Coffs Harbour to see my parents, I drove to Sydney to take up my new job, and I was glad to be there. Kath and the children remained in Brisbane until they were eventually allocated married quarters in Mosman across the Harbour Bridge in late August 1967. We were separated and I was living in the Commando barracks at Georges Heights, a modern building compared to 2 Commando World War II barracks at Ripponlea. But I got sick of cooking for myself in the large kitchen which was only used when we had courses and weekend parades. So I moved down the hill to the Engineer Watercraft Unit at Chowder Bay for a while. Subsequently, I transferred into HMAS Penguin barracks at Balmoral on Middle Harbour – great sailing territory, and the new home of the RAN Diving School, which had moved over the harbour from Rushcutters Bay. Because of my work with the Diving School the Army gave approval for me to be rationed and quartered with the Navy only a kilometre from the Commando barracks. I had the use of a self-drive Army station wagon and I also had my own VW 1500 station wagon, although it was admittedly getting on in age.

I had come back from Vietnam with a few dollars saved from the year there and I was determined to get my estranged family settled so they could enjoy stability with schooling and friends rather than having to move around every two years, or sometimes less. Our relatively meagre salary was tax-free and we got a whole 75 cents a day combat pay. With my savings, a War Service loan and second mortgage I bought them a nice new modest split-level three-bedroom brick house at Campbelltown, west of Sydney, and then we went through the formalities of divorce. We were given a Decree Nisi, with five years for Decree Absolute, and of course I had to provide house mortgage repayments and maintenance for the children.

Meanwhile I was savouring working with Commandos at Georges Heights up the road from Penguin and alongside the Sydney WRAAC (female soldiers) barracks which provided a target for odd Commando raids by the soldiers on full-time courses at our barracks, but that is another story. I was trying to come to terms with the unit I had taken over. I had a very good Regular Army cadre with several experienced warrant officers like (late) Danny McClymans, (late) Ray Smith, (late) Gary Holmes, Ron Jarvis and others specialising in the various activities of diving, parachuting, underwater and surface demolitions, small-scale raids and unarmed combat. It seemed there were about 380 reservists on the books yet not that many regularly attended the parades. I asked my adjutant, Captain Bob Supple, to work out how many men would be available if we had to go to war. Bob told me we had about 150 effective men, not even a third of a battalion. I saw no reason why we should not be an independent

Commando company like 2 Commando in Melbourne and concentrate on Special Forces work.

In order to see just how good these CMF officers and men were, I organised an amphibious raid in Sydney Harbour one weekend using the legendary MV *Krait,* now in the Maritime Museum, as the mother vessel. In 1968 she was still seaworthy. *Krait* was originally a Japanese fishing vessel based in Singapore called *Kofuku Maru.* Following the outbreak of World War II the ship was taken over by Allied forces and reached Australia in 1942 where she was handed over to the Australian military. In Australian service she was renamed *Krait* after the small but deadly snake. One of our roles, like the World War II Z Special Force *Jaywick* raid on Japanese shipping in Singapore in September 1943, was to plant limpet mines on ships, by approaching silently in canoes before diving under ships to place the magnetic mines.

Commando training.

Almost everything went wrong because most of my men were 'weekend warriors', many of whom either didn't have much of a bloody clue or didn't do what they were supposed to do. Mind you, the problem was due mainly to the different roles of the unit, being both an Infantry battalion of the Royal NSW Regiment, part of the 2nd CMF Division, and a Commando unit. Senior CMF Divisional HQ officers in Sydney were not supportive of the Commando role, nor of the Green Beret men who attracted special equipment and training. Jealously always came to the fore. And my wearing the distinctive MC white-with-purple-stripe ribbon and a Green Beret did not auger well for good relations with many staff officers sitting in their offices at Victoria Barracks and Moore Park.

On the parade ground at Georges Heights I dressed down the Commando Company after the dismal canoe and assault boat raid exercise up Sydney Harbour. This was about the time I temporarily lost my 'Ratcatcher' handle and became known as 'God'. I told them the exercise had been an absolute disaster and, 'If we were at war you would have lost 150 men. You have to do exactly what I tell you, one singer one song, and that includes walking on water if required.'

'Yes Sir God' was the unanimous reply. Later, the men quietly put up a plaque under my photo in the officers' mess. It read 'GOD 1967–1969'.

These same CMF men were later to become excellent soldiers when I reorganised the unit from a non-effective battalion to a Commando Company. In today's Army many

Commando soldiers have served in Afghanistan and we now have regular Commando units. Some of 1 Commando officers such as Ian McQuire and Mike Wells served on full-time duty in Vietnam in 1966–67. Mike was the ARVN Liaison Officer at Ba Ria in 1966, and Ian was a platoon commander in Charlie Company 6RAR and when promoted to captain became my company 2IC in 1967, taking over when 2IC Captain Mick Weaver was wounded by the NZ artillery fire. Ian also served with AATTV and later, after studies in the UK, became involved with weapons research at Port Wakefield and procurement in AHQ, and was awarded an AM for all his good work.

I submitted to Army HQ that we should delete our battalion status and just go it alone as a Commando Company and this was approved. I then cleared the books of all non-effectives, and moved others out to 2nd Division. So away went those who were either not regular attendees, no bloody good or wasting time because they were in reserve industries and couldn't be called up. It may have been a bit savage but

I had to get rid of all those men. One of the officers I moved on, Joe Brain, hit the headlines in recent years for claiming he had been to Vietnam, obtaining the appropriate medals and then a Department of Veterans' Affairs (DVA) Pension. He fabricated Vietnam service with false letters and records to show he had served in war, but in fact he had never left Sydney. I believe he escaped repayment of some $90,000 in pension benefits that he had fraudulently obtained on the ground that the DVA had approved the medals and pension, so it was not his fault! One would hope DVA has now instituted better checks on other 'wannabes'.

About the end of my time with Sydney Commandos we enlisted the now infamous Hines twins who were in court in 2014 over marching on Anzac Day 2012 with Green Berets and pseudo US Army uniforms and more medals than Korean generals, claiming they served in some secret US unit. More 'wannabes', as recorded with others on the Australian & New Zealand Military Imposters (ANZMI) list on the Internet. Just before Anzac Day 2015 a police officer who had served in the army noticed a would-be commando officer in uniform in a supermarket and that his various badges did not seem correct. On questioning it seems he had served two months in the reserves. He was then formally charged with impersonating an officer.

As sailing was a necessary skill for canoes and amphibious work, I became involved in trials to replace the heavy RAN Bosun dinghies and provide sail adventure training in the RAAF and Army, as well as small-scale raids sail training for SAS and Commando units. I sailed with the RAN at HMAS *Penguin* and tested De Havilland 16-ft Corsairs made in Sydney against the user requirements specified by Canberra, written by SAS and Commando from a synopsis I had drafted three years before when in 2 Commando in 1963–65. We had a trial yacht on loan from De Havilland Bankstown. The old Bosuns were 4m long and terribly heavy slow yachts. In 1970 they were replaced by the Corsairs for all three services. I had enjoyed doing the research for that change on behalf of the Army, Navy and Air Force.

It was during this sailing period that I met a pretty WRAN officer, Anne Sheehan. I was sailing with the Navy most Wednesday afternoons in those heavy Bosun dinghies. We had a three-person crew and Anne was often a member. I had seen her in the Officers' Wardroom in passing and, yes, she had certainly caught my eye. Anne was the daughter of dairy farmers from Cooroy in Queensland and was the officer-in-charge of all WRAN girls in the Sydney area, working mainly at HMAS *Watson* at South Head by day. Anne and I became friends, often meeting at the bar after work and dining together in the wardroom, with me usually heading back for night work at the Commando barracks until late.

I continued to live in the Navy wardroom. Female officers were accommodated on the top floor of the barracks. Male and female quarters were separated by a flight of stairs. Anne was a petite lady with a soldier brother in the SAS, Peter, whom I knew. He served in Vietnam with SAS and was later promoted to captain quartermaster. Anne was a couple of years younger than me, a quiet and attractive young lady.

The RAN did it rather well in those three-storey barracks above the wardroom and dining room, with all the lady officers and nurses on the third floor. Some of the 'inter-service cooperation' would certainly be frowned upon today. It was a pleasure to live there and we ate and partied very well in leisure times. I used to dive with the RAN School, often at night across the harbour near Balmoral. I have a vivid recollection of swimming along the bottom with one eye on the compass and one arm extended to locate any obstacles, and then feeling this large animal – probably a bull or shovel-nose shark. Luckily it swam away rather than attack as one did with a RAN diver in Sydney Harbour near Garden Island, taking his leg off. He recovered and had the courage to return to diving with one good leg.

I was able to dive with the RAN clearance diving teams on oxygen rebreathing sets which had been removed from Army Commando after a fatality in Melbourne around 1959. With the advent of modern rebreathing sets I then sought approval for new oxygen sets for Commando units and Defence later procured Drager sets for trial in conjunction with the RAN Diving School at HMAS *Penguin.* Oxygen, unlike compressed air, leaves no telltale bubbles on the surface to indicate divers below but it can only be used safely to a depth of about 10m, one atmosphere of 14 psi, lest the CO_2 (carbon dioxide) breathed into the sodasorb (CO_2 absorbent powder) be forced into the bloodstream, which is fatal. I was to later parachute into water at Port Stephens with a new Drager rebreather set, on its very first use, and after leaving the chute harness just above the water, I swam below but not deep. Very soon I felt very ill and luckily was able to get up to the surface and be pulled out by the RAN diving supervisors into their inflatable assault boat. Luck has played a big role in my survival to a ripe old age. When we checked the set we found the required sodasorb powder had not been put in the canister, so I was breathing my own exhaled CO2 air back in! Thereafter we always checked our own gear before diving and had no more problems.

One of our excellent RAN diving school instructors, Lieutenant Ken Haynitz, who also instructed 1 Commando courses in underwater demolitions at Port Stephens using their Patrol Boat as a base, was to set sail in a yacht on an around-the-world trip when he had served his time, but he disappeared off the east coast of Africa in 1985 while I was cruising along Cape York. Storm, pirates or just sunk? We'll probably never know.

While at 1 Commando we received the first two 26-ft alloy motorboats to replace the virtually useless old 18-ft Bell Boy boats. They had been requested for SAS and Commando units when I was in 2 Commando in Melbourne during 1963–65. We used the new boats as dive-and-rescue boats during diving courses and amphibious exercises. Rather than having to launch the boats from trailers towed by three-quarter-ton US Dodge trucks for every use, wasting time, I persuaded the Army to keep ours moored at the nearby Spit Bridge Marina. Army HQ engineers told me my request for anti-fouling painting below the waterline was not approved because barnacles would not grow on aluminium. Unbelievable! It took me some time to convince them otherwise. I remember telling the Canberra engineer officer that barnacles would grow on your fingernail if you left your finger in the water long enough. I had learned that if one kept arguing with the public service and officers in Canberra and could quote facts, eventually you won out, but it was a frustrating process, and it seems no different today.

Having the boats moored at the nearby Spit Bridge Marina was handy for maintenance and, conveniently, necessary maintenance runs often included Warrant Officer Class 2 Danny McClymans and me trolling for pelagic kingfish outside the Sydney Heads, mostly with success. But the boats had problems and, typical of Defence procurements, the contract had been given not to a recognised boating firm, but to a caravan firm which had never built a boat. The quote was no doubt cheaper. During our first diving exercise, with the boat loaded with divers and heavy air bottles, the cockpits, which were supposed to be self-draining and watertight, leaked water down into the bilge, almost sinking the boat and damaging the twin inboard engines.

We then found the hundreds of pop-rivets in the alloy cockpit floor had small pinholes where the rivet pins had been pulled out, through which the water poured in like rain. Our boats and another four being constructed for SAS and 2 Commando had to be repaired by the manufacturer plugging all the rivet holes with nylon pins. So what happened to any pre-delivery trials by Army procurement officers? The floors should have been welded sheeting. During amphibious exercises around Broughton Island off Port Stephens, we often fed the boys with fish caught by using hand grenades – easy, and rewarding, but no doubt illegal, if not plain dangerous. But we got away with it in those days and we all ate lots of fresh fish.

The Spit Bridge Marina manager was Keith Thiele who I met again around 1990 sailing his Ahrends 33 yacht *Spitfire* along the coast. Keith was originally from New Zealand and served in Spitfires with the NZAF in the United Kingdom during World War II. He also joined the Dambusters, but after their famous raid. Awarded the DSO and DFC with three bars, he was something special. He had been shot down over France and did a Steve McQueen in *The Great Escape,* stealing a motorcycle and escaping. I often wondered how McQueen got into that story because no Americans were actually involved in the real escape from Stammlager Luft III, more commonly known as Stalag Luft III, a Luftwaffe-run prisoner-of-war camp. After the war Keith became a Qantas pilot then a marina manager then turned to sailing the oceans between Sydney and Auckland and once to Raine Island in the Coral Sea to establish an amateur radio base. He then kept his yacht at Mid Town marina in Bundaberg and we saw him during our trips north.

His ill health ended sailing and in 2012 I visited Keith in the RSL nursing home in North Bundaberg. He was 92 and needed a walker to get around but he still had a sense of humour. His front doormat was inscribed with 'If I don't answer the door I am having sex.' Keith was writing a biography and had wonderful stories to tell. One of his World War II memories was of being given approval by a husband in London to live with his wife when on leave! Although most unusual this is no fairytale and Keith has shown my wife Felicia letters and photographs from the late lady and then her daughter. He was flown back to London by Qantas as part of Bomber Command ceremonies in 2012 and while there returned a special picture his squadron had purloined from a local pub. I gather the RSL home was flooded in the big Burnett River floods of 2013 and Keith went to Sydney and is still alive in 2015.

At 1 Commando Company we finished up with an elite team of men. They did as they were told and we had a wonderful relationship. They ended up qualified in all sorts of skills. These fit men were ready for war if needed. Reserve forces now are being used in war. The unit is part of 4 Battalion Commando based at Holsworthy NSW. 1 Commando Company exists still and I was immensely proud when they asked me to go to Sydney and march with them and other special forces on Anzac Day 2011 and of being made a life member of the 1st Commando Regiment Association. Afterwards, at the Customs House bar of the Marriot Hotel near Circular Quay, I enjoyed meeting many of the fit, slim, current Commando soldiers all dressed in black suits, their issue civil attire. Many former Rhodesian African Rifles men were there in their Green Berets and more rows of medals than I had ever seen. One explained to me they served under two or three governments, so two or more armies, so two or three lots of similar medals.

 The 1 Commando Company base was an hour-and-a-half's drive from the Parachute Training School north of Newcastle and as Commando training other than full-time courses took place over weekends and nights I was able to drive up for jumps on off days, sometimes taking a couple of warrant officers with me. I also got myself onto a Free-Fall course and qualified, although I had some initial problems getting stable in flight until one instructor, Captain Tom Marshall, jumped alongside me and told me that I had one leg out of whack which caused me to slowly spin, and that I just had to hang in there and relax. 'Boss, just relax, you're too tense,' he said. That did the trick and thereafter I enjoyed free-fall jumps and learned to fly around and link up with others. But until Tom sorted me out I was prepared to give up freefall parachuting, hating to fail at anything that was a personal challenge. Another glitch was a badly bruised heel that could have stopped me completing the course. I prevailed on the local RAAF doctor for help and he injected cortisone with a huge needle which killed the pain and let me finish the course. That qualification opened the way for me to jump free-fall with UK, US and Canadian units when I was overseas in 1972-73 after which I came back to Australia and was posted as the Army Chief Instructor Joint Warfare School at RAAF Williamtown as well as CO of the Parachute School, then to Chief Instructor of the new Army Parachute Training School.

Freefalling at Salisbury Plain, UK. Photo courtesy RAF Parachute Trials Unit.

I was also involved in work with RAN Submarines based at nearby Neutral Bay, thanks to RAN Commander Tim Duchane, including attending a Submarine Familiarisation Course which included using submarines to launch and recover canoes, inflatable boats, and divers. This incorporated divers going out of torpedo tubes, although we did not have the type of diving sets to actually do that, but we went through the motions of getting into dry tubes, which were flooded, and then exiting through the outer front hatch.

While at 1 Commando we had fun with local Navy people from HMAS *Penguin* and the Dive School and they used to get involved in our helicopter rappelling, parasailing and parachute water jumps. When we conducted helicopter rappelling from Iroquois choppers on our barracks oval we invited RAN people to join in. We inherited the first parasail in Australia from the RAAF Parachute School which was obtained for possible parachute-jump training with a 300-m rope behind a Land Rover, but it was all too dangerous for the RAAF, so they gave it to us to use on the water. I had unsuccessfully tried to use an old parachute behind our boats when at 2 Commando in the sixties, unsuccessful because it had no steering slots and rolled around. I recall first using the new parasail behind one of our dive boats in Sydney Harbour; it was probably the first use on the water in Australia. Parasails are now popular and used off various tourist resorts, towed by commercial boats. But on our first run we were pulled up by the NSW Water Police who wanted to know just what we were doing; they considered that whatever it was, it had to be against the law. They said we could not use it within 1000ft (300m) of the shore or other boats, so we reserved it for use in leisure time up at Nelson Bay during various courses we ran up there, such as underwater demolitions, blowing up old sunken timber barges, having been qualified in such demolitions by the RAN Diving School.

In early 1968 I was sent over to 3RAR base near Adelaide to brief them on my Vietnam experiences. One day I was called to the CO's office to find I was to be interviewed by the top Army legal officer, Brigadier Ewing, and one of his legal eagles. They had flown over from Canberra to try and pin me for the water torture of a Vietnamese girl we had captured after Long Tan. The media had got hold of the torture story and there was hell to pay. I was completely innocent and all we did was capture the girl and send her back to base with the regimental police we called out. Whatever went on, it took place back at Nui Dat. But only in 2004 was I to discover it was not our prisoner that had been subjected to water treatment but a girl captured by Bravo Company 6RAR in the Nui Dinh hills in a cave protecting a radio transmitter. In 2010 a local Maryborough ex-serviceman who had been involved with the 'torture' confessed all to journalist Toni McRae, then working on the *Fraser Coast Chronicle,* who helped me start putting this book together in late 2012 just before a serious medical problem intervened with her work. Toni persuaded me to expand my family life story and have it published. She spent considerable time recording and typing my tales of military and civilian life.

But in early 2014 Toni had a heart problem and then breast cancer which required a double mastectomy. After surgery and treatment she worked with our Hervey Bay RSL Committee on a book relating to the 2015 Anzac

Centenary and was active with a camera at the dedication of the new Lighthorse statue on 11 October 2014. Then, on 29 October 2014, after working all day at the RSL on the final chapter, she went home and died in her sleep at only age 67. I continued to put this book together as best I could with help from the publisher. Toni and I had met at Mooloolaba some 25 years ago and as then, she pursued me for Long Tan media coverage after I moved to Hervey Bay in 2003. Born in New Zealand, her contributions to journalism will be remembered. She was buried with her parents at Mooloola on the Sunshine Coast. There was a memorial service for her at our RSL organised by Nancy Bates and attended by about 300 people. In 2015 Nancy led the casting of a bronze statue of Maryborough's Major Duncan Chapman, the first Anzac soldier to go ashore at Gallipoli, to be killed in action in France 1916.

Back to 1968. In October I was selected to lead a group of 50 Army officers and men, mainly Vietnam Veterans, as part of a combined 150-strong Army, Navy and Air Force group to go to Paris for the 50th Commemoration of the World War I Armistice on 11 November, Remembrance Day. The overall Contingent Commander was the late Colonel Eric Smith DSO, former CO 7RAR Vietnam 1967–68, with a nickname of 'Idle Eric', a gentleman. His 7RAR Charlie Company was involved in heavy fighting in Operation 'Coburg' now narrated in the book *All Day Long the Noise of the Battle,* published in 2011 and telling of the problems with the appropriate recognition of officers and soldiers. Shades of our Long Tan medals disgrace.

For the Armistice Day commemoration we assembled at Ingleburn to get new uniforms, slouch hats and parade ground training before flying to Paris on a Qantas 707. We were each issued with two first-off minted Vietnam Medals to wear on the trip. Someone else noticed in 2006 that my two were unnamed and suggested that my originals had been stolen. After some trouble I eventually got Canberra to admit the fact that the hurriedly issued medals had not been named and it was suggested I could return them for engraving, but by a different process to that in 1968. Canberra finally gave me documentation to support their advice, but I was advised by medal experts to leave them as issued, unnamed. I noted a recent email warning about medal-mount scammers who are stealing and selling originals, especially miniatures, and warning owners to take photographs of their medals and note any marks. If there are no marks, the email suggested the owner make a small personal mark on the reverse side.

Me in 1968.

Marching through Paris behind French mounted cavalry was an experience, especially trying to avoid slipping on the large mounds of horse poo dropped on the street. Next day we travelled out to a ceremony at Villers-Bretonneux, the site of a large but costly World War I battle where Australians counter-attacked resulting in the town being handed back to the locals on 25 April 1918. The site of an

Australian National Memorial, Australians are still feted by the locals. They turned on a great dance and fine food before we returned to Paris to our ancient barrack blocks where the water taps were locked off and you had to get a key before showering. Circumstances were similar when I toured Paris en route to Army exchange duties in Italy, Greece and Germany in 1972.

Marching through the streets of Villers-Bretonneux.

In late 1968 I went over to SAS in Perth and became a rappelling instructor, rappelling being the name for sliding down a rope (abseiling) from a helicopter. It was used by Special Forces in 'hot insertions' in jungle or in areas where the nearby enemy needed to be fooled into thinking the chopper had not landed and unloaded a patrol ('hot' meaning 'dangerous'). The same rope was used for 'hot extractions' with soldiers clipping on to the rope while the chopper lifted them up and flew to a safer area where they could get on board. One SAS soldier, Trooper Fisher, unfortunately fell off during one Vietnam hot extraction in 1968 and was killed on impact. Despite searches by 3RAR his body could not be located, but his remains were finally found and repatriated to Australia in 2008.

One day during the course a 9 Squadron Vietnam pilot, Geoff Banfield (whom I was to meet again at Yandina around 1995 when he was terminally ill and came to say goodbye) jokingly dangled me on the end of a helicopter hot extraction rope with my feet just touching the sewage in the huge Perth sewerage farm. I also managed to be attached to SAS Perth for various parachuting activities and I recall jumping on a very hard drop zone at Derby in northern Western Australia that must have squashed my spinal discs several millimetres. Apart from old age shrinking, I am sure my lesser height in 2015 is mostly due to my 499 live parachute landings, plus all the thousands of practice landings during hangar training as a student and instructor aimed at perfecting the landing roll to absorb impact shock.

Also, in 1969 I was sent up to Vanimo in Papua New Guinea on attachment to SAS who were patrolling the Indonesian border. Their activities were and are secret but Commando unit commanders were familiarised with SAS work as part of the Special Forces system. We were also involved in the then top-secret establishment at Swan Island near Queenscliff where we attended briefings and special training activities. I had hoped to command the SAS Regiment one day and get to wear the elite sand-coloured beret.

It was in late December 1969 that I was offered a year's course at Quetta Staff College in Pakistan, a condition of which was that my wife accompany me. Being separated I had to reject that offer – that perhaps would have been a great overseas trip. So instead I was posted to the Australian Staff College at Queenscliff Victoria as a student on the 1970 course – I imagine that it was a bit like going to university, pouring over reference books, studying, listening to lectures and writing papers about warfare.

Anne obtained a posting to RAN HQ in Melbourne so that we could see each other at weekends. Money was a problem as usual. I was still paying off the family-house mortgages and paying maintenance yet somehow we managed to rent a cheap small old-fashioned furnished bedsitter flat and I moved into it on weekends when Anne drove down. I used to jog to and from the college where I also had a room during the week, and also run daily as I had given up smoking and put on a little flab. Nevertheless I started smoking again on just one small cigar a day, then two, then three, and then found it was cheaper to go back to cigarettes anyway, until I quit at age 43 when I had a bad cough and it was suggested I might have throat cancer. I recall ditching two cartons of Winfield Menthols and never smoking again.

Anne had an old Vauxhall car which needed gearbox repairs and my VW was near the end of its life. We sold Anne's car to a dealer who put banana skins in the gearbox to quieten the noise. We also traded my old VW for a new VW 1500 sedan after adding the proceeds from the Vauxhall and a nice stamp collection I had started at an early age. I had been left some fairly good old Australian stamps by my grandfather and I think we only got about $500 for the collection worth a lot more, but another car was necessary.

At the end of the 1970 course I had achieved good results. Studying there was an exercise to prepare you for promotion and be able to command at a higher level of rank. The course acquainted you with military management, and in my case it equipped me to become a lieutenant colonel and therefore hopefully be a competent officer in tactics or staff work. Some at Queenscliff were good at fieldwork while others couldn't find their way around a train. We learned to speed-read and to write our own battle plans. Everybody was expected to be learned in the basics of managing war – which I thought I'd actually done at Long Tan, though with a company of three platoons, not a brigade of three battalions plus support units! We had to study military history and dissect battles like Tobruk, Normandy, El Alamein and Kokoda. You were marked on your knowledge and how you assessed the battle. You learned how to avoid failure in future battles by discovering what had failed in the old ones.

We also studied Gallipoli. I hadn't known the full terrible details before those classes. I found World War I battles particularly horrifying and often unnecessarily so had skilled and sensible generals been in charge. Gallipoli was a disaster caused in the main by the ships anchoring 5km to the north of the lower terrain. Some landing boats moved further north and others also got units mixed up, facing cliffs defended by just a couple of hundred Turks at the start. The defenders could see the ships anchoring and their few artillery guns and machine guns were ready for the landings at what became known as

Anzac Cove. It was a disaster which resulted in 21,000 casualties with 8500 men killed by the time of the very successful secret withdrawal in December 1915. The Turks were fooled into thinking the allies were still in their trenches by the clever use of water dripping into cans with a cord to pull rifle triggers. Overall losses by NZ, UK, Indian and Canadian units were horrendous. My wife Felicia's uncle, Private Lawrence Mobilia of the Queensland 9th Battalion, aged 24, was killed on the beach on Anzac Day in the first wave ashore at what is now known as Queensland Point

In our tactics studies we were reminded never to attack the enemy unless we had a superiority of at least five to one, but preferably 10 to one. Superiority that day at Long Tan was 20 to one on the enemy's side, so they knew that principle of war! And of course we did not know the enemy was out there – and the brigadier failed to tell his battalion commanders. I still think that, like Gallipoli, it was a disaster that should not have taken place. But a similar lack of foresight was to be shown at the Coral-Balmoral battle in 1968 where an enemy regiment attacked the first night, before the Coral Fire Support Base 45km north of Saigon was properly established, the enemy intelligence similarly not properly assessed and passed down to battalions and units moving up from Nui Dat.

My next posting was to HQ Western Command at Swan Barracks in Perth as a personnel staff officer, which did not overly please me but I accepted I had to sit behind a desk at some time in my career. It could have driven me nuts if I'd let it. I prefer work in the open air. Anne left the Navy as there was no posting for her in Perth. In January 1971 we drove to Adelaide and put the VW 1500 on the train across the Nullabor. We found an affordable small but nice unit just outside the city and Anne located work as a finance clerk with a car firm.

I had about 20 Army and civil staff in my branch but I spent much of my time organising an Army Sailing Club. SAS, RAN, RAAF and Army in Perth now had six Corsairs each, purchased after my Commando-RAN Sydney trials, and they made up most of the Corsairs in the Perth Flying Squadron Club on the Swan River, allowing for serious racing each Saturday. Anne's brother Peter sailed an SAS Corsair and it was here I also met SAS Trooper Greg Pullin who sailed another and was to sail with me in Mooloolaba on Queensland's Sunshine Coast in later years on a fast Lyons 40 racing yacht *Midnight Special.* She sank in the 'Fatal Storm' of the 1998 Sydney–Hobart race, just after I had sold her on. Greg sailed on our Cavalier 395 *Cavarlo* on the delivery up from Sydney and in the local Kingfisher Regatta a few years back. We had named an earlier Cavalier 345 *Tamika* after his adopted grand-daughter, a very small girl with a congenital growth problem. When sailing *Tamika* in Trinity Inlet, Cairns, Japanese tourists onboard passing charter boats would look and wave excitedly as *Tamika* is apparently Japanese for 'small people'.

In Perth I was to beat the top RAN skipper Ken Goodsell and take out the WA Corsair Championship in 1971 before getting involved with Rolly Tasker's 48-ft *Siska I,* a converted metre yacht, previously the fastest yacht in Australia. Rolly had built a new yacht and could not sell *Siska I* so I suggested he loan her to the Army. We tried to do a deal on buying the yacht for the Army Sailing Club as was done in Sydney with the yacht *Ballandra,* involving a donation to a 'charitable club', with a tax discount for the seller. But Rolly pre-empted the deal in a media release about the donation, indicating he had 'donated' the yacht to the Army, so the tax man said no way, and Rolly was happy to have us look after his yacht while he sailed *Siska 2* to far places provided we were able to cover mooring and maintenance costs.

With eight Army crew we raced *Siska* every weekend and also took many families out on twice-weekly twilight sails, with a small charge, like one dollar, going towards costs. We did well, beating some of Rolly Tasker's records, such as for the 1972 Fremantle to Bunbury annual race. We also obtained lots of good publicity for the Army.

One night, as we sailed into Bunbury Harbour to the turning mark at about midnight, I was hit in the right eye by a flying fish that was attracted by a torch I flashed onto the buoy. I was knocked out and carried below while scales and slime were cleaned from my eye. Twenty-five years later that eye was diagnosed with a problem due to some 'trauma'. 'Yes Doctor, an argument with a flying fish'!

My immediate boss, Colonel Alec Smith, and the Perth commander, Brigadier George Larkin, were both very supportive of the sailing activities and I was able to delegate much of my staff work and spend a lot of time away from my office organising the boat and crew and doing much of the maintenance work myself.

48ft Siska with Bondy's Apollo in background.

We used to sail against Alan Bond and his new *Apollo I,* although Alan steered by instrumentation, not by experience. We could beat him in light weather but with any breeze *Apollo* disappeared over the horizon. Downwind sails were a problem as most of *Siska's* had been lost in a Tasker sail-loft fire, and we only had one large symmetrical balloon spinnaker, which was unusable on tight reaches. Alan took pity on us and gave us several used spinnaker sails from a yacht he had sunk in the Swan River, the *Panamuna.* Bondy was a top fellow in those days and, still is, in my humble opinion. When he launched and bankrolled his first quest to race for the America's Cup which he eventually won in 1983, he offered the Army a deal whereby our crew would be able to sail a Pace yacht and be considered on merit for crew positions on the race yacht. He asked Defence for administrative support for the challenge but that was denied by government ministers in Canberra. In later years the Forces were permitted all sorts of 'adventure training'. The RAN has had several yachts in Sydney–Hobart races and many servicemen sailed in bareboat rentals in the Whitsundays. But back in 1972 that idea was all too much for politicians who worried they might be accused of wasting money on sail training. RSL Queensland now has a former 'round the world' Volvo 65 'Spirit of Mateship' crewed by disabled servicemen as part of the RSL Mates for Mates program.

TWELVE

A BATTLE WITH A PARACHUTE: PLUNGE TO EARTH AND CRASH OF DREAMS

During 1972 I was told by the Military Secretary Office in Canberra that I had been selected to command the first Army Parachute Training School, taking over from the RAAF Parachute Training Flight at Williamtown RAAF Base, initially as the Senior Army Instructor at the Joint Warfare School. This would entail promotion to lieutenant-colonel and an 'accompanied' (with wife) posting overseas for 13 months to study parachuting in the United Kingdom, United States and Canada and suggest the future role and equipment required by our airborne units.

Although the five years of Decree Nisi were not finished I was able to impose on the court and obtain a final Decree Absolute. Anne and I were then quietly married in the registry office in Perth in time to get our passports and travel orders and to travel by train to Adelaide, then drive our VW 1500 car to Sydney to say farewell to our parents at Coffs Harbour and Ballina and to sell the VW in Sydney. We needed the cash knowing we would have to buy a cheap car in London for our time in the United Kingdom. The 13-months posting gave us eligibility to bring a new car home duty free, as other service people had done, but we did not have the financial resources for a new Mercedes or Jaguar.

We flew out of Sydney via Qantas on 26 July, first-class travel in those years, with paid rest days in Hong Kong and Rome, arriving in London and occupying a delightful plush UK Army rental unit in Mayfair while we were briefed by the Australian Army staff. We had to buy a car and we quickly settled on a lovely old silver Jaguar 1964 sedan for £500 from a town outside London, unaware of salt being put on icy roads. It looked good for the price and we drove it back to Mayfair in the rain and parked it outside the unit. The next morning there were long lines of red rust on the road and a friendly neighbour was quick to tell me about salt. The Jag was rusted along and under the doorsills. I later fibreglassed the bad areas and repainted the silver car with spray cans – looked good.

We were allocated a two-storey cold old brick married quarters house at Wilton outside Salisbury near the Boscombe Downs Royal Air Force base where I was attached and we drove there. We had no problems with the old Jag – it was a nice comfortable car, but the same could not be said for the house. In winter we had to shovel coal for hot water and heating and there were no double-glazed windows.

I was involved in parachute trials and techniques with the RAAF Trials Team at Boscombe Down, all very competent and hospitable people. I jumped with them often, including an oxygen free-fall jump from a C130 Hercules flying on radio beacon beams at 25,000ft (or 8km up) over Salisbury Plain. We were well rugged up in RAAF-issue cold-weather jumpsuits, along with a small oxygen bottle for use above 12,000ft. Raining on the ground, the cloud was all white from above, just like a sheep's back, and after going out over the Hercules ramp, it took near four minutes to get on the ground, pulling the ripcord inside dark cloud at 2500ft. We had been briefed to then steer the parachute on a compass bearing and, sure enough, at about 400ft we came out of the cloud and there was the target, spot on. You can get lucky falling out of the sky. The very next day one SAS section was inadvertently dropped into the water off Bournemouth when the C130 deviated from the radio beacons. I did many other jumps from 10–12,000ft and often used a new type of steerable parachute that would become the issue in Australia.

Me during a free fall jump at Williamtown.

Anne got an office job at the Salisbury Brewery and, while this did not augur well with some of the British wives, not being the 'right thing' for a colonel's wife to work, it helped our pocket money. I recall Anne jokingly telling a UK Army wife, when asked what she did, that she trod on the grapes! The allowances in the United Kingdom were no better than in

Australia and we wanted to tour the British Isles during our year there. I wasn't allowed to travel to Ireland because of the IRA heightened violence with bombings, executions and even murder of children; and an Australian Army officer visit was politically banned. We did see a lot of the UK country and even looked for the Loch Ness monster in Scotland before we went to the United States for three months' duty in late November 1972. This limited time did not provide for taking a wife under Australian Army rules but I was able to privately cash in my own first-class fare with the airline and get two economy return tickets at little extra cost and so Anne went with me, and why not. I think our bureaucracy later removed similar first-class air travel, so we were fortunate.

In the United States Anne was fully accepted to travel with me and our embassy in Washington paid top-dollar allowances. We needed a car to see the sights en route to attachments with the US Special Forces at Fort Bragg, North Carolina, and the USAF Joint Warfare School and Parachute Trials unit at Fort

Walton Beach, Florida. We bought a nice used dark blue 1964 Mustang coupe for US $500 and drove south to Fort Bragg to be met by a snowstorm during which we found most local cars could not handle the conditions. The Mustang, with my experiences from snow in Tasmania, did it beautifully. I add a brand-new Mustang in 1973 was only $4000 in the United States, but up to $14,000 in Sydney. And a good 1964 Mustang is now a collectable worth up to $75,000. In 2015 I see new Mustangs are soon to arrive from the USA, priced at only $45,000 for the four cylinder (turbo), but more for the eight cylinder.

The US Army Special Forces men were a very friendly gang and I enjoyed jumping with them, even though I was not that happy they packed their own parachutes and had me do the same. I was used to having trained professional parachute packers. On my first free-fall jump the jumpmaster gave me a tomahawk and told me to strap it on my leg. Innocently I asked why, to be told, 'Man, you could have to cut yourself down from the tall pine trees around the drop zone.'

But I survived the trees and landed the steerable Para-Commander chutes onto the drop zone each jump. I did over 10 free-fall jumps and was presented with a US Master Parachutists' Badge and a small silver free-fall trophy which now resides in the Maryborough Military Museum on the Fraser Coast.

One of the benefits of being attached to US Forces was that accommodation was always available on base in Bachelor Officer Quarters even with wives and at just $2 a day for the lady. Army staff in Washington, more cooperative than their London counterparts, authorised air travel for me, and agreed that I could trade the fares into cash for petrol costs for the car between cities. That might sound profitable, but air fares were only something like $15 between cities. Petrol was just 25 cents a US gallon.

We drove on to Florida and I joined the USAF Joint Warfare School at Eglington for a course. I also jumped free-fall with the USAF Parachute Trials Team at Fort Walton Beach. Then we drove east towards Daytona. The only problem with the Mustang was that west of Daytona when we stopped for 'gas', the water pump was leaking badly, spilling water onto the ground. Being Sunday, the man said we should fill the radiator up and keep driving as it would not leak while the engine was running and the pump was working. We got to Daytona Beach, booked into a motel opposite a service station and on Monday morning got a new water pump fitted while we waited – parts and labour $17. They were the days! We then drove along the beach, complete with traffic signs, then to Disney World on the way back to Washington, from where I had to fly to Edmonton in Canada for an attachment to the Canadian Parachute School.

In Washington I left Anne with friends Peter and Anne Smeaton. Peter was our Alpha Company commander, then operations officer, in Vietnam between 1966 and 1967. I went on to Canada for three weeks in the snow. We returned the accommodation favour for several months in 1982 when Peter's Adams 45 yacht *Gemini* nearly sunk en route in the race to Japan and then came to Mooloolaba for repairs. Peter was to prematurely die from prostate cancer a few years later. I went to his funeral at Buderim and my wife and I helped Peter's widow Anne move into a house they had recently bought near Eumundi.

The Canucks were also very friendly and I jumped several free-falls into snow – lovely soft landings. In the heavy cold air, their small plane could only get up to about 8000ft. But what a lovely view it was of snow-covered country with the chimney smoke from Edmonton factories spiralling up in the still air in the distance. Social life was very good and I was taken to dinner several times and one night to a dance, where one of the 'spare' wives whose husband was away came on strong until I told her my lovely wife was just over the border. I had obviously learned to behave myself in the presence of attractive women. I flew back to Washington via a day in Montreal to re-join Anne and then we flew back across the Atlantic to London after selling the Mustang to an incoming Army officer for what we paid.

After more jumping with the RAF Parachute Trials Team and visits to the Special Air Services Regiment the next trip on the Army schedule was to the Continent to UK and US Army bases in our old Jag, one at Bielefeld on the Russian border and then down to the underground nuclear NATO HQ at Vicenza in Italy just inland from Venice, which we visited often with our US Army hosts whom we were staying with and we shared many meals in canal cafes. Leaving Anne with the US friends, I flew from Venice to Athens for a NATO amphibious exercise. At Athens I boarded the UK Commando Carrier HMS *Bulwark* and sailed in a NATO fleet to a beach assault landing in Sardinia. One of my pleasantest memories was watching thousands of dolphins having 'fun in the sun' as they daily swam and jumped between the ships. I then flew back to Venice.

In Athens a memory that I would rather forget is having drinks in a bar in company with two British Commando officers and being conned into buying drinks for the usual lovely local bar ladies, shades of Vung Tau bars. There were no ulterior motives other than drinks, and while we wanted to pay as we went, the clever barman insisted we pay when we left to rejoin our ship. Well, did we get ripped off! When we argued about the enormous bill he threatened to call the police so we just paid and left rather than get involved in an international legal incident. Very expensive drinks!

Anne and I had driven down through France and Switzerland into Italy and, loaded with souvenirs, we later drove back from Vicenza into Germany to the USAF Base at Heidelberg, a lovely castle city, then into Rheindahlen Military Complex, a British forces base in Mönchengladbach, North Rhine-Westphalia. At the German border the corrupt guards wanted to confiscate our souvenirs, but suggested we could pay to keep them. I pushed my Official Passport under their noses, said my piece and they reluctantly let us through. After visiting various bases in Germany we drove on through Holland to Calais and jumped the ferry back to

England, sold the old Jag for what we paid, and packed our bags for home. Many Jag owners tell me you need two cars, one for spare parts, but apart from body rust we had no problems with our old girl. Some years back one of my former 1 Commando officers Peter Collins AM QC had sent me a 1:18 scale model of a similar 1959 Mark II Jaguar which has found a home on my desk. In 2014 he picked me up from my daughter's Sydney home in a brand-new Jaguar S – very nice.

What a great overseas trip we had, with thanks to Gough Whitlam! We flew back to Sydney via a rest day in Singapore and moved up to RAAF Williamtown on 15 August 1973 to settle into married quarters on the base after visiting Anne's family at Kin Kin in Queensland. Back to reality. We looked at a used Jag in the Sydney dealership, but all too dear, so we spent all our savings on a new $4000 Datsun 240 coupe and borrowed money from the Army Canteens Trust Fund to get furniture for our married quarters.

Getting the Parachute School organised the way I wanted it was not easy and the RAAF base commander the (late) Air Commodore Jim Fleming was perhaps understandably reluctant to see it go to the Army after all the years with the RAAF. I eventually got it sorted with Army Headquarters and moved in as Chief Instructor and CO, having had Army Instructor Major Ian Gollings promoted to take over my desk at Joint Warfare. (Ian and his wife Shirley retired to Canberra and we have seen them during various visits.) We organised the school with a Training Wing, a Trials Wing, a Parachute Packing Wing and the Airborne Platoon. We were approved to train some 650 students a year, including free-fall for Special Forces.

Working direct with Army Headquarters for policy, we were able to order RAAF support aircraft when we wanted it, direct with RAAF Operations Command Penrith, much to the disgust of Army brass who could not get the same support. The generals did not like me when I wore a Commando Green Beret, and they had no better respect for me with an Airborne Forces Red Beret. What is this thing in the Army with old soldiers who come down on anyone having earned a Special Forces beret? But I am content that I always got the job done, and done well, and I am pleased to see our Special Forces have earned more respect in recent years. Indeed, most Army Generals of 2015 have seen service in Special Forces. The SASR and Commando's have provided many of the fighting units in Iraq and Afghanistan.

While at RAAF Williamtown I looked at sailing opportunities. First I bought an A-Class 16-ft fast racing catamaran which frightened Anne and was all too much trouble to launch and recover from the trailer. We checked out other options with our limited resources and located a nice timber Nordic Folkboat at Lake Macquarie for $7000. She was named *Svenska* and we sailed her up to Port Stephens and started racing her with the local club. An Army mate and still a close friend, Brian Hayden, the Army Ground Liaison Officer (GLO) on the RAAF base, bought a Colleen-Class sloop *Amber K* and we enjoyed friendly contests in Port Stephens Sailing Club races. Brian still sails and has a

Beneteau 50 which he bought in Hong Kong and had reconditioned in Phuket. Brian sailed in *Great Britain 2* from England to Sydney in 1976 with an all-Army crew paid for by the Army, a change from the 1972 attitude. Indeed, when at 2 Commando I had suggested a yacht be chartered for the 1964 Sydney–Hobart with a Commando crew but that got nowhere, as did my suggestion of entering Army Land Rovers in the 1965 Redex Trial. Things have changed for the better over the years and the Services are now involved in these sorts of activities, and why not?

At Williamtown on one holiday break we cruised *Svenska* from her Port Stephens Lemon Tree Passage mooring 100 nautical miles (160km) to Sydney but found the lack of headroom was a problem. So we sold her for a slight profit and bought the hull and deck of a Swanson 32, a much better proposition, although she had to be fitted out and rigged. We had the yacht trucked up from Newcastle and placed in our married quarters backyard which could be seen from the Officers' Mess.

We were a source of curiosity to others on the RAAF Base – an Army officer married to an ex-Navy officer, living on an RAAF base, with a yacht in their backyard?

    RAAF people could not resist offering services to an Army man whom they thought obviously knew little about fitting out boats. I was quite happy with the challenge and with my teenage carpentry skills did a good job on the timberwork fitting out but I was very happy to accept RAAF advice and help with mechanical items, like keying the prop shaft and Radio Officer Kevin Maddox doing the wiring with tinned wire from old 'mothballed' aircraft. An old surplus Sabre Jet compass came my way. I was up and jumping most days at dawn and was able to stop work at lunchtime, hand over to my staff and then work another eight hours on the yacht at home.

    Anne and I saved enough money to cover the outlays over the year it took before she could be launched. We were able to get bare extrusions for the mast and boom and fit the rigging, but we could not afford the sails. I prevailed on my father for a loan of about $6000, with agreed monthly repayments including interest. After I paid back the capital a few years on, Dad generously dropped the interest payments. A couple of years later my retired father, who had never been that generous with money, called all us three Smith children and spouses to Coffs Harbour for a gathering on a wedding anniversary and presented us each with a cheque for $10,000. That unexpected gift sure helped our budget.

When the yacht sails arrived we had to hire a large truck, trailer and crane as we had done when we bought her, to get her launched in Newcastle Harbour. The RAAF transport officer suggested it would be good training for his crane and truck drivers, so we were happy to agree, and they dropped her into the harbour at zero cost other than a few slabs of stubbies. We christened her with the traditional bottle of champagne, naming her *Soolaimon* after the Neil Diamond song with the words 'Lord of my night, God of my day, taking me home, safely'.

We were invited to moor at the Water Police dock. Next day, with several RAAF colleagues as crew, we sailed her north to her Lemon Tree Passage mooring. Two of that crew, Ken Johnson and Dave Bowden, are still sailing today in their own yachts and I saw Ken on his Swanson 36 in the Whitsundays a few years back. Dave sails a 14-m catamaran named *This Way Up* and recently returned from a cruise to Phuket, Thailand. Dave used to fly me up to Coffs Harbour in a RAAF Winjeel when I needed to visit my parents.

Swanson 32 Soolaimon being lifted into back yard.

We had a C130 Hercules to take the 12-man Red Berets Free-fall team, which I had formed, to the Perth Air Show when all Army support was on hold due to finance. That did not endear me to Sydney staff officers but too bad. When we ran a free-fall course at Dubbo I had a Hercules attached, and it so happened that I organised it to fly me and my attached RAAF LO 'Bomber' Brown back to Williamtown for two days when we sailed my sold Folkboat yacht *Svenska* on delivery to the new owner in Sydney. The official reason was to get more parachutes. 'Bomber' and I sailed the 26-ft Folkboat south to Neutral Bay, Sydney, overnight, where Anne met us and drove us back to Williamtown. We flew back to Dubbo the same day. Some said the C130 was my very expensive taxi, but we really did need more parachutes as the forecast weather suited more jumps, so that coincidentally worked in well with the yacht delivery.

When the Australian Army decided to teach its own soldiers to jump out of aeroplanes, I was honoured to be the first Army chief instructor. My new posting was wonderful. For nearly three years I was almost autonomous, responsible with my instructors to decide on how to train people to parachute and being able to order aeroplanes with direct access to the HQ RAAF Operation Command. The ability to be free to call up and get hold of a Hercules, Caribou, Chinook or Iroquois for whenever I wanted one for courses was awesome, but you had to have aeroplanes to jump out of!

We trained over 600 students each year, initially males; then I introduced the training of females, particularly those packing our parachutes. My philosophy was that if you packed a parachute you should jump with one and so they did the eight jumps to qualify for wings and we fitted most females into spare slots in future jump sorties. They were very happy to be part of the team, and students were also happy and more confident to see packers jump the chutes they packed.

We also trained the Army's first Infantry battalion to be a parachute battalion, 3RAR. That idea was conceived with Army HQ where a couple of fellow officers, Colonels Tony Hammett and Owen O'Brien and I all agreed that the Army should have its own parachute battalion. After training several companies we did a parachute drop at Shoalwater Bay, the first ever up there. I recall I flew in with a few of my staff in an Iroquois chopper and we jumped freefall to set up the DZ. When the Hercules C130s arrived the mass drop from 1000ft (300m) was excellent but I remember one tall soldier was badly injured in his landing, unable to hold his long legs together as is required.

I also formed the Parachute Display Team 'The Red Berets' and we once jumped at Tocumwal, a town in the southern Riverina region of New South Wales, near the Victorian border where the original Parachute School was set up in World War II. In New Guinea in World War II the Army made some soldiers into parachutists the same day; they were given a parachute and had to jump into a drop zone close to Japanese forces, and from only 200ft (60m), just time for the chute to deploy. I think the record low was US

Army paratroopers in the Philippines from just 90ft, (30m). All those men had more than the accepted dose of guts.

The first intake of women into the Parachute School.

Most Army parachutists were Commando and SAS recruits and did a basic course with our school for normally four weeks before moving on to serve with their units. While my basic course in 1954 used old Dakotas, in 1973 the basic jumps were made out of Caribous and Hercules with the chute pulled out by a static line attached to a steel cable in the plane. It was known as 'dope-roping'. Like the Dakota, it was out the side doors of the Hercules, but out over the ramp in Caribous. With free-falling we used the Hercules door or preferably the ramp, particularly with team drops where it was best to have many jumpers go out close together so as to link up quickly. Special Forces jumped with packed-up canoes and outboard motors strapped to a leg, as well as stores valises which were all lowered on a rope after the chute deployed. Many, like me, who attended free-fall and instructor courses had done basic training earlier in their Army career, a pre-requisite, before we added Chinook and Iroquois helicopter jumps.

The Red Berets 1975.

Original Red Berets badge.

On every basic course I usually went out the door first as the 'drifter' so that I got to the ground first and could watch and coach those to follow with a loud hailer. The aeroplane would come over and let the drift streamer go over the target and it would be told by the DZ officer what offset for wind was needed. We had no GPSs in those days and had to drop the streamer from 1000ft (300m) for basic jumps or 3000ft (900m) for free-fall which was the height we pulled the ripcord. For free-fall the pilot would then climb to 10,000 or 12,000ft (3 to 3.5km) and adjust his run to the streamer site and we would hopefully land on the target, but we sometimes went into trees and scrub round the drop zone. The wind would often change and upset the streamer calculation but modern free-fall chutes had some steering capability so mostly we were able to land on target.

The common catchcry was 'If in doubt throw the CO out', referring to me going out first to confirm the drift, but I always maintained I wanted to do things before I asked others to do it, which was to be my literal downfall later.

Williamtown was home to the RAAF's fleet of Mirages and the only time I have ever been airsick was in the back seat of a dual Mirage in 1974. The Mirage III was a beautiful supersonic fighter aircraft designed by Dassault Aviation during the mid-1950s, and manufactured in France and other countries. The versatility of its design enabled production of trainer, reconnaissance and ground-attack versions.

'Come up and have a fly,' said RAAF pilot 'Tubby' Wilson one day when we weren't jumping due to high winds. Kitted up in G-suits we flew around the coast and even did a few barrel rolls. I got to play with the joystick and was having a lovely day. The Mirage came back to the airfield and the pilot decided he wanted to do touch and go's. The air conditioning wound down and it got hotter and hotter and I was finally sick into my oxygen mask. On the ground I apologised to the Safety Equipment people, who no doubt were fighting not to grin. They graciously said, 'Sir you can have the mask, all yours.' I washed and kept the face mask as a souvenir. That was the first time I had ever been airsick or seasick and it has never happened again.

Around this time in 1974, my first wife Kath was to remarry and thus I was to receive half the net proceeds of the sale of the house I had built the family. The house value had doubled since built in 1968. Her husband-to-be rang me and said I had to continue to pay maintenance. I told him I had news for him and that while the mortgages would be settled after sale, if they married the family would become his financial responsibility. Not happy about that he told me they would not then get married or sell the house, but they did. After paying off the house mortgages Anne and I were left with a nice kitty to pay off some of our debts. My two daughters, Debbie and Sharon, married and left home and son Brett left after clobbering his new stepfather Basil, who sadly for Kath passed on a few years later from a heart attack.

Kath now aged 81 lives alone at Campbelltown and is unable to drive because of eye problems but is supported by her three children. Son Brett, who lives near his mum, has always worked and has been with De Havilland Bankstown for many years and has been to post-war Vietnam to service helicopters. Brett's first wife joined the Army and met someone else. His second wife was Mandy and they had son Jacob who is now a mechanic. Mandy left home one day with baby Jacob, a new car and most of the good furniture as Brett discovered after arriving home from work. He was left with almost nothing but a single bed, a desk and mortgages on the car and house. At work he met third partner Christine — following in Dad's footsteps? They are still together. His main hobby is jet-powered dragsters and making small helicopter drones.

Sharon has always worked and is now with E-toll as a finance manager and lives with husband Greg at Camden in a lovely house. They have no children so are able to afford to travel overseas a lot and enjoy fishing on the southern NSW Coast. Debbie's first marriage produced daughter Kylie, who is now a teacher in Melbourne, and son Damien, an underwater photographer, last heard of in the United States. Debbie has worked ever since the two children from her second marriage to Frank could be left alone; daughter Charlotte is now at university; and son Christopher is a mechanic with Volvo. Debbie is now customer relations manager with Estee Lauder and lives at Kyeemagh just south of Sydney's Mascot airport in a nice but older style house in a quiet street opposite a Chinese market garden. I see my daughters quite often, either on trips to Sydney or on their visits up here. We get on well. Son

Brett is a loner, like his dad. We were all together in Canberra in October 2014.

In my times at Williamtown I had the good fortune to fly as co-pilot under supervision a Vampire, a Hercules, a Victor trainer, an Iroquois, a Winjeel and, briefly, a Mirage, but of course was never permitted to land or take off, except in a Victor trainer one day. Flying as co-pilot on a Hercules coastal at 500ft (150m) back from Perth to Adelaide after a jump display was great and flying that big plane was just like driving a car. Back in the sixties I had applied to join the new Army Aviation Corps but was rejected on age as 22 was the limit, so I continued to jump out of planes.

In October 1975 I was jumping a new French free-fall Papillon parachute, my policy unchanged – always trial new gear myself first. That was my downfall. We had received the new parachute to try out; I had requested it to compare it with our Para-Commanders, a French Papillon – ironically Papillon meaning butterfly, as smart as the birds when it comes to flying on the wind. What I hadn't considered was an omen that butterflies live on average for a month, the smaller ones for a week. Their little lives are very short.

    I decided to jump that Papillon parachute early one morning because there was less wind. I was up at 4.30am for breakfast at 5am. At 5.30 I kitted up and went out to the chopper at around 6am. Nothing out of the norm in good weather; I often did three, four or sometimes five jumps before lunch, especially with Iroquois and Chinook helicopters which could land and take off on the Salt Ash drop zone with fresh sorties using parachutes taken out to the DZ by truck. With normal aeroplanes we had to return to the base to refit chutes and if the wind had not risen we might get two jumps in. The wind limit then was 13 knots or about 20 kph, although the Air Force and Navy use knots, and they also use nautical miles at sea, and feet in the air.

    Just after 6.30am I jumped from the Iroquois chopper at 10,000ft (3km). I pulled the ripcord at the regulation height of 3000ft (900m). Nothing happened. Shit! No problem – I had a small reserve chute. Still falling towards earth at 120mph (193km/h) I rolled over on my back and recall seeing my two altimeter pointers passing through 1500ft (450m). I went to pull the reserve parachute on my chest at 1200ft (365m) – doing everything as I had been trained. Your actions are instinctive. But I didn't get to actually pull the ripcord because the main chute just then came out of the backpack and up between my legs rather than up over my shoulders. Being attached to capewell release clips on the front of my shoulders it whipped me backwards dreadfully when it filled, coming to a stop from 120mph terminal velocity. It was trying to drag my shoulders back and up through my rear end. Then I remember terrible pain and blacking out. I came to on the ground. I couldn't walk easily and was driven to hospital.

As luck would have it I did not pop the reserve. If I had it would have probably entangled with the main which is usually fatal. It was the only jump of 499 where I had a major problem. I had lots of very hard landings in high winds but, unlike tall people with long legs which were often broken, I was always able to roll up and was never badly injured. But this time I was in the RAAF base hospital for a day and night. X-rays could find no broken vertebrae. Later, doctors discovered I had two prolapsed discs in the lower spine and another two in my cervical spine.

It was on that 497th jump that finally something went terribly wrong. The chute was repacked and jumped by others and it worked. What went wrong with mine I'll never know. Maybe the pilot chute was caught up in a vacuum on my back. Then maybe I was a little head down on my back when it came out and it went between my legs. It still haunts me.

Never one to give up, and frustrated by my injury, I tried a couple of free-fall jumps three months later in January 1976 but they caused me acute pain in my back and legs, and I had to say to myself my jumping days were over. I was then medically boarded as 'home only' which meant I was no longer able to serve in the Infantry corps in an active role or ever become the CO of a battalion or – as I had dreamed – command the SAS regiment. And I was pinged off that I did not make 500 jumps – only 499. That number is miniscule to the thousands of jumps logged by many warrant officer parachute instructors, but not too bad for a 'half colonel'. Friends suggested I do another jump, tandem free-fall, on my 80th birthday in July 2013, but I would only jump if allowed to go solo, which was rejected, because my old qualifications had been replaced by new techniques and Workplace, Health and Safety laws. But with the new type wing parachutes landing on local beaches, there should have been no problem with a hard landing.

After my parachuting injury, my efficient adjutant Captain Wayne Shannon had me sign the normal D11 Injury Report form. Just as I was leaving the Army a couple of months later to start civil work, he insisted I sign a standard Claim for Compensation form. I was reluctant but he explained that down the track I could have problems and that the form could pave the way for costs of any medical treatment. In those days peacetime injuries were not covered as I discovered when I left the Army in May 1976 and later applied to the Repatriation Department (now DVA). I was referred to Defence Compensation. As my form was already in the system Defence agreed to pay me compensation of some $44 per fortnight for 'loss of earnings' due to injury, my civil salary being less than half that of my Army pay.

I had a big battle with back problems from my back injuries in the years after I left the Army. At times I was often unable to walk properly, sit down for meals, or bend over. To walk up slopes I had to turn around and walk slowly backwards to take the pressure off discs when leaning forward. In 1980 I was destined for fusion surgery until the surgeon told me a slip of his scalpel cutting a spinal column nerve would mean life in a wheelchair. I reneged on surgery and, on advice, wore a prescribed nylon corset and set about doing push-ups as I used to do, slowly but surely strengthening the muscle train along the spine. It took a couple of years until I was able to jog again. These days I don't jog unless I have to and I still have to be careful not to lift anything heavy lest a swollen disc pinches a nerve and puts me in bed for a week or two. Too much sitting or bending also causes problems but I am still able to walk well and sail – standing behind the wheel rather than pulling on ropes.

Around 1982 when peacetime injuries were incorporated, DVA awarded me a small disability pension which was not affected by Defence compensation payments. Then in 1993 Defence Compensation advised it wanted to pay me out based on the actuarial assessment of my life expectancy which was then, I think, age 73. They offered me a lump sum of $27,000 tax-free compensation, supposedly no strings attached, rather than continue fortnightly payments.

What a mistake I made in accepting that very usable lump sum! Almost immediately DVA advised that I would suffer a deduction from my disability pension for the rest of my life at the rate of some $52 per fortnight, but with no increase on that rate. So the money reverted from compensation to a repayable loan! Then DVA advised of new legislation that provided the repayments would increase with CPI! Five years ago, in 2010, with the repayments having increased by 30 percent since 1993 I calculated I had already repaid the original $27,000 sum in full and submitted to DVA it was unfair to ask me to pay compensation to the Commonwealth. No joy – and the Ombudsman would not get involved in arguing the DVA policy. It means that if I live for another five years to 2020 I will repay the Commonwealth about $10,000 more than I was paid in 1993! The DVA philosophy is that the compensation would have been invested and would thus earn interest which then caused a larger loss of pension. That might sound logical to public servants, but I used the 1993 lump sum to assist in reducing a home mortgage. So that lump sum from Defence was not in my bank still gathering interest, but I still have to pay for life, currently $1800 per annum.

A similar situation applies to Armed Services' Retirement Superannuation where the 'Fair Go' campaign has been lobbying the government to increase retirement fund pensions to the rate paid to public servants and age pensioners, given that a past government took all the money from our fund and placed it in the Commonwealth's general revenue bank. It is also asking that once a commutation amount has been repaid the lesser pension reverts to the full amount, otherwise we are again paying the government more than received. The system rejects that but notionally our payments made while in the service are still gathering interest in the government's bank.

These two issues might indicate the attitude of the Commonwealth to those who have sacrificed in war. In my own case I am still paying off the interest on a grant, albeit having repaid the capital sum five years ago, and having passed the actuarial age I am not receiving the pre-commutation amount of my Defence Forces Retirement and Death Benefits Scheme (DFRDB). As with awards justice, the bureaucracy continues with a strange, even suspicious, attitude which appears embedded in the minds of public servants who have never seen combat. I fully support the 'Fair Go' campaign – yet another David and Goliath battle.

And thanks to that campaign we were advised the Abbott government is to index our DFRDB pensions at the same rate as the age pension from July 2014, although it will only be fully beneficial to those who served to retirement. People like me who left early with smaller payments and then became entitled to a DVA part service (age) pension have to suffer reduced payments when DFRDB fortnightly payments – 'income stream' – are increased. They claim we will be slightly better off? I note the government is suggesting the new rate could be indexed back to CPI rate again in 2017? Nevertheless, I am very happy that I paid into the original DFRDBF scheme and that even though it was changed to Comsuper, a payment is in my bank every fortnight.

After the parachuting accident I could have changed to another corps and pushed paper but that didn't excite me and protracted sitting was bad for my back. On advice from a senior RAAF medical officer I decided to resign and leave the Army rather than take a medical discharge. I obtained civil work as NSW sales manager for Beaufort Air Sea Rescue Pty Ltd at Brookvale north of Sydney. But before I left the Army in May 1976 the RAAF medical system enabled me to have a vasectomy in a Newcastle private hospital. Anne and I had agreed we did not want children, and I volunteered. That was my first ever surgery since a child when I had ingrown toenail and tonsil operations.

Thereafter, when doctors asked about surgical history I used to say, 'Three operations Doctor, three Ts'. It normally got a smile when I explained 'Toes, Tonsils, and Testicles'. But in 2007 I had surgery for an inguinal hernia caused by very bad coughing after catching an Asian flu germ on a plane, and that was followed by prostate cancer surgery in 2008. So my 'three Ts' have gone by the board.

Recently I saw on TV some of the current Red Berets Team jumping at an Enoggera Open Day, using the new 'square' parachutes that were just coming along as I left in 1976. Some of my instructors at the Parachute Training School formed a civil team, the 'Green Machine', and jumped 'squares' in competitions in Europe in 1975. I supported them with jump planes now and then but they used their own private chutes. One day when attending a conference in Sydney, I was shocked when I was told one had ploughed in, perhaps having stalled, and instructor Warrant Officer Col Colough was killed, the first death at the school since World War II. I was caned by HQ for authorising the team to jump with 'squares', although I had not known of the jump that day. The team had just returned from overseas and Col was accidentally killed. All very sad. We gave him a military funeral at Newcastle. Since formation in 1951, the school has never had a student killed, although there have been a few other paratrooper deaths in the SAS and in a plane crash at Jervis Bay where the school is now located.

When I left the Williamtown gang they gave me a great farewell party in the Parachute School canteen, presenting me with a large chromed steel shackle which I have kept on my desk to this day. I'll always be shackled to the fellows I worked with at the Williamtown Parachute School. The school later moved to a new site near Jervis Bay in NSW. I still miss them, the school, parachuting and all the adventures with the RAAF even though their favourite saying was, 'Nobody in their right mind jumps out of a perfectly serviceable aircraft.' In May 2014 I was invited to attend an Airborne reunion at Tweed Heads and it was wonderful to see many old faces, including Craig Legget, Matt Faulkner and Bill Harvey. Like Commando postings it was one of the best times in my quarter of a century in Aussie Army life. Apart from adventurous service in action in Malaya and Vietnam, I had a very different military lifestyle from the norm of most Infantry officers and I am very grateful for that.

THIRTEEN

BATTLING THE BRASS: AUSTRALIA'S SHAME EXPOSED

Delta company returned to Nui Dat late on the afternoon of 21 August 1966 and, at midnight, the Commanding Officer Colin Townsend rang me to request I submit urgent recommendations for awards, said to be required by Canberra.

So began what became a bizarre lifelong battle with officialdom that raised its head again in 1996 and still continues as I write today. I do not wish to unnecessarily demean former 1966 senior officers, all now deceased, but the facts need to be told.

Half the 16 men I cited for Imperial awards were scrubbed and some of the other half of the awards I recommended were downgraded. But Brigadier Jackson was cited, in addition to meritorious service, as having 'personally directed the battle' and he was awarded the DSO in December 1966, at the top of the Long Tan awards list. In some Australian media reports a subhead ironically said: 'Medals for bravery'. Incredibly his DSO citation included:

> In one action on 18 August 1966 he personally directed the engagement which accounted for 245 enemy dead by body count with very light comparative losses to his own troops. His able personal direction was a decisive factor in obtaining an extremely favourable outcome in very difficult circumstances.

He gave me no direction and neither did my Commanding Officer Townsend and frankly, throughout the Battle of Long Tan, Delta Company was pretty much alone out there and we accordingly acted as though we were alone, and organised ourselves and the support that was very reluctantly made available to repel the hordes.

The CO of 6RAR, Colonel Colin Townsend, was also singled out even though that accolade was postponed to January 1967. He was cited by Brigadier Jackson as 'moving out immediately and taking over command from me and fighting his battalion in action'. Frankly, that is a serious porky that has been allowed its legs for far too long.

Colin Townsend's DSO citation, written by Brigadier Jackson, additional to statements about 'meritorious service', which is not applicable for an 'Immediate' gallantry DSO, reads:

> During the battle at Long Tan during the 18th and 21st August 1966, his battalion comprised the infantry element in the action against a regiment comprised of three North Vietnamese and Viet Cong mainforce battalions. As soon as the initial heavy contact was made by his Company on patrol he moved immediately with a relief company in armoured personnel carriers to join the Company which was then heavily committed and took firm and effective control of the battle during which a major defeat was inflicted on greatly superior enemy force.

Given that he did not move out immediately and arrived after the enemy had left the battlefield, and that Jackson did not direct the action, I believe their citations were written for these two men by their senior officers after listening to the recipients' versions of what they claimed to have done, and can be considered very inaccurate. They were perhaps made up to indicate command in action to avoid criticism from London that had earlier been levelled at the 1965 DSOs for Colonels Serong and Brumfield. It is recorded on file in the National Archives, Defence Minute No. 42 of 8 February 1966, that London queried the recommendations for DSO for Lieutenant Colonel Ted Serong, Commander Army Training Team and Lieutenant Colonel Lou Brumfield, first CO of 1RAR in 1965, who was sent home on medical grounds after six months, to be replaced by Lieutenant Colonel David Preece, who served the remaining six months of the 1RAR tour and also got a DSO. The London query stated: 'They were not in accordance with the standards normally expected here', and '...it is suggested the

Brumfield citation is similarly not very specific, and is hardly conspicuous leadership under fire'.

The Honours and Awards Regulations for the DSO at levels below Colonel required 'conspicuous leadership and gallantry in combat with the enemy' and, for more senior officers, 'leadership over a period under fire entailing gallantry is also necessary'.

As revealed years later, Commander of the Australian Force in Saigon, Major-General Kenneth Mackay CB, who had arrived in Vietnam that same year was back in Australia for the CGS Exercise at the time of the battle and on return obviously believed Jackson who no doubt told him he had directed the battle.

Also, as Brigadier Jackson had delegated control to CO6RAR and gone to his tent, literally head in hands to bemoan his future at the possible loss of a company and an attack on his base by 274 Regiment in the north, he really did not know just what Colin Townsend did. Jackson was happy to believe Townsend went out immediately and took over command from me and fought the battle to an end. This insults the courage and sacrifice of so many men on that day.

Another file, Defence letter of 17 June 1966, indicates earlier DSO citations should only have been given for exceptional acts of gallantry and notes '...however, this has not been the case'.

Nevertheless, no doubt lobbied by the 'Generals Club', as many of us have long called the close-knit cluster of big Army brass, Canberra was able to persuade London that the DSO awards should be approved. That set in place a precedent that allowed the DSO to be approved for every one of 17 Infantry Battalion COs, an Artillery Regiment CO, six Task Force commanders and a Training Team major commanding an ARVN Battalion and a CO AATTV. Indeed, 37 DSOs were approved in Vietnam, 26 for Army, one for RAN, and 10 for RAAF. How many of these commanders were involved in conspicuous leadership and gallantry in combat with the enemy? I have not researched all of these but suspect many were not a result of combat.

There were a number of well deserved DSOs, such as for Lieutenant Colonel Colin 'Genghis' Khan DSO, CO 5RAR, of the Binh Ba battle against 33 NVA Regiment troops in June 1969, and the DSO for Major Pat Beale DSO MC, of the Training Team, who fought a very gallant action with his South Vietnamese battalion in the highlands. Other majors, such as our excellent former Governor-General Mike Jeffery MC, and Major General Peter Phillips MC, who as majors both commanded significant company actions in Operations Hammersley and Coral–Balmoral respectively were perhaps prevented from getting DSOs because the DSO went to their COs. Their 'good service' might have been better recognised with the OBE (Order of the British Empire, albeit often called 'Other Buggers' Efforts') as in Malaya. This would have permitted proper recognition of those who commanded companies in action with more than a third-level MC award, generally awarded to platoon commanders and captains as happened in Korea, Malaya and Borneo and with three 5RAR platoon commanders in

1966. And it would have permitted more platoon commanders to be awarded the MC rather than just the MID.

Observers suggest there was a policy in Canberra to 'decorate' up-and-coming RMC generals, as they regarded short-service commission officers and those from OCS and National Service as not being around for the long haul. Of the 726 awards approved in the 10-year Vietnam War, only 22 private soldiers of the up-front cannon fodder, and just one from Long Tan, were given gallantry medals while some 150 officers were decorated with various medals, with several Brigadiers at Task Force Headquarters getting DSOs.

Author Ian Barnes, in his 1974 book about Vietnam awards, *Australian Gallant and Distinguished Service, Vietnam 1962–73,* published by the Military Historical Society, states: 'Those furthest from the action were the first to claim awards', and 'The DSO was awarded for just meritorious service or simply commanding a unit.' Barnes also said '...the lowest award for gallantry should have taken precedence over the highest award for meritorious service.'

Ian, who had served in the Volunteer Defence Corps in World War II, told me at our second meeting in March 2015 that the book was written in support of overtures by Vietnam Veterans to obtain the normal End-of-War (Awards) Review. But that did not take place until 1998, another 20 plus years, 26 years after the war. Why? While Vietnam was an unpopular war, soldiers still placed their lives on the line for the government of the day and those who were denied awards because of the quota should have been recognised as soon as possible after the end of the war.

When Colonel Townsend called me on my field telephone in my tent at midnight on 21 August and asked for citations for gallantry awards to be ready for his signature by the next afternoon, on the correct forms, known as Army Form (AF) W3121, which also required personal details of the individual, I did wonder at the lack of understanding. We had just fought a major battle, lost 17 young soldiers killed, with another 23 wounded, and I had other things to think of, other than awards. No doubt he was under pressure from above and could not or would not defer the matter. In hindsight, it is quite inexplicable that there was no after-action battalion or Task Force conference to discuss which units and which soldiers had done what and when, and who should be recognised for gallantry.

I argued with him that my thoughts were primarily focused on all the men we had lost and the others in hospital; reorganising the platoons and company; and writing to next-of-kin. To do justice to any awards, I said, I needed time to fully investigate the acts of outstanding gallantry which should be recognised. He said to me Canberra wanted to urgently announce gallantry awards to placate the public outcry at, particularly, the loss of so many young National Service conscripts at Long Tan. Delta's dead and wounded included 25 National Servicemen, with 11 killed. He told me to just do what he asked. Yes, Sir!

In contrast to the supposed urgency, it was later revealed the Long Tan gallantry awards were not sent back to Canberra immediately as was required by the regulations but were held over in the Task Force and Saigon HQs for at least seven weeks until mid-October while they were 'moderated' by senior officers. Moderated is the term used by the 2008 and 2009 Awards' Reviews to explain the alleged right of senior officers to change awards recommended by field commanders. Frankly I prefer the term 'manipulated' or even 'tampered with'. Personal opinion and politics often took over from fact and it is worth stating here that the US Army has Honours and Awards Units that investigate awards, a system that could well be adopted by our forces to eliminate the influence of personal opinions of senior officers who were not at the actions.

Early the next morning (22 August) I called a conference with my three platoon commanders, Company Sergeant Major Jack Kirby and Forward Observer Morrie Stanley. I explained the situation and that, while I believed everyone should be recognised, there was a strict quota for awards which meant platoons could only cite about three men each and that I could add others. The rule was that all names were to be secret. We came up with a list and brief facts for citations qualifying the selected men. The platoon nominations were an MM for 11 Platoon's Corporal Bill Moore and MIDs for Privates Geoff Peters, Ian Campbell and Bill Roche of 10 Platoon; Lance Corporal Barry Magnussen, Privates Allen May and Ron Eglinton of 11 Platoon; and Noel Grimes and Neil Bextrum of 12 Platoon.

After a subsequent private discussion with my CSM Jack Kirby, whose opinion I respected, and who was perhaps my mentor, having moved around platoon areas and seen other gallant exploits, I added a few more soldiers who had been killed: Max Wales, Glen Drabble and Paul Large. I also then privately added the three platoon commanders, Geoff Kendall and Dave Sabben for the MC, Bob Buick for the MM, plus the officer killed, Gordon Sharp for a posthumous MID; my CSM Jack Kirby for DCM Medical Orderly Corporal 'Doc' Dobson for MID, Sergeant Paddy Todd for MID, and Signaller Bill 'Yank' Akell for MM. The total was 20 men cited, most soldiers just for a Mention in

Despatches, not for a medal. During my deliberations I had rung the CO and suggested the CSM should be cited for a Victoria Cross but Townsend's reply was that 'he would only sign a DCM', which is what went on his form.

By noon I had given the company clerk, the (late) Corporal Tony Green, the draft citations to be typed on the official forms and at 4pm I took them up to the CO for signature. When I handed him the 20 forms, the CO's immediate response was, 'You have far too many for the battalion quota. What if we have another big battle next month? And we don't have quota numbers for dead men.'

I argued, with some knowledge of the awards system from my experiences with periodical awards when I was adjutant of the Infantry Centre at Ingleburn in 1963, that the quota was based on the total strength of the force in theatre, not just the battalion, and that the action warranted proper recognition. I was aware that 3RAR in Korea had been given 38 awards for the Battle of Maryang San, with similar casualties on both sides. But I was not then aware the Korean quota of one per 100 for Infantry per six months had been cut in half just before Long Tan by our esteemed Chiefs of Staff in Canberra (Ministerial File 133/3/26 of 17 June 1966), who claimed 1965 – early 1966 awards had been excessive for the operations in Vietnam to date, considered 'less intensive' than in Korea. Some earlier 1RAR Group and AATTV recommendations had been struck out or downgraded in Canberra, but the citation forms were still filed in Defence archives.

The new six-month quota was only one medal per 250 men and one MID per 150 men. So the new six-month quota for a battalion of 850 men was only about nine awards, say three or four medals and four or five MIDs. In hindsight, I can understand the CO being concerned that I had submitted 20 citations but I do believe he could have sought more than the 'battalion quota' if the will had been there. Certainly the Commander AFV could have provided more awards from the Force quota, but he had not been in the country for Long Tan and, as stated by the 2008 Review, did not understand the nature and ferocity of the battle.

I was also not aware in 1966 that in Vietnam the awards quota had been already notionally distributed to units based on personnel strengths, rather than to the most gallant actions in the Force during the period, in this case July to December. This unusual system was set in place by General Mackay and obviously approved by AHQ Canberra. I was not to find this out until after the end of the mandatory 30 year secrecy period in 1996 when I launched redress.

In our post-1996 search for evidence on what happened in Vietnam I was to learn from Ian Barnes's 1974 book that because of the very limited quota or ration 'all COs had demanded their fair share of the available numbers'. Thus administrative units like the HQ AFV in Saigon and the Australian Logistic Support Force at Vung Tau were able to get the same percentage of awards, albeit for meritorious service, as Infantry battalions which fought the combat actions on the front line!

So after the Training Team with 112 Imperial Awards, the next most decorated unit was HQ Australian Force Vietnam Saigon with 37, where, forgive me being blunt, the only gallantry displayed was to escort lovely local ladies to the cinema in peaceful downtown Saigon. Perhaps that is being overly cynical as soldiers who performed outstanding service in those rear areas should still have been recognised. But not at the expense of, and in the same ratio as, combat units, and contrary to the Military Historical Society's view that the lowest gallantry awards should take precedence over the highest awards for meritorious service. The system did not differentiate between the gallantry awards awarded 'Immediately' and 'Periodical' meritorious service awards. Both types were counted in the same six-month quota.

Incredibly, my company of 105 men was theoretically not entitled to one award for the iconic battle. The three Kiwis of the attached Fire Control Team, of whom two were recognised, were under their own NZ system. In the new 1991 Australian contemporary awards system, there is no ration on gallantry. This is well illustrated by awards given in Afghanistan, such as the present-day Delta Company 6RAR getting five: three gallantry medals and one commendation among the 20 men in the courageous action at Derapet in August 2010, headed by a Victoria Cross for Corporal Daniel Keighran. The platoon action with Air Cobra gunship and APC gun support against Taliban insurgents led to a withdrawal after one Delta Company soldier was killed – the only casualty. And there have been two other Victoria Crosses to SAS Troopers Mark Donaldson and Ben Roberts-Smith, plus another to Commando Corporal Cameron Baird, killed in action. Wonderful to see, given that, inexplicably, not one Victoria Cross was awarded in the 16 Australian battalions who fought in Vietnam over 10 years, despite major actions like Long Tan, Coral– Balmoral and Binh Ba, with many individual acts of outstanding gallantry and heroism. Although not well known, the Victoria Cross can also be awarded for 'extraordinary performance of duty in the presence of the enemy'. I quote Sir Roden Cutler VC.

Keith Payne VC, Ben Roberts-Smith VC and me at Maryborough 2011.

Afghanistan awards highlight the inadequacy of the awards system in Vietnam, especially for Army combat troops, as the RAAF and RAN were allocated a higher percentage of awards. Paul Ham said in his book that the RAAF received awards on the basis of one to 17 men while the Army was only one to 61 and he quoted Admiral Sir Victor Smith, Chairman, Joint Chiefs of Staff in 1972 who said:

> I find it impossible to accept the RAAF is always more gallant ... than the other two services, and that in Vietnam, which was essentially an

infantryman's war, the Army was the least distinguished ... it seems the basis of the scale must be wrong...

But back to 1966. The CO quickly looked through the forms, scanning the brief citations. He instructed me to remove several names, including those of the dead, but I insisted the platoon commander killed, Gordon Sharp, should still get a posthumous MID for his command of 11 Platoon and putting himself in danger by raising up to direct gunfire before he was shot. Those killed could only get a MID or VC posthumously, whereas under the new 1991 awards system, all gallantry awards can be posthumous. The CO also said that the Military Medal for Signaller Bill 'Yank' Akell had to be downgraded to MID as I already had 11 Platoon Sergeant Bob Buick and Section Corporal 'Bluey' Moore cited for MMs.

I argued as usual but this time did not win and in the end I reluctantly withdrew, by direction, the forms for Sergeant Paddy Todd, wounded, and Max Wales, Paul Large and Glen

Drabble, all killed, and I downgraded Yank Akell from MM to MID. I left 16 citations with the CO. Although not that happy, he gave me the impression that he would sign them and send them up the line as immediate awards to be approved as soon as possible, as in the past; for example, the squadron commander, Major Scott, of 9th Light Horse in the Sinai desert during World War I in 1917, was awarded a DSO when he arrived back after a battle two days' ride away. And in Korea, an immediate DSO was awarded within three weeks.

There was absolutely no further discussion with me about these awards by the CO or anyone else and I therefore assumed they had all gone up the line, to be sent to Canberra and then signalled to London. I expected them to have been approved in a month. I add that although it was the prerogative of their own unit commanders, I gave the CO informal but typed recommendations for both Lieutenant Adrian Roberts, APC Troop Commander, and Captain Morrie Stanley, 161 NZ Artillery FO. It was my opinion both should be considered for the Military Cross. I note here that an APC troop officer and a NZ FO were both awarded MCs for action with the 1RAR Group at Bien Hoa in 1965–66, so this was not an unusual request. And an Australian 106 Fd Bty FO Lieutenant Neville Clarke was awarded an MC for his control of the artillery during a savage Alpha Company battle in 7RAR's Operation Ballarat 6 August 1967. That four-hour battle, with a reinforced company of VC 274 Regiment left six company soldiers dead and 20 wounded for seven VC bodies plus an estimated 200 casualties taken away. Morrie Stanley should have got an MC.

I was not made aware until many years later that over a beer in the canteen my company clerk had advised most of the proposed recipients of their recommended awards. Like leaks in Canberra government circles, I guess this was pretty natural and, of course, the soldiers told their families and loved ones who have never been able to comprehend why they were not approved, given the legendary status of the battle and the undisputed gallantry of their men. And, further, why they were not then approved in the Vietnam 1998 End of War Review with 81 others who had been downgraded or scrubbed, nor the 2008 and 2009 Reviews.

A few days later, I was asked by the CO to nominate 12 people for South Vietnamese gallantry awards, as President Nguyen Cao Ky planned to visit Nui Dat on 2 September and present the medals. After discussions with my officers and CSM I submitted brief typed citations, mostly the same as for the Imperial awards, as we believed the individuals might then get one or the other, given that we had found out by then there was no guarantee any would be approved. The CSM told me he had 'heard' on the RSM-CSM 'grapevine' that the CO had not signed half the ones I had submitted to him.

Details of the Vietnamese awards parade were announced on the 1st September and I was to be with the President at the medal table. But about half an hour before the parade assembled on the airstrip at Nui Dat the next day, the word went around that Canberra had refused to accept the foreign awards because they did not have Her Majesty Queen Elizabeth's approval – and therefore no medals would be presented, just gifts, thank you very much.

This led to the bizarre circumstance where the angry president, his nose out of joint at the Australian rejection of his offer of awards, then delegated his Commander of the Vietnamese Armed Forces and Head of State, Lieutenant General Nguyen Van Thieu, effectively the Vice-President, to attend. We believe his officers had to go to the local markets and buy gifts and national dolls to replace the medals. In addition to the general, there was a large entourage comprising Lieutenant General Vien, Chairman Vietnam Chiefs of Staff; Lieutenant General Khang, Commander 3rd Corps; US Army Corps Commander Lieutenant General Seaman plus a host of other big wheels and a noisy 40-man Vietnamese Army band – a lot of important people to hand out just a few '$1 dolls and cigar boxes'!

In 1999 in AWM Archives I located a cable from our ambassador in Saigon,

Lewis H Border, to Canberra, dated 1 September 1966, suggesting the president be permitted to present the awards but they not be worn until Royal approval was obtained. Canberra declined, which did little for international relations or for my gallant men. Canberra rejected the suggestion that night and the ambassador told HQ Army Force Vietnam Saigon and then ATF Nui Dat next morning there would be gifts instead of medals on the big parade that day.

President Ky had a reputation for being an angry man and this event did nothing to cement relations with Australia. Indeed, it is rumoured he said his piece to our ambassador, who sent another cable suggesting that in future similar awards be accepted. We believe Malcolm Fraser, then Minister for the Army, was sent to Saigon in October to smooth the troubled waters. But while Fraser was known to have been in Vietnam, recorded in a Training Team history book *The Team,* a search of National Archives in 1999 mysteriously failed to locate any details of his visit. An NAA file relating to Fraser's air travel was advised as 'having been destroyed'. Fraser at home in Melbourne around 2000 refused to discuss it with one of my former platoon commanders, Dave Sabben, who was assisting me with research into missing Vietnamese award documentation. Vietnamese and US Army awards were approved from about 1968 onwards but there was no action to give retrospective approval for Long Tan.

So, instead of military decorations and awards befitting warriors, the officers received lacquered wooden cigar cases, sergeants and corporals were given similar but smaller cigarette cases and the lance corporals and privates were handed Vietnamese dolls in national dress. This became well known as the 'dolls for medals' debacle. Some Australian media reported 'Dolls for Heroes'. What a shameful disaster! The VIP entourage then went to the Task Force Officers' mess where Brigadier Jackson was given a plaque for the Task Force and a lacquered screen for himself.

Vietnamese medals were rejected by Canberra, so dolls and cigarette boxes for Heroes!

The Australian media published the medals that were to have been presented, having been given the official press release just before the awards were cancelled. The Australian HQ in Saigon had been given the documentation by the GRVN, the 'offer' if you will, and passed it back to Canberra for release to the media. I later learned a Unit Citation was also offered; also rejected by the Australian government on the grounds it had to have been first approved in London by Her Majesty. The post-war Canberra bureaucracy vehemently asserted that the offer of awards had been rescinded. It also came to light from files we located in 1999 that a US Army Honours and Awards Team visited Nui Dat to offer individual US awards, but was sent packing by Brigadier Jackson who fired a signal to Australian Force Vietnam, on file in AWM archives, that he had rejected the US Army offer 'because of the lack of clear policy on foreign awards'.

In May 1968 America's President Lyndon Johnson announced the award of the prestigious Presidential Unit Citation to my Delta Company, as had also been awarded to 3RAR for the battle of Kapyong in Korea. No other units, just Delta Company, because the Americans considered Delta to have fought the main battle, which it did. The Citation and Streamer for the Colors, a blue badge known colloquially as the 'blue swimming pool', said equivalent to each man being awarded a US Distinguished Service Cross medal, was presented at 6RAR Townsville on 18 August 1968.

With many of my former soldiers and their families I was seated in the audience, while the serving officers of 6RAR took the credit, as if it had been awarded to the battalion. In fact the speech by CO Lieutenant Colonel David Butler DSO recorded in the memorial book suggested the whole battalion had been involved: 'With magnificent artillery, air and armoured support, the Battalion inflicted a bloody defeat on the enemy, forcing him to withdraw.' This followed a similar theme to Colonel Townsend's words in 1966 that: 'Delta Company's performance was admirable. 6RAR won a great victory.' I realise it is a problem to have just one company highly decorated but this attitude has been fostered by successive commanding officers of 6RAR from 1966 to the present day and it is an attitude that is based entirely on keeping the battalion family happy and not elevating their Delta Company onto a pedestal. Now the same company has been elevated to Victoria Cross level – from Afghanistan!

The evidence relative to our foreign awards points to the Department of

Foreign Affairs and Trade (DFAT) having the documentation but being persuaded to reject the offer of GRVN awards on the ground of Royal approval, although the Generals Club did not want the 'noggy trinkets', and 'American confetti'. This was an actual quote from Brigadier Jackson's statement to me around mid-September of 1966 when he patted his chest and said, 'We only wanted our prized Imperial awards.' He had been commander of the Training Team in late 1965 and objected, after combat actions, to the manner in which Vietnamese commanders liberally handed out medals on a plate, which he considered 'trinkets'. But over the 10-year war the Training Team was to receive some 650 Vietnamese and Cambodian awards and 300 US awards, in addition to over 100 Imperial awards including four Victoria Crosses, among 990 officers and men, which looks like everyone got a medal. I have no doubt members of the Team working mostly with ARVN units, deserved this recognition but it highlights the lack of recognition in Task Force battalions.

Apart from the dolls and cigar cases presented after Long Tan, the only Vietnamese awards to members of the Nui Dat Task Force were the formal presentation of a Unit Gallantry Citation and some 22 medals to 8RAR for successful but costly actions during Operation Hammersley in the Long Hai hills in early 1970.

AATTV and 2 Squadron RAAF (as part of the USAF 35th Tactical Wing) were to receive the Vietnamese Unit Citation. 2 Squadron also received the US Air Force Outstanding Unit Commendation, with V for Valour badge, and 50 men of the AATTV were to receive the Presidential Unit Citation for being attached to the 5th Special Forces Group although none fought as a unit. On the other hand, 1RAR was attached to 173 Airborne Brigade at Bien Hoa in 1965–66 and was awarded the Brigade's US Meritorious Unit Citation ('red swimming pool') but the Vietnamese Unit Citation awarded to 173 AB did not flow on to 1RAR because the Defence bureaucracy claims 1RAR was not attached to 173 AB – in contradiction of its award of the US MUC, yet 173

AB Brigade unit structure diagram shows 1RAR as their third battalion.

I am aware that argument has lingered on for many years but in May 2015 the Vietnamese Citation for 1RAR was finally approved. One wonders just what politics or personal influence of senior commanders played a part in the various US and Vietnamese awards awarded to some units but not to others. In 1972 the Vietnamese Government was to award their Cross of Gallantry medal to all those who fought in South Vietnam under MACV but Australia refused to accept that offer on the basis our troops were under the command of AFV Saigon. But we were under FFV2 and MACV for operations. In more recent years foreign awards from France, Belgium, Malaya and Timor have been accepted and as with Contemporary Awards since 1991, highlight a change in attitude to awards.

At Nui Dat we got on with life, reorganising the company with reinforcements and patrolling local areas. On 2 December 1966 we had another disaster, with one NCO killed and 11 men wounded by a mine on a track out near Xuyen Moc. Claymore mines had initially been distributed by the Americans to ARVN units and the Viet Cong captured a few and also had Chinese mines. That day the Claymore that killed and wounded our soldiers was similar to what is known today in Afghanistan as an IED (Improvised Explosive Device).

We had to move along a dirt track in single file, not my choice, but the jungle each side of the track had been defoliated by the USAF spraying chemicals (Agent Orange) and there were dead trees on the ground out to 150 m which made it impassable. My gut feeling was that we could be hit by the Viet Cong and sure enough there was a large explosion up front in 11 Platoon, the leading platoon. Corporal Colin Lithgow was cut to pieces and killed, Private Peter Ainslie lost a lower leg and there were 10 others wounded. We called for Dustoff choppers and the casualties were flown to Vung Tau hospital.

We located command detonation wires from the jungle edge leading to a Chinese mine which had been exploded as the leading troops went over a small culvert. This then caused the sympathetic detonation of the Claymore mine carried by Colin Lithgow, killing him and causing more casualties.

Critics in another Company claimed that Colin Lithgow, a very fastidious NCO, had failed to disarm his Claymore in the morning as he should and he had thus contributed to the disaster by his own Claymore mine wounding others. But I was able to tell them that after the disaster CSM Jack Kirby had taken the matter up with the engineers who conducted tests and found that even a disarmed Claymore could still be exploded by sympathetic or mutual detonation. On a similar tragic note it is recorded that an VC RPG round hit a box of unarmed Claymores on top of an APC during Operation 'Overlord' June 1971 and the resultant catastrophic explosion killed seven soldiers and wounded three.

More weeks flew by and nothing was mentioned about approval of the awards I submitted on 22 August. But In late December, I think it was the 22nd, four months to the day I had submitted them, the word came down the line that Long Tan gallantry awards had just been announced, the List unbelievably headed by the award of DSO to the Task Force Commander Brigadier Jackson for his 'able personal direction of the Battle'. Media articles said 'Medals for Bravery'.

I was very proud to have been given the MC on behalf of my men, although normally a platoon-level award in past conflicts, and given to 5RAR platoon commanders in previous months, but in Vietnam it became used to decorate majors who might otherwise have been awarded the DSO if that had not become a good-service award for battalion and some Task Force commanders. I was pleased to see Jack Kirby get the DCM and Bob Buick the MM. But I was not pleased to see a soldier cited for MID being upgraded to the MM which should have gone to Corporal 'Bluey' Moore, who was not mentioned, while the two surviving platoon commanders were only given a MID, with nothing for the (late) Second Lieutenant Gordon Sharp.

Of the 16 awards I had cited and which had supposedly been accepted by the CO, plus the award cited for me by the CO, we only received eight: four medals (Kirby DCM, Smith MC, Buick MM, Eglinton MM) and four MIDs (Kendall, Sabben, Akell and Dobson). Those not approved were the MM for 'Bluey' Moore and MIDs for Bill Roche, Geoff Peters, Ian Campbell, Barry Magnussen, Allen May, Noel Grimes, Neil Bextrum, and Gordon Sharp. Only one front line soldier of the 80 or so who gallantly fought the enemy at the coal face had been recognised. As the Official History remarks 'insulting for the heroism displayed'.

We were out on Operation 'Duck', a battalion patrol operation over Christmas 1966 when the awards were announced. I went to see the CO and made my displeasure known but all I could get from him was that he 'had nothing to do with the lesser awards', that 'it has all been done up the line' and that 'awards matters are secret so nothing can be done for 30 years anyway'!

In January 1967 we were paraded at Nui Dat and presented with the ribbons of our awards by Brigadier Jackson. The medals had to come from London and were not presented until later, my MC at an Investiture at the Australian Embassy in Saigon in May. Bob Buick got his MM from the Governor in Brisbane when he came home.

Medal ribbon parade January 1967: Smith, Kirby, Buick, Rutherford and Eglinton.

Brigadier Jackson presenting presenting my MC ribbon January 1967.

In 1999, the former Task Force liaison officer and personal assistant to Brigadier Jackson, Lieutenant (later Major) David Harris, stated in a letter to me that awards citation forms had arrived at HQ ATF from CO6RAR and that he recalls the recommended awards included the DSO for myself and MCs for Geoff Kendall and Dave Sabben. He believes the original Forms for the lesser MC and MIDs may have already been up to HQ AFV in Saigon and upgraded. He said that when lesser awards were announced in December, with the DSO going to the brigadier, many of the officers at Task Force were dumbfounded. His gut feeling was that there was 'a cosy little deal' done between the commanders at AFV, ATF and 6RAR to decorate senior RMC officers at the expense of those junior OCS and Scheyville officers who fought in the battle.

The evidence is that the original inadequate officer MC and MID awards first recommended by Colin Townsend had gone through to Saigon and were directed to be upgraded, with me then cited for the DSO and Geoff Kendall and Dave Sabben for the MC. Then in October, they were downgraded back to the original recommendations to pave the way for the DSO for the brigadier, with the forms retyped in the Saigon's AFV HQ and sent back for signatures, although my own DSO Form was just amended. The forms went up and down like 'Harlot's Drawers'. At the start of the next six-month period on 1 January 1967, Jackson signed Colin Townsend for the Immediate DSO, not near the end of his tour in June as would be expected if a meritorious service award.

A 'cosy little deal', indeed. Townsend's Army Form (AF) W3121 for the DSO was notated an 'Immediate' award, which suggests it had been drafted in September but postponed when I was upgraded to DSO and postponed again in October to pave the way for Jackson's DSO. The 2008 and 2009 Reviews said senior officers had the right to 'moderate' awards, but this sort of nonsense was clearly 'manipulation'.

In March 1967 'Bluey' Moore was given a belated MID signed by the CO on 10 December 1966 but without mentioning it to me. The postal officer at 1 Australian Logistics Support Group at Vung Tau was also given an MID for outstanding postal services, despite the tongue-in-cheek catchcry in late 1966 being 'Punch a postie for Christmas'. How can anyone compare the postal officer MID for service on the beach at the Vung Tau resort area with the lowly MIDs given to the officer platoon commanders or soldiers at Long Tan? Assumptions that awards were examined and adjudicated fairly by senior officers were baseless.

The AWM Official History Volume 3 notes that while my platoon commanders were given only the MID, a similar MID, apart from the one for the postal officer, was also awarded to a Vung Tau officers' mess cook, clearly indicating problems with the awards system in Vietnam and the lack of a clear policy which allowed approving officers to sign off such anomalies. How could anyone in a recommending or adjudicating role at HQ AFV Saigon or in Army HQ (AHQ) Canberra compare a cook at Vung Tau with a soldier in combat action at Long Tan? This has to do with General Mackay allocating awards to units based on strength rather than to the most gallant combat actions over the six-month period and the lack of proper arbitration by senior officers at all levels, right back to Canberra

I got on with life with my company, although I was very annoyed by the lack of Imperial recognition for my men and the giving of Vietnamese dolls instead of medals, all indicating a negative attitude and maladministration by our highly decorated masters.

After Jack Kirby and others were killed by friendly fire in February 1967, there was a memorial service parade for these men and I was appalled that the NZ artillery commander, the (late) Major Harry Honnor, to become brigadier and who passed away in early 2012, a 1948 Duntroon classmate with Colin Townsend, chose not to attend and placed the blame for the tragic incident on a plotting error by a recently arrived and inexperienced OCS officer whom he had permitted to control the gun command centre that day without supervision.

At Long Tan, to the best of my knowledge, not one friendly round of over 3500 fell on us although I often reflect that the death of Max Wales 10 Platoon may have been caused by me requesting the guns drop 50 m closer in the face of a huge assault. But I can't dwell on that nor the loss of all the others as being my fault otherwise I would not be able to face the dawn of another day. I have to tell myself that I did what I did for the Army and government of the day, and to the best of my ability, and that had I not trained our company the way I did and demanded all the support I needed, then we might have lost a lot more at Long Tan, maybe the lot of us.

I regard the loss of 23 men and another 47 wounded from my company, 70 casualties from a nominal company strength of 125 men over the year in a war we could not win as very sad. I have tears in my eyes on Anzac, Remembrance and Long Tan Days, and I obviously suffer Post traumatic Stress Disorder although we were not aware of that problem in Vietnam. But as I get older, perhaps because I sometimes have more time on my hands, my thoughts tend to linger on the sadness. If things are going okay I can cope, but if there are any problems I fly off the handle very quickly, as my good wife knows. I guess sailing is my best therapy.

While we had been given just the ribbons of our Imperial awards at Nui Dat in January, in May 1967 I was called up to Saigon to be presented with the medal of the MC by our ambassador, Lewis H Border, along with a few other officers and soldiers. My

'Bluey' Moore and Alpha Company Frank Alcorta got their MIDs. Frank, nicknamed 'The Mad Spaniard' for his brave exploits without regard for his own safety, thought the MID was for his dismounted assault en route to Long Tan. But no. It was for capturing a VC officer on Operation Vaucluse in September 1966. He was recommended for an MM for Long Tan by his platoon commander, Lieutenant Peter Dinham, and an MM also for the disaster that was Operation 'Bribie' in February 1967 by the (late) Major Owen O'Brien. He went forward under fire and attacked the enemy with grenades to rescue his badly wounded machine gunner, the (late) Ron Brett, who had both legs shattered by machine gun fire. Still under heavy fire, he carried him out, which might well have earned him a Victoria Cross if in Afghanistan (like Jack Kirby). A soldier in Alcorta's platoon, Private Bill Reynolds, is on record in the Alpha Company book as saying:

> The bravest soldier I ever saw was Sergeant Frank Alcorta. What he did in Operation Bribie was unbelievable. He didn't seem to care

for his own safety. Like I said, unbelievable.

Ambassador Lewis Border, Major General Vincent and me with the MC medal in Saigon, 1967.

Neither recommendation for the MM for Frank Alcorta was processed in 6RAR. Owen O'Brien was to tell me in 2012, just before he passed away from the lingering effects of prostate cancer, that Townsend rejected the MM for Alcorta for 'Bribie', saying 'He already has an MID'! Similarly, there is a citation form in the AWM for an MC for the second of two White brothers. One had already been awarded an MC and the signing brigadier had downgraded the next one to MID and written on the form the words 'One brother already has an MC. You can't have two in the same family – so just the MID.' These examples typify the attitude and personal opinion of many senior officers who were involved in 'moderating' awards.

Frank Alcorta and I are good friends. In 2000 we visited his home in Bicheno, Tasmania, my childhood seaside holiday town and we often see each other in Bundaberg where he moved after losing his first wife to breast cancer. Frank in 2013 received an Australia Day award of the OAM for Services to Journalism for when he was working in Darwin after Vietnam. Frank, alone except for native porter parties, also walked the Papua New Guinea border from north to south, unarmed, in areas frequented by cannibals and where several past explorers had been killed. The 'Mad Spaniard', a truly brave man, in both war and peace, wrote a great book on his adventures, *Journey into the Stone Age.*

I am told Ron Brett, his M60 gunner, who lost both legs after Frank carried him out at Bribie, met his death in Townsville years later when, on crutches, he walked off the footpath in front of a truck.

In Saigon in May 1967 as I was leaving the ambassador's residence with my MC medal, I was met by a GRVN officer who asked me to go with him to the palatial home office of Tran Van Lam, Ambassador to Australia, President of the Senate and Minister for Defence. Tran Van Lam was a diminutive but very pleasant man who explained to me that his government had been embarrassed and annoyed by the Australian Government's September 1966 decision to reject their awards for Long Tan as offered by President Ky. He told me he had just been advised in early 1967 that retrospective formal approval was underway but that as I had been given my UK MC medal that day, he wanted to present me with the unique National Order of Vietnam, 5th Class (Knight), that I was to have received on 2 September as a token from his government for my company

– pending formal approval of all the proposed awards. He also gave me an original Cross of Gallantry Citation with Palm (CGCP) badge, a large early version with a clear plastic cover to stop the colours running in the rain, for the unit citation mentioned by an ARVN colonel at HQ Field Force Vietnam eight months before. He claimed that award was also about to be approved by Canberra.

But not so, Defence advisers were to claim the Vietnamese goverment had withdrawn the offer of awards, which was not the version told by Tran Van lam in 1967 and in 1999 when I contacted him in Canberra. Also, the medals had been published in the media! It sounds typical of bureaucrats not wanting to change previous decisions, albeit incorrect at the time.

One Canberra bureaucrat, a former adviser in Defence, who wrote a Military History Society paper in 2010 under the pseudonym of 'Missio', critical of our awards, was quick to point out that the CGCP was not formally introduced until 1968 and therefore I could not have been given a badge in 1967. My response was that the new unit award must have been known by the GRVN and that Defence Minister Tran Van Lam had very obviously obtained an advance issue of a badge in 1967, perhaps a prototype, later to be replaced by smaller weatherproof badges, which I gather were then made in the United States. Indeed when the unit award was finally approved on 'proof of offer' in 2008, we had to order the badges from the United States and initially pay for them.

Cabinet Secretary Senator Faulkner's letter to me dated 11 August 2008 said:
> Foreign awards protocol prevented the government conferring awards of another nation but the approval will enable the insignia that the men obtain themselves to be worn, and I understand the emblem is available commercially.

I had been given advance verbal advice of this by Alan Griffin MP, Minister of Veterans' Affairs, and so our company association ordered the emblems from the United States. I think they were $8 each. One of my former soldiers leaked this to the media in Sydney asking why we had to pay for the badges, and the ensuing media embarrassment for the Labor Government saw the $800 costs reimbursed while the emblems arrived just in time to be worn on Long Tan Day 2008.

But the approval denied the Vietnamese award be officially recognised as a unit award and so the normal Streamer could not be flown on the Battalion Colours alongside the USA Presidential Unit Citation (PUC) Streamer, and the serving Delta Company soldiers could not wear the emblem badge. I located Streamers in the United States and had the matter re-appraised by Canberra. 6RAR Regimental Funds paid for a Streamer and it is flown on the Colours. But I could not get approval for the enduring award for current and future serving members of Delta Company. Oh well, our efforts finally saw the 1966 award approved in 2008, after 42 years, but the government had to have one final say. Can't win 'em all! Delta Company of today wears our PUC and UCG and some who were there wear the Meritorious Unit Citation (MUC) from Afghanistan. Contrary to popular opinion the MUC went to all the Mentoring Task Force units, not just 6RAR, and I gather is also not an enduring award.

I mentioned earlier that in mid-1967, the CO, Colin Townsend, was awarded a DSO. At the time I was not aware that Long Tan was included in his citation.

It was not until the end of the secrecy period in September 1996 that I was to be gobsmacked by the mythical statements that he commanded the battle. Then in 2007 Prime Minister John Howard sent me a 150-page dossier about Long Tan awards, which contained Townsend's citation for a GRVN Cross of Gallantry with Palm, as given to others in September 1966, a lesser award than my National Order of Vietnam.

In this citation it said, in part:

> His personal presence and calm control of the battle inspired confidence in all ranks and enabled the battalion to inflict an overwhelming defeat on the enemy

despite their greater strength as is attested by the large numbers of enemy dead, weapons and equipment left on the battlefield.

This is untrue; he did not control the battle as he was not there. It was a complete fabrication.

A similar citation was the one he wrote for Charles Mollison for his Vietnamese Cross of Gallantry with Palm medal:

> He quickly mounted his Company in carriers of 3 Troop 1 APC Squadron and sped to the scene of the battle. On its way the force brushed aside enemy opposition. Captain Mollison then advanced his company through D Company forcing the remaining enemy to withdraw thus permitting it to reorganise and collect their casualties. The timely arrival, quick and aggressive action by A Company under the leadership of Captain Mollison contributed to force the enemy to withdraw leaving behind over two hundred dead.

Alpha Company did not mount the carriers until over an hour after the warning order was given at 1630 hours, because they were delayed by the brigadier. It did not advance through D Company but arrived on the southeast frontal flank after the enemy had left, and was ordered to move across our front as a screen – no enemy was there and not a shot was fired. The timely arrival and aggressive action en route was due to the APCs under Adrian Roberts' command. Adrian told me he was offered a GRVN medal but passed it on to one of his Troopers. He later went back to Vietnam with AATTV and came home with several GRVN awards.

One has to ask just how very senior officers come to write these citations, which contain false statements then higher officers in Canberra go on to have the awards approved.

6RAR ceremony on 18 August 1969 at Long Tan.

FOURTEEN

ANOTHER WAR: THE BATTLE FOR RECOGNITION

It was not until September 1996 and the end of the mandatory 30-year secrecy period that I could seek various files under what was then called Freedom of Information Act to try and ascertain what had happened with the Long Tan Imperial awards and Vietnamese awards. When I examined the purported original MID Citation forms for Geoff Kendall and Dave Sabben, I saw the date in blocks for each HQ was in the same handwriting, suggesting their MC forms had been rewritten down to MID at Saigon HQ and hand-carried by an officer back down for new signatures by CO6RAR, Colin Townsend, and Commander, Australian Task Force, Oliver Jackson.

After advice from former Captain Peter Harris, adjutant of 6RAR in 1968, to get my own citation from archives, I discovered it showed I had been downgraded from DSO to MC on 5 October, the same day the brigadier was cited for the DSO. On Colin Townsend's DSO form, signed 7 January 1967, it was an immediate award, yet the 2008 Review panel was to claim it was simply a periodical good-service award. But I have a copy of the form notated 'IMMEDIATE', which is for gallantry, and probably first drafted in late August then postponed when I was re-cited from MC to the DSO and further postponed when the Long Tan DSO went to Jackson, signed in October.

While I was sailing up north as in most winters, and not at Enoggera for the usual 6RAR Long Tan commemoration in 1996, some of my soldiers' wives made it known to VIP visitor Bronwyn Bishop MP, then Minister for Defence, that she should do something to get our awards approved and she agreed, and soon after there was a media statement to that effect. But I gather her advisers quickly put an end to that press release being followed up.

Bob Buick wrote letters to the media about a unit citation, while I tried to get the unapproved and downgraded individual awards listed on the 1997–98 belated End of War List (Vietnam) Review. Ms Bishop wrote to me explaining our awards could not be reconsidered in the End Of War Review as I had requested. The excuse was that the awards had been properly considered at the highest level in Vietnam by the late General Ken Mackay, COMAFV, and that was therefore the end of the matter. 'Properly' considered? The 1998 Review approved 81 other recommended awards that had then been struck out or downgraded back in Canberra, and then another review, the 1999 Tanzer Review, obtained by former Vietnam Veteran Graham 'Stumpy' Edwards AM MP, who lost both legs to a mine, upgraded six of those recipients to higher awards, MGs, more compatible to their originally recommended MMs.

Aided in my battle for 'medals justice' by my loyal former officers and soldiers Dave Sabben, Bob Buick, Bill Roche and Bill Akell, I pushed for a special review, which was supported by the Tanzer Review. Panel member Major-General Peter Phillips MC (Retired), who had fought his Delta Company 3RAR at Coral-Balmoral and was highly respected by all, told me there was to be a special review for RAAF FAC pilot Gary Cooper who had been recommended for a Congressional Medal of Honor by the US Army, which translated to a Victoria Cross, for rescuing a US general under fire, and that we should also obtain a review for Long Tan. But other than for a brief mention that the foreign Vietnamese awards should be revisited, nothing more was said in the Tanzer Review report and ministerial advisers were quick to reject my overtures that Long Tan awards should be reconsidered.

In hindsight, given the broad-ranging 2011 Valour Inquiry going back to the Boer War, the 1998 Review should have encompassed all awards that had been struck out or downgraded during the Vietnam War and, like the Terms of Reference for the 2009 and 2011

Reviews, called for other awards that perhaps should have been recommended but were pushed aside because of quotas. The 1998 Review terminated the quotas for Vietnam awards so numbers were no longer an issue. Observers suggest the 1998 Review did not wish to publicly discuss all awards as it could open up unwanted criticism of the large number of awards that went to officers 'far from the action'.

In 1999, Dave Sabben and I went to stay with former war photographer the (late) Denis Gibbons AM in Sydney to help with the draft of our *Long Tan Commanders* book. Denis, our initial editor, had spent five years in Vietnam (1966–71), much of that time at Nui Dat but also in dangerous areas up north, wounded six times. His wonderful collection of photographs is now in the AWM Canberra and in his obituary he was cited as being the Frank Hurley of Vietnam. Denis claimed he had a mate in DFAT who had told him the documents relating to the offer of Vietnamese awards were locked away in files with a 'D Notice' (meaning 'not to be released'). After a few weeks' work, with me incorporating contributions into the draft, and Dave concentrating on maps, Denis, who suffered from PTSD, quit after a bitter phone argument with Charles Mollison who apparently claimed Denis was not qualified to be our Editor. We drove to Canberra to search Australian War Memorial and National Archives for anything that might be of use. I got to see AWM Director General Steve Gower AO AO, who had been my artillery FO captain in Vietnam in 1967 after FO Captain Barrie Winsor was wounded in the tragic NZ friendly fire accident in February 1967. Steve, an RMC graduate, seven years younger than me, was a tall handsome man, later nicknamed the 'Black Prince' and awarded an Order of Australia (AO Mil) for military service. He was to be awarded another AO (Civil) for his wonderful work as Director AWM, and some of his staff were heard to quietly sing, 'AO, AO, and off to work we go.'

In discussions about awards with General Steve Gower, who was always supportive of my former company, he told me that former Vietnamese

Ambassador to Australia and Minister for Defence, 'Charles' Tran Van Lam, had escaped from Saigon with 'boat people' and was running a coffee shop in Canberra. He gave me his address and later I wrote to him and reminded him of our meeting at his home in Saigon in May 1967. I asked him if he had any information that would confirm the offer of awards by his former government. He replied in two letters his government did offer the medals and unit citation and that he had presented me with the National Order Medal and Emblem of the Citation. He also gave me the US address of his former President Ky, but my letter to him was returned with a note he had died. These Tran Van Lam letters I passed to Graham Edwards AM MP, the ALP Shadow Minister for Defence, and I also presented them at the 2008 Recognition of Long Tan Review in Canberra, which then stated in their report they were not official documents from the Vietnamese Government of 1966–67 and thus could not be accepted!

In 2004, while in Canberra for the launch of our *Commanders* book, retired Colonel Peter Dinham AM, formerly 2 Platoon Commander Alpha Company in the APC Reaction Force at Long Tan, advised me he had nominated former Sergeant Frank Alcorta for the MM and his M60 gunner, the late Ron Brett, for an MID in his After Action Report, for their gallantry in their brief dismounted attack en route to the main battlefield, but that no formal citations were drafted by the Acting Company Commander, Captain Charles Mollison. I added them to my list and noted that in the Mollison 2005 book he claimed the CO told him that due to the quota, any awards for Alpha Company would have to wait until near the end of the tour. That was contrary to the regulations that gallantry awards *were to be urgently forwarded and approved as immediate awards as soon as possible after the act of gallantry.*

It is further contradicted by a gallantry MID for Frank Alcorta in September and several awards for Bravo Company for Operation Bribie in February 1967. In fact Second

Lieutenant John O'Halloran's Bravo Company 5 Platoon became the most decorated platoon of the RAR. None of these were deferred to the end of the tour in May 1967. Further, Charles Mollison was the adjutant of 6RAR when a special HQ 6RAR awards review was held in May 1967 and several awards were recommended for meritorious service, but he did not push for gallantry awards for his men from August 1966, whereas Major Brian McFarlane obtained an MM for his Private Winterford backdated to Operation Hobart in July 1966. I was not invited to attend this review. Obviously the CO had no intention of reconsidering the Long Tan awards. I have to say, reiterating a statement from Ian Barnes's book, that scrubbed Long Tan gallantry awards should have taken priority over the good service awards.

Former senior officer observers have suggested that Mollison, knowing the quota was tight, did not forward the two recommendations as they might impinge on his own chances of getting an award for Long Tan. As to Alpha

Company awards, Colin Townsend was to tell me in 1999 he saw no reason why Charles Mollison or any of his men, protected inside APCs, in their brief encounter as part of the APC Reinforcement/Reaction Force, deserved any special recognition compared with the protracted action by Delta Company which sustained all the casualties bar one APC corporal who died of wounds nine days later and one Bravo Company soldier accidentally wounded by friendly fire from Alpha Company men atop an APC.

But Townsend, as in December 1966, continued to claim unapproved awards for my soldiers had been downgraded at higher HQ. He did not tell me that 'he personally had downgraded and scrubbed awards for my men', which was to be revealed in a confession when he was terminally ill with prostate cancer published in Paul Ham's 2007 book, *Vietnam: The Australian War.* He did suggest the MID upgraded to MM for Private Ron Eglinton by Brigadier Jackson was because it was politically expedient for a National Service soldier, the first, to be decorated with a medal to take the heat off the loss of so many others. This embarrassed Ron Eglinton, the only platoon soldier to be recognised.

I also ascertained he never passed my citation recommending Lieutenant Adrian Roberts for the MC to his APC Squadron unit commander Major Bob Hagerty. Bob, who retired as a Colonel AM, was to tell me in recent years that when he raised the subject of awards immediately after the battle, he was told by the more senior Colin Townsend that Smith was to get an MC and thus Adrian had to be restricted to the MID that had been cited for the two Delta Company platoon commanders.

Adrian Roberts had been unfairly criticised by Charles Mollison and this was taken up and published by Townsend in the 6RAR After Action Report, although it was ordered to be removed by Brigadier Oliver Jackson, along with an apology, published in November 1966. I am sure Adrian was not the flavour of the month for refusing to stop his advance and wait for Townsend, who, although he claimed otherwise in various articles, was not with the APCs when they left Nui Dat, having told the Operations Officer to tell Adrian he would fly out later – in a monsoonal rainstorm? The APC force was delayed by over an hour in leaving Nui Dat and there was ample time for Townsend and his HQ party to get on board.

After the 1999 Tanzer Review advisers in the Department of Prime Minister and Cabinet and the Directorate of Honours and Awards, as well as several generals, opposed any review, quoting all the usual tales that GRVN awards could not be approved as it would usurp a government no longer in existence, that we could not go back in time and approve Imperial awards that had been properly considered and so on. They claimed this would set a precedent for World Wars I and II.

But in 2004 we did have a rare win. Ex-Army officer, Liberal MP Mal Brough, holding the portfolio of Assisting the Minister for Defence, was able to obtain approval for the 1966 individual Vietnamese awards of which 12 were for some of my men in 1966, but not for the Unit Citation. He told me the new foreign award legislation provided for approval of offered individual awards but not unit (group) awards. Although they had to buy replicas from medal shops for about $40, the recipients were now able to wear their Vietnamese awards. I of course had my original National Order of Vietnam given to me in Saigon and could then wear it. I continued to push for approval of the Vietnamese Unit award and the unresolved Imperial awards.

Minister DVA Bruce Billson MP was supportive. On 17 August 2006, when we were in Canberra for the Prime Minister's memorable 40th Long Tan Day/Vietnam Veterans' Day, John Howard called Adrian Roberts, Dave Sabben and myself to his modern office with a grand view down the long Memorial Drive to the War Memorial.

John Howard agreed that the 1997-98 End of War List Review should have included the unapproved and downgraded Long Tan awards and he listened to Minister Billson's claim there was documentary evidence to support the offer of the Vietnam Cross of Gallantry Citation, as with the medals approved in 2004. Because of the requests by Vietnam Veterans who had been given Vietnamese awards without appropriate documentation, especially people from the Army Training Team Vietnam, legislation had been passed in 1999 that provided for approval of foreign awards if evidence of offer could be produced. Breakthrough at last! Thepm directed the Minister to seek opinion for a review from Defence.

A year later, in September 2007, John Howard sent me a hefty 150-page dossier for my comment, which consisted mostly of formerly secret documents relative to Imperial and Vietnamese awards. It was delivered to me by a local Cairns MP in a government car to our Cavalier 395 cruising yacht *Cavarlo* in the Marina Mirage at Port Douglas while my wife Felicia and I were en route to Lizard Island. Apart from many files relative to my push for a review of awards, it contained the briefs and comments of various advisers. On page 4 one adviser criticised my claim that I had cited platoon commanders for the MC, saying they were only recommended for MIDs, and that I said Townsend had arrived after the battle terminated. He then went on to say, 'It is recorded that CO6RAR moved out immediately and took firm and effective control of the battle, contrary to Lieutenant Colonel Smith's recollections of the events!' That sort of negative opinion from advisers sitting in their Canberra offices based on reading fraudulent citations was of little benefit to justice being done. The dossier also contained negative opinion from 8RAR Association suggesting we should not get the Vietnamese award they had, and even a quote from Charles Mollison that to approve any more awards for Delta Company would be detrimental to the harmony within 6RAR.

These comments and similar opinions were signed off on 30 April 2007 file CDF/2007/390, by Air Vice-Marshal Angus Houston, Chief of Defence Force, below a note that '...he did not agree with any additional awards or a Unit Citation to force elements involved in Operation Smithfield in Vietnam during August 1966'. Appalled, I wrote back to John Howard, vehemently opposing

Houston's view and asked for a formal review. I asked nothing for myself but insisted my officers and men be reconsidered for the awards I had recommended in 2006, plus the awards to two Alpha Company soldiers and the APC officer, and the offered Vietnamese Unit Citation for my company.

My main argument was the awards should have been considered and upgraded in the belated 1998 Review and the citation approved with the Vietnamese medals in 2004. Opposition to this theme had come from Defence advisers to their ministers and generals who really did not comprehend nor were genuinely interested in the problem, the rhetoric being you can't go back in time and risk setting a precedent for earlier wars.

Then Chief of Defence Force (CDF) Air Vice-Marshal Angus Houston, had himself accepted five high foreign awards from Malaysia, France, Singapore, East Timor and the Netherlands – along with a Commander of the Order of Australia for meritorious service as CDF. I am not saying his awards were not deserved, but think it's hypocritical that it was good enough for him to accept foreign awards, yet he tried to deny appropriate awards and the Vietnamese citation to my soldiers who fought and sacrificed in combat at Long Tan!

I met Angus Houston at the 2006 Canberra Long Tan Day and more recently at the March 2012 Caloundra dedication of the second Iroquois helicopter that resupplied us with ammunition at Long Tan, recovered from Nyngan in western New South Wales, refurbished and now a monument outside the RSL. Angus was the last CO of 9 Squadron. He had been replaced by Lieutenant General David Hurley as CDF in July 2011 and, no longer serving, he was very friendly but I did not discuss awards with him although we did briefly discuss our respective prostate cancer surgeries. In any case we had seen his 2007 opinions in the John Howard dossier overturned in 2008 with the approval of three officer awards and the Vietnamese Unit Citation.

In October 2007 Felicia and I had to climb halfway up the Cook's Look hill at Lizard Island to get mobile phone reception from the mainland aerial near Cape Flattery after receiving an SMS. While looking down at the stunning reef around Mrs Watson's Bay, I received welcome advice from Minister Bruce Billson that Prime Minister John Howard had read my comments on the dossier and had approved a review of Long Tan awards to start in December, chaired by Retired Major General Peter Abigail AO, the former Land Commander of the Australian Army, and including Retired Major General Steve Gower AO AO (mil), Director of the Australian War Memorial, plus Retired Brigadier Gerry Warner AM LVO. I wondered how General Gower had been chosen as he had written articles supporting more awards for Long Tan in AWM Wartime magazines and even in the foreword to our 2004 *Commanders* book. He may well have been perceived as biased but I welcomed him being on the panel. On the other hand, Canberra colleagues told me to beware of General Abigail as he had the 'mind of a barrister' and if the paperwork was not there, with the I's dotted and the T's crossed, he was unlikely to approve anything.

In addition to providing a written statement I was called to give verbal evidence at a very brief two-hour Canberra interview on 13 December and the report was published in March. It became known as the Review of Recognition for the Battle of Long Tan March 2008. The panel did not seek to interview my three platoon commanders and discuss the awards they had cited for their platoon soldiers. I must say I was warmly welcomed by the generals and they accepted the main documents I tendered relative to the Vietnamese citation; two letters from Tran Van Lam, and an 18 December 2000 Defence letter to my colleague Bill Roche signed by adviser Brad Fallon advising yes, the government did admit the Vietnamese Government had offered medals and a unit citation in 1966.

I thought all that would see the Vietnamese award approved by the Review panel, but no. We discussed the Imperial Awards, but while General Abigail made me aware of many former secret files, such as the use of the DSO as a senior officer good service award, and the reduction of the Imperial awards quota by half in 1966, we really did not get down to detail in the brief interview before I had to leave to fly home at noon, the booking made by Review staffers. I followed up the interview with another written submission but I felt the outcome of the Review had been decided before the interviews. Colleagues claim that all Canberra reviews simply confirm decisions that have already been taken!

The Review report was then delayed by a late request for the upgrading of an RAAF MID to DFC for one of the helicopter pilots, the late Cliff Dohle, who flew in ammunition at Long Tan, although not under fire, and was directed to the drop point by the leading helicopter piloted by the (late) Frank Riley DFC.

The March 2008 report recommended that only three original 'officer' awards be upgraded to the new equivalents of their recommended 1966 awards: to the Star of Gallantry (SG) for myself and Medal for Gallantry for Geoff Kendall and Dave Sabben, contemporary equivalents of the DSO and MC. While a former Alpha Company soldier has recently claimed we should have only received Meritorious Service Awards, thus suggesting we did not demonstrate personal gallantry, he is obviously not aware that good service awards do not apply in combat, and that our awards were for 'conspicuous gallantry – command and leadership in action', not personal heroism. No other men on the list, nor pilot Cliff Dohle, were to be upgraded and the other individual awards and the Vietnamese Unit Award were not recommended on the grounds of 'no official forms or evidence on file'. The RAAF MID award upgrading was denied on the basis that Cliff Dohle was led into Long Tan by Frank Riley and was sent home injured after crashing a helicopter in October, thus failing to complete his tour and qualifying flying hours, apparently an RAAF requisite for the DFC.

The Review panel was quick to point out that Brigadier Jackson's 'Long Tan' DSO was warranted by his good service over his 18 months in Vietnam and his able personal direction of the battle, and said it was a periodical award, despite heading the Long Tan Gallantry Awards list. The DSO is undoubtedly an immediate gallantry award and is so stated in the Imperial Honours Regulations (Modified for Australia) which applied in 1966.

On page 21 of the report it compared our awards with other battles. It showed 17 awards, but only nine of those were given to my company which fought the main battle. To pad out the figures to aid their negative findings, it included the two DSOs for Jackson and Townsend, the two awards for the NZ gunners, the two awards for the RAAF pilots, and the two awards for the APC Troop, another eight.

As to further blatant inconsistency, on page 26 the report denies the 1967 DSO for Colin Townsend was an immediate award for gallantry as on the citation form, just a periodical good service award, but on page 17, it includes the 1967 DSO award as being a gallantry award for Long Tan, August 1966! One would have expected the authors of the report to have at least got it right.

Much of the report dealt with various claims of conspiracy and manipulation of awards in order to dispel an image that senior officers not in action had decorated themselves at the expense of the combatants. It dwelt on my submissions about the interview in Saigon 1966 and letters from Tran Van Lam and dismissed them as being unsupported by official documents, despite being given a copy of the written admission by Defence adviser Brad Fallon in 2000 that the Vietnamese awards 'had been offered'.

The final bullet was on page 10 where the report extended the time of the end of battle from 7.10pm to the midnight casualty evacuation, to cover the Commanding Officer, Townsend being in a hostile area. This is like saying that World War II ended when the troopships arrived back in Australia!

It also said the victorious company battle 'was also due to a product of planning, decisions, and actions by other participants including the commanders at battalion and task force level'.

The old schooltie club blatantly shows up here. What planning? What decisions? And what actions? I am on record stating the brigadier did little other than delay the reinforcements, causing more casualties, and the colonel did nothing but argue with my requests for reinforcements and regimental artillery, arriving after the enemy had withdrawn.

The report also stated the opinion:
> ...that if General Mackay had not been back in Australia at the time, his attitude to awards might have been more liberal, whereas the awards approved did not conform to the level of recognition which might otherwise have been expected.

So why therefore did they not approve all the awards that I had recommended for my men?

The change of my company's Operation 'Vendetta' into 1 ATF 'Smithfield' and its dates from 17 to 21 August created a scenario which suggested Long Tan started with the mortaring of the Nui Dat base on the 17th, and ended on the return to Base on 21 August, yet not one shot was fired before 3.40pm and after 7.10pm on the 18th.

The five-day Operation 'Smithfield' then became a vehicle for the Task Force and battalion commanders to be seen as being involved at Long Tan and they certainly made use of that. It was also noted that General Mackay was recommended for a Commander of the British Empire (CBE) by AHQ which was upgraded to Commander of the Bath (CB) in Canberra.

The 2008 report decorated just three officers and none of the soldiers. It was illogical, inconsistent and unjust but there were no original forms for other than myself for the DSO downgraded to MC, and MID forms for my two officers, plus those for the few approved awards, totalling nine.

The unapproved soldiers' forms were supposedly not on file and there was no evidence to show whether they had been destroyed or secreted. But the Review accepted testimony under a principle of the 1994 Committee of Inquiry into Defence Awards that 'where documentation was not available as is often the case, testimony of recommendation can be considered'. I stated I had cited Geoff Kendall and Dave Sabben for MCs and this was accepted. I gather former assistant to Brigadier Jackson, David Harris, testified he had seen those awards on the original forms sent up the line, confirming my testimony. It was then suggested by the panel that the original forms had been rewritten, down from MC to MID after I was downgraded from DSO to MC, a domino effect, and the originals destroyed. But while the officers were upgraded the same principle was not then applied to the soldiers.

The report also required Geoff, Dave and me to return our Imperial awards in order to accept the new Contemporary Australian awards. As Australia had excised itself from Imperial Awards with the 1991 Contemporary system, this direction was queried by protocol experts as the original Imperial Awards were from Her Majesty the Queen and could only be withdrawn by de-gazettal in London, normally for being guilty of offences, like Rolf Harris who recently lost his CBE. Besides, apart from some of the 81 people upgraded in the 1998 Review who were permitted to keep their original Imperial awards, there was precedence from World War I where Australian soldiers awarded MIDs in 1914–15 were upgraded to the new MM when issued in March 1916 and they were permitted to keep and wear both awards. The 1854 MID was originally just a mention of good service in a message dispatched to higher HQ. It was gazetted during World War I, then became a Metal Oak Leaf Clasp attached to the campaign medal ribbon from 1919.

I discussed the 2008 Review report with the new ALP Government Minister for Veterans' Affairs Alan Griffin MP, whose portfolio then included Honours and Awards. Alan Griffin had been supported by Graham Edwards MP in suggesting favourable approval of awards in their ALP election platform. Dave Sabben and I both threatened not to accept new awards if the soldiers' awards were not similarly approved. And apart from that principle, we were not overly impressed by the design and appearance of the new contemporary awards compared to the gilt and enamel DSO and the silver MC. Walk into any RSL with a DSO or the distinctive white and purple MC ribbon above the silver cross and heads turn. Some who look at my SG, unaware of what it is, say it looks like it was stamped out of a beer can and sprayed with gold paint! Many say we kept the Victoria Cross for Australia, so why did we not keep the other UK gallantry medals? The 2014 reintroduction of Knights and Dames adds to the argument. As my Vietnam National Order is a Knight order, some of my former soldiers have said 'Boss, tell Tony Abbot to call you Sir Harry.'

Alan Griffin, an impressive Minister for Veterans' Affairs, whom I admire for his support and good advice, persuaded Dave and me to accept the upgrades because they added lustre to the platoons and company. He suggested the other unresolved awards should be approved by the ALP's new Defence Honours and Awards Tribunal on the 1994 Committee of Inquiry into Defence Awards' principle that it would accept testimony they were in fact recommended in 1966. The government told me it established the Tribunal in late 2008 because of many other claims for awards justice. The new ALP government then approved the recommended new officer awards which were gazetted immediately. It also approved the Vietnamese Unit Citation 'on proof off offer' and referred the unresolved awards to a new 2009 Tribunal inquiry. We wore the new Vietnamese Citation emblems on Long Tan Day 2008. In 2009 Mike Kelly AM MP told me the original documentation for the offer of GRVN awards had been located and was used in 2008 to approve the unit citation, CGCP.

General Steve Gower rang me to suggest my MC would be welcome in the AWM, but I rejected that idea on the basis I could still wear the elite silver cross that was given to me by Her Majesty. The government then withdrew the requirement that we hand in our 1966 Imperial awards, given the new awards were from a contemporary system launched in 1991. If the original DSO had been issued then I would have returned the MC, but as we had our own medals system from 1991, two decorations from two systems became legitimate

Both awards and the postnominals are clearly stated in my Defence Central Army Records Office Statement of Service and I now get letters from generals, including Steve Gower, addressed to me with postnominals SG, MC. I have no qualms about wearing two medals from two different systems given I should have had the prestigious gilt and enamelled DSO. And wearing the SG inspires me to continue waging the war for the unresolved awards for my soldiers, along with Frank Alcorta and the late Ron Brett of Alpha Company, and APC officer Adrian Roberts.

For the new Inquiry, I met with Minister Griffin and Defence Secretary Mike Kelly in Canberra in December 2008 when I was there to present ADF Long Tan Leadership Awards to students at Burgmann College. The Headmaster asked me to present the Leadership Awards as Defence had sent them a Navy Petty Officer in 2007.

Alan Griffin and Mike Kelly considered that the Terms of Reference to be written for the Honours Tribunal would provide for acceptance of testimony about the original awards and that they would therefore be approved, as had happened with Dave Sabben and Geoff Kendall in the 2008 Review.

The awards train then ran off the track in early 2009 when 'medals' went from DVA to Defence, with Secretary Mike Kelly AM MP, a former Australian Defence Force legal officer, replacing Alan Griffin in the medals portfolio. His Terms of Refernce required documentary evidence. I argued this but Kelly referred it to the Defence Honours and Awards Tribunal Chair Dennis Pearce AO who essentially told me he ran an independent authority and could do what he wished. In hindsight, the original Tribunal was simply an extension of the Defence Office and was not legislated until mid-2010. Our legal advisers suggested its legality to operate until then could be questioned in the Federal Court. Our pro-bono barrister Michael Sumner-Potts and Canberra solicitor John Orr both prematurely passed away in 2012 but we have been offered legal advice by a former 1

Commando officer who is now a barrister. The support from almost everyone out there is wonderful. At the RSL on Anzac Days I am embarrassed by the number of Veterans who want to shake my hand and congratulate me for pursuing justice for my soldiers.

The Tribunal also confused the issue by advertising the Review nationally in early 2009 and while it stated it was to inquire into 'individual unresolved awards recommended after the battle', it left the door open by using other words such as 'unresolved concerns about awards'. I was told by Mike Kelly's office that many more claims were received, albeit names were not given to me, including three from Bravo Company; five from the APC Troop, and others, none of which had been recommended after the battle. But given some thousands of Vietnam Veterans claim they had something to with the battle it is a wonder there weren't more. I had several meaningful discussions with Mike Kelly's office and the Tribunal chair to suggest the Inquiry would become confused, exacerbated and delayed if the 12 unresolved awards mentioned by the 2008 Review and in my very detailed submission were to be expanded by others jumping on the bandwagon.

At my subsequent brief Tribunal panel interview on 1 April it was announced many more claims had been received, and that many other soldiers had probably not been recognised during the war, so what was I on about? I recall retorting that was the business of other unit commanders and I simply wanted justice for the men who fought at Long Tan as cited in my submission. I also mentioned that in 2006 I was told by Minister Billson that there were no other outstanding claims for Vietnam other than a claim from Gordon Sharp's brother, as all others had been considered in the 1997–98 Review.

The April 2009 Defence Honours and Awards Tribunal panel was inexperienced with only the chair and two junior members of the 13 available people being on the panel, one a former RSM who had never served in Vietnam, the other a former captain, adjutant 3RAR in Vietnam. More appropriate senior panel members like retired Brigadier

Gary Bornholt AM CSC were not included to interview four former colonels which, apart from the lack of courtesy, would suggest the Review was simply an exercise to produce a result that had already been decided. We believe it bowed to the wishes of the Chief of the Defence Force not to approve more awards for Long Tan, as he had already made very plain to Prime Minister Howard in his 2007 Brief.

No personal Army awards were approved because no forms were on file, and the testimony of former officers, including four former colonels and my three platoon commanders, that the awards were recommended in 1966 was not accepted. One reason given was only the CO6RAR was authorised to recommended awards as the regulations stated an officer was to sign citations, normally the unit CO. But as the CO was not there I suggested I should have been able to sign. Another excuse was 'the passage of time', suggesting our memories were unreliable and that to accept our testimony would 'impinge on the integrity of the Honours system', implying we all suffered from

Alzheimer's or were likely to be liars. That was the panel's view of the testimony of Colonels Bob Hagerty AM, Peter Dinham AM, Adrian Roberts OAM, Harry Smith SG MC, and three decorated former platoon commanders Dave Sabben MG Geoff Kendall MG and Bob Buick MM! The panel did not comprehend that our memories were more vivid in recent years because of discussions with our former enemy in 2006 and involvement in several videos and books in the period 2000 to 2009.

But the late Cliff Dohle, the RAAF pilot, was upgraded from MID to the DSM for 'leadership and command in action' and the Honours Tribunal recommended Delta Company 6RAR be awarded the Australian Unit Citation for Gallantry (UCG), which was not recommended by me, the leading advocate for the Review. I did say in my submission that *if* the Tribunal was to consider unit awards then all the other sub-units, including the APC Troop, Alpha Company, the Bravo Company platoon, RAAF crews, USAF Crews and all Artillery units which supported us should be considered and that unit awards should also recognise the battles of Coral-Balmoral and Binh Ba.

We gathered the Tribunal policy was to recommend approval of the UCG for all my men, as if 'to silence the noisy peasants' or to match the USA and GRVN Citations? But the UCG did not abrogate the 1966 individual awards and it was unfair to reject the individual awards cited, shall I say, 'for being more gallant than others', in an attempt to create a level playing field. Furthermore, the two members of Alpha Company and the APC officer, not being Delta Company, did not get the UCG!

I advised DHAT and DVA that we would not rest until they were approved and I wrote an appeal to Prime Minister Kevin Rudd supported by letters from Colonels Peter Dinham and Bob Hagerty and also Graham Smith, President 6RAR Association, my former Signaller. Rudd sent a belated reply six months later, stating the government was obliged to accept the findings of the Tribunal and that nothing could be done. I replied to Rudd saying I could not accept that the RAAF pilot, never under enemy fire, being upgraded while my officer killed, Gordon Sharp, and other men who fought the enemy in combat were not so recognised. I made the point the 1998 Review removed any impediment relative to the quota that applied in Vietnam, so the number requiring approval was acceptable. No reply.

At about the same time, in March 2010, the Tribunal was legislated as a statutory authority. The legislation included a right of appeal to the courts and Ombudsman, which I tried to access, with little success. My appeal to the Ombudsman was denied because no charter had yet been set down to investigate awards, as the new 2010 Tribunal legislation amendment to the Defence Act had not yet been incorporated in the 1976 Ombudsman Act!

The October 2009 Tribunal report was flawed in many areas. It claimed I had simply submitted a 'list' of names for awards when I had actually submitted typed formal Army citation forms (AFs W3121) ready for signature of the CO. It also claimed I had moderated the awards cited by platoon commanders, when in fact I had added more, but worst was the statement that the panel 'had conducted an exhaustive search of AWM Archives for any forms thought to have been seen in 6RAR archives'. This was a blatant lie. The panel never conducted such a search! This untruth was unearthed by a Canberra witness, former 6RAR Warrant Officer Rod Armstrong, corroborated by the AWM Registry Officer who said the panel never went to the AWM, and is now on a statutory declaration, which is part of the evidence being used to seek further review. This matter alone would be enough to overturn the Tribunal Review if we went to the Federal Court, which could be our next move if the new Tribunal is prevented from reconsidering the unresolved awards in the Valour Inquiry Part 2.

My main interest now is that the 2013 Valour Inquiry Part 2, still awaiting Chief of Defence Force approval in 2015, is supposed to reconsider all other outstanding gallantry awards raised during the 2011-12 Victoria Cross inquiry. In 2012 I tendered my late CSM Jack Kirby for the Victoria Cross as I had suggested in 1966, and there are another 11 men with unresolved awards from the 2008 and 2009 Reviews to be reconsidered.

However, as a result of public submissions arising from advertisements the Honours and Awards Tribunal has tendered a list of 140 names, including 20 more for Vietnam, and is waiting for instructions from Defence as to how they will inquire into these submissions. I requested that the 12 unresolved Long Tan awards be removed from the list and be considered separately. I have since been advised the list will be broken down into appropriate groups and that testimony will be given on oath or affirmation.

But in March 2015 I was advised by Defence's Darren Chester MP that they have not been approved for reconsideration and that my next move is to request the Honours Tribunal to overturn that decision as is provided in the Defence Act Honours Tribunal amendment 2010. So the battle goes on, around and around. Adrian Roberts suggests Defence is part of an 'office of circumventolution' which makes things go around without resolution. In my latest March 2015 submission I indicated that the quota was removed in 1998, and that there is no ground for refusing the awards on the basis of retrospectivity given the number of awards recently approved back to World War II and Vietnam. Another objection raised by Defence was that the senior officers who moderated the awards in 1966 are all deceased and their decisions cannot now be questioned. I countered that by saying that if their decisions can be shown to be based on untruthful citations, as with those mentioned earlier, then their decisions have to be overturned in favour of the awards first recommended by the officers who commanded their subunits in battle. I told the Tribunal Chair in 2011 I would not embarrass Defence and former senior officers in the media, and have stood by my word, but after another four years of dithering in Canberra, perhaps it is about time to tell the full story on the ABC's *Australian Story.*

    Presentation of the October 2009 UCG then morphed into another drama.

It was normal for the Governor-General to present such awards almost immediately and it was agreed with Defence Secretary Mike Kelly MP to take place as soon as possible in late 2009 or early 2010, and in Canberra.

The then current CO6RAR and Mentoring Task Force in 2010–11, Lieutenant Colonel Mark Jennings, whose battalion was to be awarded a predicted Meritorious Unit Citation (MUC), made it known in Army circles in Canberra, supported by the Long Tan Veterans Association, that the presentation should be postponed from late 2009 and take place at Enoggera in August 2011 when the battalion returned from Afghanistan.

I objected to the near two-year delay for the presentation of the UCG and near three years for the medals and wrote to Defence Canberra and the Governor-General's office. The Governor-General then agreed to a presentation at Government House in Canberra on 17 August 2010, but required Defence to provide transport and accommodation. Defence rejected this, and bowed to the wishes of 6RAR to have the presentation at Enoggera on Long Tan Day the following year, 2011, but said that the officers could still have their medals presented by the Governor-General in 2010, although our soldiers would not be there to receive their Unit Citation. Dave Sabben and I wanted our men to be there with us to get their UCG, and we upset the system by requesting our new medals to be posted to us, which they were. Veterans at large bemoaned the government funding travel and accommodation for immigrants yet not seeing its way clear to pay for the Long Tan Veterans to be in Canberra. Two RAAF Hercules aircraft would have been able to take everyone to Canberra and return that same day. I ascertained most of my men were happy to pay for any accommodation in Brisbane.

Geoff Kendall and the RAAF pilot Cliff Dohle's widow had their medals presented in Canberra by the Governor-General in August 2010. I had my Star of Gallantry presented by my local Federal Member Hon Paul Neville MP at the Maryborough Military Museum on 8 March 2011 in front of a large audience of my former soldiers. It was a great day that meant a lot to me. I wear the medal for their gallantry as well as my leadership and command at the battle.

Having sold the Cavalier yacht and bought a Fleming 39 timber cruiser, *Melaleuca,* I motored to Townsville in Winter 2011 in company with David Collins in his Clipper 34 *Bad Habits.* We had fun fishing and crabbing and sharing meals, but David is the better cook. I took my medals and suitable clothes to fly back for Long Tan Day and the UCG presentation at Enoggera but I had to have surgery on my right ear because of a skin cancer in the ear canal and I was told not to fly.

In Townsville I went to the local Long Tan Day service in the Memorial Park alongside the Breakwater Marina while Enoggera's normal Long Tan Day was turned into 'Afghanistan Day' for the Governor General's presentation of the Mentoring Task Force Meritorious Unit Citation and individual awards for 6RAR from Afghanistan. It was a let-down given all my men were already wearing their UCG badges since the gazetted in March 2010. But at least

Dave Sabben was able to get the Governor-General Dame Quentin Bryce to present his 2008 Medal for Gallantry that day. Dave is a fighter, as he was at Long Tan, and has been invaluable in helping me in our struggle for proper recognition. But I am critical of a system that takes three years to present medallic awards. The 2008 upgraded medals and the 2009 UCG should have been presented in late 2009 as originally mooted by Defence's Mike Kelly MP.

For me, the Enoggera UCG farce was just another sad event in the long saga since 1966 of senior officers not providing, or worse, even properly acknowledging awards for the men who had earned them. While we could do nothing until the end of the secrecy period in August 1996, we have certainly pushed the envelope in arguing with the Canberra bureaucracy for more than 18 years and the battle still goes on in 2015. But we have had some success, and our efforts are positively acknowledged by the veteran and public community.

With the UCG awarded in 2009, on top of the 1968 Presidential Unit Citation and the 2008 Government of the Republic of Vietnam Cross of Gallantry Citation with Palm, plus individual awards headed by the SG, Delta Company 6RAR 1966 is the most decorated company of the Royal Australian Regiment. And it seems I am the most decorated National Serviceman as has been recently pointed out to me. But I see some two-year NS men are complaining that the NS medal was minted to recognise their two year conscription and people like me got it for just three months in the first system launched in 1951. *Bad luck.*

While I did not succeed in my appeals to Defence and to Prime Minister Kevin Rudd about the failure of the 2009 DHAT to approve the unresolved awards, I had an assurance from the 'new' 2010 Defence Honours and Awards Appeal Tribunal Chair, Alan Rose AO, that the unresolved awards would be represented to the Valour Inquiry Part 2. In April 2015 that is now in limbo while the Tribunal decides whether to overturn the March Defence verdict not to approve them being included in the Valour Inquiry. But on 8 May 2015 I received good news. I was told the Tribunal Chair would now review the recent Defence decision not to approve the reconsideration of the awards, and I look forward to justice being done in the near future.

My 2009 claims to the Tribunal also include unit awards for other units that supported us at Long Tan, along with Coral-Balmoral and Binh Ba, which would go a long way to providing better recognition for other gallant actions in Vietnam as well as putting jealousies to bed. I have also been assisting 1RAR Association in seeking approval for the Vietnamese Cross of Gallantry Citation which should have been approved in 1967 as part of US 173 Airborne Brigade at Bien Hoa in 1965-66. If it is good enough for RAAF 2 Squadron and Australian Army Training Team Vietnam members to get unit citations for being attached to US units, it is good enough for 1RAR to get similar approval. In late 2014 I heard the Tribunal had recommended approval of the GRVN Citation for 1RAR and on 7

May 2015 it was approved by the Governor General. Another successful battle for an award which should have flowed to 1RAR about 40 years ago.

The 2011 Valour Inquiry Part 1 was mainly concerned with 13 Victoria Crosses for RAN Officers in particular, but also for Private John Simpson Kirkpatrick (Simpson and his Donkey). In 2013, the government announced that none of the 13 proposed VC recipients were to receive any awards, but that HMAS *Yarra* would receive a Unit Citation for Gallantry retrospective 71 years to 1942. It suggested that awards for the crew of the *Yarra* were poorly handled and that all hands be now recognised for their gallantry.

Yet another awards process gone wrong – shades of Vietnam. As to the Victoria Crosses, it seems the main reason for rejection was the lack of live witnesses to testify to the gallantry now claimed. Also, that some of the nominated RAN officers had already received very high and multiple awards, such as one officer with two Imperial (Navy) Distinguished Service Crosses.

It was also advised that another 140 names had been received by the Valour Inquiry as the result of the national advertisement for submissions from the public as to other servicemen who may have been entitled to recognition. One was for the Boer War. Defence was to examine those submissions and advise those which might be considered for an award. In May 2015 I heard words which suggest few might be considered. Under the Act, that could lead to more reviews by the Tribunal.

Irrespective of the absence of 1966 documents, the unresolved Long Tan awards were recommended by the platoon commanders and myself, and a principle of the 1994 CIDA Review was that in the absence of documentation, testimony they had been recommended could be accepted. It is completely unacceptable for the 2009 Review to claim we were not authorised to recommend awards and that our memories have faded with time or Alzheimer's and our testimony cannot be accepted. The Review had rejected my request for testimony on oath, saying it was not a judicial inquiry, but that is now covered in the new Procedural Rules.

I want to say that Long Tan was just one of many significant battles fought by Australian forces in Vietnam. Some say it did not compare with Coral-Balmoral or with Kapyong and Maryang San in Korea and I am often embarrassed by the way it has become the iconic battle of the Vietnam War. However, let us remember it was chosen by the Vietnam Veterans Association of Australia in 1987 when they named their special annual day as 18 August.

Meanwhile I have never backed down from an honest and fair fight in the pursuit of justice. I will fight this to the end and we will win the rightful honours for the brave men who fought in the 'unacceptable' war in Vietnam. The Official History on page 564 states: 'The number and degree of awards for Long Tan were little short of insulting for the heroism displayed.'

The matter is not over – far from it. As I told Prime Minister Howard in 2007, 'I did not withdraw at Long Tan and I will not withdraw from this fight'.

I owe my life to my soldiers and I will continue to seek their just recognition.

FIFTEEN

BATTLES IN LIFE BEYOND ARMY

When I left the Army in May 1976 after 24 years, my career had been cut short by serious injury after an argument with a faulty free-fall parachute opening, and away went my ambition of heading the illustrious SAS Regiment or at least becoming a battalion commander. Medically downgraded to 'Home Only', I could only serve in non-combat corps. As advised by the RAAF Medical Officer at RAAF Williamtown I decided to resign, leave the Army and look for some other career.

I was 43, had no money in the bank after paying the house mortgage for my family since 1968, maintaining three children, and then buying and fitting out our 32-ft yacht with my half of the proceeds of the house sold when my first wife remarried in 1974. Relatively new wife Anne and I moved from RAAF

Williamtown to Bilgola Plateau on Sydney's northern beaches just above the Royal Prince Alfred Yacht Club at Newport. We used a second dip into the handy War Service Homes Loan scheme, added Long Service Leave pay, commuted $10,000 from my Defence Force Retirement and Deaths Benefits Scheme (DFRDB), and negotiated a second mortgage to get a nice but modest house. It was more than we could really afford at $56,000, but it was a nice home with a glimpse of the ocean north of Manly through trees in the backyard. But it had concealed gutters which filled up with 40 cm of rain in a storm one day and the water overflow went down inside the walls and wet the carpets. The insurance would not pay to clean and dry the carpets unless the water got in through something like a broken window. The representative winked and suggested we look for a broken or cracked pane. So we broke a ground-level window panel, claiming a tree branch had fallen on it, and all was fixed. I think the costs of a new window and cleaning were less than $200 in 1976 so we were not talking big money and the insurance firm was way in front with our premiums.

Despite the back problems from my parachuting injuries, I took up a sales job with Beaufort Air/Sea Rescue Pty Ltd in Sydney selling marine life rafts, lifejackets and rubber dinghies, and operating a sales/service centre at Brookvale. Beaufort had also been awarded the contract to import and supply US Army T10 parachutes to the Army based on my recommendations to Army HQ Canberra after my UK/USA tour with airborne units. The expat manager from the parent UK firm believed I could be of some use, and he already had former 1 Commando Warrant Officer Class 2 Danny McClymans in the factory service centre. Apart from parachuting my experiences with Commandos and yachts had left me with a good knowledge of marine safety.

The manager was not generous and told me that as I was already getting $10,000 p.a. Army superannuation my job would only pay $10,000 p.a. However, it did come with a nice Falcon wagon and a small expense account for food, so we ate out every Friday night with friends. I was able to use the car for personal use but the most mileage was in frequent trips from my sales/service centre at Brookvale to the Beaufort factory way out at Cabramatta, often a two-hour trip each way. Anne found clerical work at the Manly Leagues Club and we were just able to meet house mortgage repayments and enjoy life, sailing on Pittwater most weekends. Since 1974 we had a lovely Labrador dog named 'PC' after Para-Commander parachutes. He used to go out to the DZ in the safety vehicle and bark at me when I was coming down to land. We gave him to Anne's sister when we started serious cruising in 1978 but he was run over and died. We have not had another dog because new wife Felicia and I sailed offshore to Cape York most years, but we would like another Labrador or a Blue Heeler at some time in the future.

I did very well with local sales at Beaufort and was promoted to national sales manager, which involved trips interstate to talk to other state managers and display liferafts at boat shows and attracted a salary increase – another $1000 p.a. – a whole $20 a week! I designed the Beaufort logo which was used on all our products and I persuaded the Managing Director to hire *Choice Magazine* photographer and yachtsman friend David Colfelt to produce a coloured brochure. David later produced a book *100 Magic Miles of the Whitsunday Islands* and I was to assist him with local knowledge and do initial work on another book *1000 Miles from Whitsundays to Weipa.* I did a season of research work up the coast to Thursday Island and into the Gulf with a computer program supplied by David that recorded date, time, latitude, longitude and water depth, but that book was never completed because the northern fishing fleets were reduced and without refuelling barges along the Cape, the previous pleasure boat fleet was also decimated, so there was no viable market for the book.

Brochure by David Colfelt with my Beaufort Logo.

Meanwhile, in early 1977 the Beaufort firm decided to cheapskate, as they had with my salary, by using a local rubber fabric made by Leggetts Rubber Melbourne instead of proven reliable imported fabrics from France and the UK, and then, without field (on water) testing, produced cheaper rectangular life rafts without the normal inflatable canopies, aimed at maximising profit. Despite my requests for trials, I was told we did not have the time to waste on testing.

The next year a life raft made with local fabric started to fall apart when it was brought in for service after a

Sydney–Hobart yacht race. I insisted that we recall all similar rafts. The managing director said to me that would cost too much and I should not worry because if a raft failed at sea 'there would be nobody alive to complain'. That attitude really disturbed me – I could not believe that money was put ahead of saving lives. I could not sell faulty products, so I resigned, but the Allied Polymer Group manager Ken Parker persuaded me to stay on with another of the group's companies, Dryclad, to sell life jackets and swimming pools. I gave it three months then gave that away in favour of a 'once only' trip to the Barrier Reef with several other yachts, one being *Kotori*, a nice HMG 31, owned by close friends Colin and Bea Howe.

Beaufort (Australia) was to go to the wall a year later when a life raft failed off the West Australia coast but the crew thankfully survived in a tin dinghy. The resulting legal action required all the locally made rafts to be replaced by UK types and that cost sent the Australian branch into receivership and extinction. So much for that reckless and irresponsible boast that if a raft failed at sea no one would be alive to tell the tale!

In 1979, having cruised the Barrier Reef coast and enjoyed it, we sold the house in Sydney and moved up to Queensland's Kawana Waters on the Sunshine Coast into a modest house just one street back from the beach – bad news for rust and corrosion from the salt air. We continued to cruise north each year in the Swanson 32 yacht but in early 1982 I had a relapse of my back problems. We sold the yacht and bought a 10m Ho Hsing cruiser which we renamed *Arpege.* It required no heavy work like pulling on ropes (sheets) and it had a good electric anchor winch. The name had to start with an 'A' to get in early on the coastal radio alphabetical position reporting list, and one of my sailing mates said you have to have a sweet-smelling name for a 'stink boat'. *Arpege* was my wife's chosen fragrance. We cruised north to the Whitsundays and Bowen most winters. I recall being befriended by Bowen fisherman Les Mann, who with his wife Gladys ran a

40-ft fishing boat *Lady Rose* and fished the reefs way out off Bowen. Les convinced me to take my boat out to Darley Reef 40 nautical miles (70km) northeast of Bowen and he taught me many tricks of reef fishing in his dory. Then we had wonderful times exploring and beachcombing all the beaches and immediate hinterland from Cooktown to Cape York.

Friends Doug and Barbie Hardy of Smithfield near Cairns, a town name that brought back vivid memories, had cruised the same areas and found a lot of Japanese glass fishing floats that held up longlines or nets, so we decided to embark on locating more. We teamed up with Jim and Mavis Purcell from Gladstone and tried our luck. We cruised up the Cape to Thursday Island and into the Gulf for each of the years 1989 to 1993, beachcombing and fishing. We walked every beach and mangrove swamp from Cooktown to Cape York and found many Japanese glass fishing floats of various sizes and colours – collectables – along with rubber dinghies and diving gear that had escaped from boats out on the reef. Wonderful times.

Mavis, me and Jim with our new found collectables.

I recall our best finds were in the mangroves behind the beaches opposite Night Island, just south of Portland Road. We would take our dinghies into the beach and leapfrog off to the north or south. Jim and I would search into the mangroves while the ladies walked the beaches. Jim and I both carried pistols in case of arguments with 'Captain Cookers' (large black feral pigs) and crocodiles; I had the 7.62mm Tokarev from Vietnam and Jim had his Grandfather's Tower .45 revolver from World War I, but we never had to use them. Sunbaking crocodiles usually ran away, as did feral pigs, unless they had babies, in which case they made us run away, usually down the beach into the water.

The plot was to follow the tideline flotsam and jetsam of lightbulbs, fluoro lights, thongs, plastic bottles and junk that had floated inland with the tides and cyclone surges. Normally at the start of the natural rise of bushland hills behind the mangroves there would be the last line of junk, and every now and then a nice glass float, which we would carry out to the beach in netting backpacks. With more than one the weight was like being back in the Army. These days I often get bad vibes about Jim and I wandering alone, often miles apart, through mangroves, along creek beds, with no radio or phone communication, and wonder what would have happened if we had been bitten by a snake or gored by a pig. It sends shivers up my spine when I think about it – our bones might still have been there. But we were confident of our bush skills, and lucky. And opposite Night Island we found about 80 glass floats of various colours and sizes in about a week – a wonderful haul.

We also found a creek where I caught my first barramundi. Of course we could only get ashore if the weather was calm enough to be able to land on the sand, so we often had to continue on and search other areas and leave some until the return trip on the way south. Over the years we located some 420 glass floats of various sizes and colours which we shared. Apart from the Japanese ones, we found smaller types made in European countries, probably pre-World War II. In the Gulf there were small blue plastic ones made in Indonesia. I still have about 30 glass floats around our house but have given most of my 200 share away to family and friends. In Port Douglas the normal 11-inch types are being sold for around $250. Plastic floats replaced glass in about 1967, but the Japanese fishing fleets had lost several million in the Pacific, many to be blown ashore on the Far North Queensland coast. Also, they were caught up in the equatorial currents and some finished up in Alaska. I have a book about collecting glass floats and it shows 1000 were once found in a bay on the Alaskan coast back in the 1970s. Odd ones still come in, and just a couple of years ago one was found floating into Gladstone Harbour.

A great barra catch in 1990.

Apart from floats and other interesting items like diving gear and rubber dinghies washed off charter boats, and PNG canoes of various sizes carved out of logs, one of the fringe benefits of cruising the Far North Queensland coast was the abundant supply of large black-lipped or Pacific oysters on rocks and mangrove roots. It was normal to carry a bucket with a large sharpened screwdriver blade and a hammer to open these huge oysters, with the flesh often as big as a pork chop. They were a bit strong raw, but Jim's wife Mavis taught us how to simmer them in fresh water and then add worcestershire sauce or fry them in breadcrumbs. The law was that they had to be eaten off the rocks, but in case of being apprehended and charged I had a note from my doctor stating I could only eat cooked oysters. A Water Police patrol came over to the shore when I was getting oysters at the Owen Channel in 2009, seeking information about crocodiles, and weren't concerned that I had half a bucket full of big oysters.

Also, pelagic mackerel fish were plentiful and with two trolling lines out, we always had fresh fish as well as oysters in the fridge. And at reef anchorages there was always coral trout, sweetlip or grass snapper to be caught. We were able to get fuel and fresh water from barges that were either moored at major trawler anchorages or that sailed up the coast from Cairns weekly. Fuel was about 30 cents a litre and 9-kg gas bottle refills were $12 back in the 1990s. If needed, the barges would bring up groceries from Cairns. At trawler anchorages like Margaret Bay a 10-litre bucket of fresh prawns was usually $50 with a few bugs or painted crays tossed in. We were able to supply antibiotics to a trawler hand with a tooth abscess, and every time we met up he gave us a bucket of prawns.

South of Margaret Bay where there were still two World War II US fighter planes corroding on the beach, crash-landed when out of fuel after being caught in bad weather, was a headland named Greenwell Point, then Indian Bay, which was another source of glass floats and empty nautilus shells, which used to float in on the tide by the dozens. I think we found around 100 floats in mangroves in this area. One night a yacht skipper failed to return from a walk and next morning we mounted a search and found him up a tree where he went to escape angry pigs. And further north we discovered that in the Olive and Escape Rivers floats had drifted in through the wide river mouths on the tides and winds and lodged in the mangroves up the river. We found quite a lot, after having worked out where the current and wind took them. Jim found a rare Olive Oil Blue float on the bank of the Escape River some 8km upstream, matching a blue one we had found in the Whitsundays.

Our first glass float was found way off Mackay in 1979 when we saw a seagull sitting on something, which turned out to be a nice float. Floats were coloured and stamped to identify the fishing company, with the Japanese Emperors' fleet floats being reddish. Doug Hardy has the only red one I have seen. When we returned south with all the floats tied to the fly-bridge handrails, we were always a source of curiosity in ports. I often dream of doing it all again, but 30 years down the track and with all the boats and 4WD vehicles now exploring the same areas, it is unlikely any goodies would be left. It was great fun in the late 1980s–early 1990s but I guess I have to come to terms with my age.

Cruiser Arpege with floats

In 1984 Dad advised that Mum was very ill, so I joined my sister Joan in flying to Coffs Harbour. We were there when Mum died in hospital and we helped Dad sort things out. He asked me to handle her will with the Public Trustee at Lismore and told me that he 'thought' Mum had a couple of bank books with small amounts in her dresser. A 'couple' was about ten, amounting to some $30,000 in savings! Joan told me Mum had always asked Dad for more money for food, but then tucked it away. Dad gave Mum's nest egg money to Bev, Joan, myself and his six grandchildren.

Sick of the sea air rusting everything, we sold the Kawana house and moved to a cheaper lowset place at Wurtulla, some 8km south, then to a Kawana canal townhouse that was going at half price where we were able to moor the boat on its small canal jetty, avoiding marina fees at the Mooloolaba Yacht Club or Lawries' Marina at the end of the main canal. I also kept a Windsurfer and Laser racing dinghy on the beach and kept up my sailing skills, although I had problems with my light stature in keeping the Laser upright in offshore Club races in strong winds.

In 1985 I decided to get a Coastal Master IV ticket with a view to earning money doing the light work of driving commercial boats. This took four weeks at TAFE South Brisbane, as well as the prerequisite four years of ocean sea time, which I had. The sea time was normally on commercial vessels, even as just a 'deckie', but I was able to persuade the Marine Board that all my private time in ocean waters skippering various yachts along the coast had to be comparable. I stayed at a seedy motel at Kangaroo Point for four nights during the week and drove home for weekends at Yandina in the Sunshine Coast hinterland to where we'd moved in 1994. Every night I poured over marine rules and regulations, flag and light signals and chart work. I passed the course, got my Master IV and was able to secure a number of boat deliveries, such as taking a cruiser from Yamba to Mooloolaba, a 57-ft Roper ketch *Pan Pacific* from Hamilton Island to Mooloolaba, and a 12-m cruiser from Brisbane north to Hamilton Island, to quote a few of many. I also surveyed a few yachts until new regulations put an end to 'amateur' surveyors who were previously accepted if they had built a boat.

The owner of the *Pan Pacific* has recently been in media headlines after being given jail time for numerous sex offences relating to conning young ladies on board his yacht as nannies to look after his son and then spiking their drinks and taking advantages. He wasn't on board during my trip as he had broken a leg falling off a buggy on Hamilton Island and was recuperating at home, but I recall seeing his yacht at Airlie Beach in later years and him being in the company of lovely female Swedish backpackers in the Whitsunday Sailing Club. After having delivered his yacht south he contracted me to do some minor repair work on the big yacht but almost every morning I turned up for work he would yell out for me to come back because he had a lady in the rear cabin. Then he delayed payment for many weeks until I drove to his home and waited for him to arrive in his Mercedes sports car with another lady in tow. That embarrassed him to write out the cheque on the spot – and I bid him farewell. In 2015 he is in the media again, facing yet another rape charge.

Back in the 1980s coastal deliveries usually paid $2 per nautical mile plus fares, fuel and incidentals. So a trip to or from the Whitsundays paid about $1000 net for about five or six days' work, but including 24/7 responsibility and often overnight trips. It wasn't a big income, but the casual trips helped my small Army (DFRDB) superannuation income. In those days I wasn't old enough for the 'Burnt Out Digger's pension' (DVA Service or Age pension) and I just had a small 10 percent Disability Pension for loss of hearing attributed to gunfire, which had started under tin-roofed range sheds at Brighton Camp in the early 1950s, exacerbated by war service.

Somewhere along the line DVA included peacetime disabilities with war-caused injuries and my parachuting injuries led to me getting the very generous Gold Card which thankfully pays for all medical costs. I understand the Gold Card is now issued to all veterans over the age of 70, and war widows. It is good that veterans and widows are well cared for by our Veterans Affairs legislation. Some try to cheat the system and I recall DVA advocate Claude Ducker MC calling me in 1997 about a TPI disability claim from a truck driver from Vung Tau who claimed he had driven his truck into Long Tan after the battle to load bodies and was still disturbed by the terrible memories of blood and gore in his truck. I was able to say the APCs had to swim over the river so no truck ever got within miles of the battlefield. The enemy bodies were buried, and all our dead and wounded went out by USAF and RAAF casualty evacuation Dustoff helicopters. A 'porkie'.

In 1988 Anne and I moved up to Airlie Beach and bought a new but un-landscaped house with a windfall 100 percent profit from the canal unit at Kawana. Life on a canal is not that good, looking into houses 30m away over the water, and we had a noisy trawler moored opposite, often moving on midnight tides, despite rules banning commercial vessels in residential canals. I enjoyed living at Airlie Beach and cruising further north along the coast and reefs to Cape York each winter, sometimes down into the Gulf to just north of Weipa, along with driving an O'Brien 40 charter game boat at Airlie Beach on a casual basis for pin money. This boat was owned by John 'Rusty' Dyson who was a National Serviceman in Centurion tanks at Coral-Balmoral in Vietnam in 1968 and who now runs a lime farm in the Gold Coast hinterland. We are still good friends and talk often. Redhead Rusty had a great sense of humour and his favourite act was to walk across the busy Airlie street, dragging one leg, hand up to stop the traffic. I also recall on one reef trip in his boat he pulled a big coral trout up through the galley window while I was hosting four charterers in the aft cockpit, baiting their lines and filleting fish, although not catching much at the time.

Rusty was to later split with wife Jan and move to the farm on the Gold Coast. With his then young son John, now a Master Mariner, we spent many hours walking offshore reefs at low tide in search of lovely sea shells. I also worked as a volunteer radio operator and safety boat driver with the Air Sea Rescue, later renamed Volunteer Marine Rescue. I recall I did not have a speedboat licence and, although my Master IV covered commercial boats to 80 tons at any speed, I had to get the lesser licence to drive the small rescue boat – civil bureaucracy at its best.

In 1989 Dad passed on, aged 80, having moved back to Glenorchy, Tasmania. Anne and I were halfway up Cape York and could not get back for his funeral. Sister Bev looked after Dad when he went back south and sorted out the funeral and his estate. He had lost most of his invested superannuation in the share market collapse of the early to mid 1980s, and my sisters wanted to leave the residue with the investment company, which did not want to divide the money, but I wanted my third share to make life easier and pay off various debts. It was a bit of a battle to get them and the company to agree.

Anne then became engrossed, perhaps obsessed, with her parents and elder sister Patricia's family problems at Nambour (her son was on drugs and would die from HIV) and in late 1993 I reluctantly agreed to sell up and move back to the Sunshine Coast so she could better support her family. We sold the motor cruiser to a buyer from Port Moresby at a loss. To sell our house in a depressed market we had to take a 34-ft NZ Townsend yacht, *Karma,* as a trade on the house and bought a home west of Yandina. When we moved to Airlie I thought it would be a win-win situation with real estate, and we could double our investment, but it all went bad in the mid to late 1980s and we lost. I returned by rail to the Whitsundays to sail *Karma* back south with my plumber neighbour Gerry Poma as crew with a view to selling her, but she sailed so well we kept her. Old yachting friend Jim Coxon, whose son Michael is now manager of North Sails Sydney, welcomed the boat to be moored free at his canal jetty and I took him sailing now and then. Jim was to introduce Etchells racing to Mooloolaba. We raced the yacht at Mooloolaba at least two days a week and I got involved with the Yacht Club Sailing Committee and Volunteer Coastguard radio work.

Also, while Anne was not that happy about it, a delightful and attractive lady with a passion for horses, Felicia Smith, yet another Smith, a friend of Anne's elder sister Patricia, became a crew member on *Karma* on fun races, often called WAGS, 'Women and Gentlemen Sailors', along with her long-time friend Elizabeth Wootton. Felicia's husband was building a 9-m Adams alloy yacht and she wanted to 'learn the ropes'. Most of the time Anne crewed as well, until she slipped and fell in the creek bed near home and badly broke an ankle, which had to be screwed in place with a steel plate, putting her out of action for the best part of a year. Her mother died and her father came to live with us at least half the year, the other months in Perth with Anne's younger sister. Her father became very religious and virtually turned our house into a Catholic church, which did not entice me to be at home all day, so I was happy to be at the Yacht Club most of the time.

After selling *Karma* I bought and sold an Elite 11 Catamaran *Purrfect Lady* in favour of a 12-m Lyons-Jarkan racing yacht going cheap which I called *On Silent Wings* because of the winged keel, which was renamed *Midnight Special* and was to sink in the 1998 Sydney–Hobart just after I sold her on. The costs of Kevlar racing sails and the time involved in running a 12-m racing yacht with eight crew were all too much so we downgraded to a smaller and cheaper fast MASRM 31 yacht called

Crow Bar and raced her with success for several years.

In 1998 I became involved in a syndicate of 'Long Tan Commanders' with the aim of writing a book about the battle as seen from commanders' eyes. While the first book about the battle written by Lex McAulay in 1986 was indeed very good, it was more about what the soldiers saw and not the overall view of what went on at unit and command level. Bob Buick, Dave Sabben and Morrie Stanley had given some good presentations in Canberra and my wife Anne suggested I and all other commanders should be involved. So 'The Battle of Long Tan as told by the Commanders' syndicate was born. I spent about four months typing the first draft after first editor Denis Gibbons quit, but that draft then went to next editor Bob Grandin for polishing, then on to Gary McKay MC. After considerable trouble with two editors quitting because of interference by Charles Mollison who was harbouring resentment about not having been decorated for his claimed personal command of the APC Reaction Force he was removed from the syndicate and the book draft went back to Bob Grandin, to be published in 2004.

With Anne's pre-occupation with her father and elder sister plus many family members and distant relatives coming out of the woodwork, and no doubt exacerbated by my time sailing and having another lady in my crew, our relationship suffered. We drifted apart and I became good friends with Felicia and her family of three sons, Paul, Marcus and Philip, and daughter – another Felicia. While we sailed together almost every week, we initially kept each other at a distance, but the chemistry between us eventually took over. After four years this led us from an innocent friendship into a relationship we could not end. In a way this was very sad after both of us had had enjoyed very long and loyal marriages, 37 and 31 years respectively.

Felicia and I enjoyed life together. I moved into her house with two acres and a lovely grey Arab-Percheron dressage horse at Nambour on the Sunshine Coast after buying out her husband Keith's half share. He had moved to Hervey Bay to live on and sail his boat which was his ambition, as Felicia was completely involved with the Nambour NAGS horse club, dressage and sailing with me. Although separated, a close friendship remained between Felicia and Keith and their family, as with Anne and me. NAGS reminds me of the Indian Chief who was asked why he called his wife 'Mrs Horse'. He replied because she just nags and nags!

Felicia and I enjoying life on yacht Cavarlo.

We were to later regret starting our relationship but we had been completely unaware that both our marital partners would be diagnosed with advanced cancers and would pass away in the near future.

Anne went for a routine eye test for glaucoma, a family problem, and an eye disorder caused her to be sent for a brain scan. She was diagnosed with a malignant brain tumour as big as a hen's egg. I organised her to have immediate private surgery at the Wesley Hospital, Brisbane, by a top brain surgeon, but there were tumour tentacles left behind and complete cure was not possible. She was given three months to live without radiation therapy. Initially she bravely rejected radiotherapy but after she passed the three-month period, she was talked into radiation by doctors. This prolonged her life for almost another year but without any quality. I saw her often and it was so sad to see her slowly slipping away. The radiotherapy simply burnt her brain and distorted her face. At about this time Felicia's husband Keith was diagnosed with oesophageal cancer. Felicia and I, still together, were involved in organising treatment and support for our partners.

I opted to go back to Anne, but, very proud, she rejected that idea. However, she wanted to get out of the Yandina home and I organised the sale and bought her a nice new townhouse unit in Nambour just down the road from the Selangor Hospital. Her two nieces blamed me for her problems. One worked for a lawyer and tried to prevent me getting my half share of the house – 'Take him to the cleaners' was the call – but my friendly lawyer kindly preserved my rights.

Felicia's husband moved back to stay with his family at Nambour while he had surgery which inserted a steel tube in his throat but, like Anne's operation, the cancer had spread and it simply postponed the inevitable. As both our spouses were supported by families and, in Keith's case, by his four children, Felicia and I decided to sell our racing yacht *Crow Bar* and go north in a suitable cruising yacht. After seven months on the market *Crow Bar* sold to Sydney. Kawana yacht broker Nick Cox sold us *Joan of Arc,* a Cavalier 345 which, although a good yacht, was badly run down and had osmosis in the fibreglass hull. But we got her very cheap to offset the cost of repairing the problems and, not wanting to 'burn at the stake', changed her name to *Tamika* after my SAS mate Greg Pullin's adopted granddaughter, and took her to Manly where the osmosis was treated with a heat process and the hull covered with epoxy. We added new sails and after some local fun racing, set sail for the Whitsundays.

12m Lyons racer On Silent Wings off Mooloolaba 1995.

Felicia enjoyed the cruising up north, seeing and exploring new places and meeting new friends on other boats. Away from the stresses of suburbia most cruising folk enjoy the life and camaraderie on the water. We still have many close friends from early cruising days and I need to mention just a few, like Les Clements, Peter Walburn, Bernie

'Breakaway', Keith and Pattie Owen, Warwick Sutor, Duncan and Nornie Thompson, Paul Swan, Brett and Debbie Swan, and Graham and Barbara Mackie. While up north we got the bad news Anne's sister Patricia had passed away, an untimely death caused by lung cancer and, sadly, Anne died the very next week from her brain cancer. I did not return for her funeral. Apart from the time it would have taken to get the boat to a marina and travel back, it was a private family funeral and I was not the flavour of the month with them. Besides I could see no valid reason to delay the funeral by the perhaps two weeks to get back. Close friends Bob Buick and wife Bev attended and he was able to obtain a large size RAN flag for her coffin. I admit I had loved Anne and been entirely faithful to her from when we met in 1969 almost to the end of our 30-year partnership and marriage. But things change. There are always two sides to the story, as my children are now well aware with regard to my split from their mother in 1965, two of them having experienced the same problems, my eldest daughter and my son 'following in Dad's footsteps' with second and third marriages.

Because of the increasing costs of living on the Sunshine Coast and sailing with the Mooloolaba Yacht Club which was going into receivership, Felicia and I sold her former Nambour home, gave her dressage horse 'Olympia' to her daughter at Eudlo, and moved to Hervey Bay in August 2003. I married my third love in the local Botanical Gardens in September 2003 and we live in a retirement-type village not far from the Urangan marina complex. It suits us ideally. Being peaceful and secure we just lock the doors and go, and for the years to 2012 we continued to go cruising every winter up the coast to Lizard Island, sometimes beyond. We sold the Cavalier 345 *Tamika* in 2008 and bought a Cavalier 395 *DejaVu* which we renamed to *Cavarlo,* a derivation of *cavello,* Italian for 'horse power', which we used to continue cruising north.

Cavalier 395 Cavarlo near Lizard Island 2007.

Lizard Island is noted for its anchorage in Mrs Watson's Bay. Sole residents in a stone cottage, beche de mere fisherman's wife 21-year-old Mrs Watson and her baby, along with a wounded Chinese cook, escaped in half a floating water tank after being attacked by mainland-based Aborigines in 1881. They died soon after on a nearby island from the lack of fresh water. The lovely anchorage is full of pristine coral reefs and we snorkelled and watched the colourful reef fishes daily. With care we could anchor the yacht in sand and swing just clear of the adjoining reefs, and it was a simple matter to roll off the boat into clear warm water right next to the coral. The large hill behind the bay was 'Cook's Look' where Captain Cook saw an opening in the reef and sailed out and north, having had repairs made at Cooktown after hitting what is now named Endeavour Reef. The private resort was in the next bay, but boaties were not welcome, except to the staff 'Marlin Bar' on special occasions, like an AFL final on TV. And around the point was the Research Station which was always interesting and it provided a mail and phone centre for us 'boating bums' known as 'grotty yachties'. Fishermen used to say you yachties get the wind for free and want everything else for free, but although that only really applied to a small number of boats it tarnished all of us.

2008 cruising was interrupted by detection of prostate cancer. Luckily I had been having an annual PSA blood check since I saw Peter Smeaton suffer and die from the disease in 1984. My count had risen slightly with age, but suddenly went very high and a biopsy revealed cancer. I was offered radiotherapy or surgery, and took the surgeon's advice to have the whole gland removed. This took place at the Wesley Hospital. DVA would then only pay for normal open-cut surgery, so I opted to pay extra for keyhole surgery and was up and walking the next day and went home the day after. My old brain could not help thinking that the several extra days in hospital for open surgery to heal would have offset the keyhole costs! I gather DVA will now pay for very expensive robotic surgery, so my former signaller Graham Smith tells me, another prostate cancer victim now cured.

But what the surgeon or my GP did not tell me was that a pre-surgery CT scan had indicated a cloudy area on the right side of the gland and that I should have been given an MRI in case it was 'local extension', a bubble on the exterior, in which case surgery is not conducted and radiotherapy is used as the cure. And in 2008 a new radiotherapy technique had just been developed to reduce peripheral damage to nearby organs. After surgery the surgeon told me the post-op pathology indicated a small piece of the cancerous gland had been left behind – because it was a bubble and was missed – but that it could die off, or regenerate later. Nothing happened for three years but then the PSA count which should have been zero started to increase in 2011 and, in 2015 as I write, it has doubled every three months in the past year. Further increase will require chemotherapy or hormone treatment. If I was younger I would probably consider suing the surgeon for failing to give me the MRI as advised by the radiographer. Doctors say it probably won't kill me, something else will get me, but it could cause chronic sickness like with 6RAR's Peter Smeaton, Colin Townsend, Owen O'Brien and many others.

Talking of prostate cancer, Agent Orange is the likely cause. In 1966–67 I do not think we had ever heard of this chemical, a herbicide and defoliant sprayed on jungle trees and rural areas. The name came from the colour of the drums the defoliant was stored in. During the Vietnam War, between 1962 and 1971, in Vietnam, eastern Laos and parts of Cambodia, as part of Operation Ranch Hand, the United States military sprayed nearly 20,000,000 US gallons (76,000,000 litres) of material containing chemical herbicides and defoliants mixed with jet fuel. The program's goal was to defoliate forested and rural land, depriving guerillas of cover; another goal was to induce forced draft urbanisation, destroying the ability of peasants to support themselves in the countryside, and forcing them to flee to the US-dominated cities, so depriving the guerillas of their rural support and food supply.

At our Nui Dat base we were aware a plane frequently flew over and sprayed mosquito repellent on the rubber trees but what we did not know was the same tanks had been used for Agent Orange and not cleaned out. Nor did we realise the chemicals were washed off trees onto the ground and found their way via the rain wash-off into creeks and streams from which we often filled our water bottles when out on patrol, so we drank water contaminated by dioxins and I am told water purification tablets we used did not cater for dioxins.

Of those men I know from 6RAR Peter Smeaton died of prostate cancer, as I mentioned earlier, also Colin Townsend and Owen O'Brien. Others, such as Ian McQuire, my 2IC in 1967; Peter Dinham, 2 Platoon Alpha Company 1966; Bob Hagerty, OC 1 APC Squadron and myself have survived after surgery. I went to former 11 Platoon Private Brian Hall's funeral after death from prostate cancer three years ago. I am aware my corporals Bill Moore and Tony Green died from cancer, and that 12 Platoon's Neil Bextrum in Perth is on God's Waiting List with leukemia cancer. Neil recently told me he is past the use by date and if his 1966 MID award is approved it should be sent to the AWM.

For years Vietnam Veterans' complaints of serious health issues caused by their exposure to Agent Orange were denied and belittled by the authorities. A Royal Commission was finally formed in 1983 to look into the veterans' case. However, the commission's highly controversial report in 1986 returned a 'not guilty' verdict for Agent Orange. My understanding is that DVA, while not admitting the cause, will still fund treatment for cancer-affected soldiers, and so they should. In the US it is accepted that Agent Orange caused a number of cancers in Vietnam Veterans, including prostate cancer, and Veterans there who develop prostate cancer and were exposed to Agent Orange during military service are eligible to receive VA health care and disability compensation.

In recent times a senior Vietnam Veteran who was in 1 APC Squadron in 1966–67 and who retired as a brigadier, a respected friend, committed suicide here on the Fraser Coast. Some said it was after being diagnosed with cancer. According to a March 2013 report by Ruth Lamperd and Patrick Carlyon in the *Sunday Herald-Sun,* the veterans' community in Brisbane alone was reeling from 11 suicides since Christmas, including former soldiers returned from Somalia, Rwanda, Timor, Iraq and Afghanistan. Veterans' advocates say the tragic tally is a fraction of a hidden blight unrecorded by authorities which highlights serious inadequacies in the DVA's bureaucratic claims process, which often stretches veterans' battles for compensation out to two years.

DVA keeps no figures on suicides of past servicemen and women. It told the *Herald-Sun* that it aims 'to deal with all claims as efficiently as possible to ensure minimal impact on the individual'. A Perth Veteran has published a list of 215 Vietnam Veterans who had suicided as at 1996. I gather there have been 200 Afghanistan veterans who have taken their own life and according to TV reports in March 2015, there are similar problems with Navy sailors in HMAS Leeuwin south of Perth. But not one of my former soldiers has taken his own life.

My personal experience, shared by many of my colleagues, is that despite no evidence of previous cancer in our parental families we contracted prostate cancer and it is a fair bet it came from drinking dioxin-contaminated water in Vietnam. The evidence is that there is a much higher percentage of this cancer and birth defects in the Vietnam Veteran community than in the public community, something like 50 percent higher. Apart from a bad temper, probably caused by continual arguments with the bureaucracy over the awards for my men, to my knowledge prostate cancer is the only possible serious health effect I've had from Vietnam, but cancer is an insidious disease which could cause cancer cells to migrate to other organs.

In recent years I have had many excisions for various skin cancers, the last one, the twenty third, a month ago, all perhaps the result of no 'slip, slop, slap' sunburn cream, shirt or hat in childhood holidays in the dry and hot Tasmanian summer sun, and no doubt exacerbated by sun damage in the Army and sailing. My dermatologist tells me that even if I hide from the sun the damage was done as a child and will still cause skin cancers to form. When sailing there is reflection off the water and unless one wears hot 'Colonel Gaddafi'-type headdress, the sun stills gets to the face and ears. But as with prostate cancer, recent USA research results announced in June 2015 indicates a 10 to 20% higher rate of non-melanomic skin cancers such as BCCs and SCCs among Vietnam Veterans who were exposed to Agent Orange dioxins.

In May 2010 I received the sad news that my Long Tan Kiwi Forward Observer Captain Morrie Stanley was terminal with a rare sarcoma cancer, and I joined Bob Buick, Dave Sabben and Red Dune Film's producer Martin Walsh in going over to visit him and presenting him with a Delta Company plaque with his UCG emblem on behalf of our company. I personally paid for it to be made by Warwick Cary's Medal Shop in Sydney which had made a nice frame for Felicia's uncle's World War I medals and his King George V memorial bronze-embossed 'death plaque' and the scroll. Our government had not advised the NZ people of the UCG award approved in October 2009 and, again, I had to chastise Defence Canberra. CDF Angus Houston then sent an urgent facsimile to Auckland to advise we would be presenting the 2009-approved UCG to Morrie and his signaller Willy Walker, the other NZ signaller Murray Broomhall now living near Brisbane.

In NZ at presentation of the Delta Company UCG to FO Morrie Stanley and his signaller Willy Walker.

Although some of his fellow officers such as Barry Dreyer believed Morrie had received the Gallantry MBE (Member of the Order of the British Empire medal) I was disappointed to find from his two sons that Morrie did not get the appropriate gallantry Oak Leaves Clasp for his 1967 MBE in lieu of the Military Cross I recommended. I then wrote and suggested to the NZ Defence Minister it be approved. In 2012 widow Alva told me that it had still not been approved. While the MBE is higher in precedence than the MC it was normally awarded for meritorious service and his gallantry at Long Tan should have attracted the Oak Leaves gallantry clasp.

I went to Auckland to visit Morrie via Sydney where I stayed with my daughter Debbie near Mascot, who organised a surprise dinner visit by daughter Sharon and son Brett who came in all the way from Campbelltown and Camden. It was very special to see them altogether.

In New Zealand Morrie's health deteriorated but although he had more radiation therapy there was no lasting cure and he passed away in September

2010. Bob Buick went over again with wife Bev for the funeral at his own cost, which was a fine gesture from a Digger compatriot and to represent our former company.

In April 2011 I was invited to lead 1 Commando in the Anzac Day Sydney march. In June 2012 I was invited to the 2 Commando annual dinner. On the way home I spoke at the Biennial National Conference of the Vietnamese Community in Australia in Sydney, most of whose members, formerly ARVN officers and soldiers or civilians whose properties were confiscated by the communist regime, had escaped from re-education camps in Vietnam in the clothes they wore. According to UNHCR reports, more than 1 million Vietnamese fled Vietnam to escape communist tyranny after April 1975, and close to 500,000 died unknown at sea or in the jungle on their escape route. Dr Tien Nguyen, ex-ARVN ranger Van Thu Pham and his wife Anh, members of the community, hosted daughter Debbie and myself. They are wonderful and sincere people, happy to be welcomed to Australia, and in the main have worked hard to live comfortably without relying on government pensions. They still admire the Australian commitment to the Vietnam War.

Dr Tien Nguyen, ex-ARVN and me, Sydney 2012. Photo courtesy Deborah Smith.

1 Commando Assn President Barry Grant and me at Anzac Day march Sydney 2011.

In 2007 I gave my medals to my family and they loaned them to the

Maryborough Military and Colonial Museum, which had Keith Payne's VC Group and Bali hero Tim Britten's Cross of Valour Group, although Keith Payne's original medals went to the AWM in June 2014, leaving the Museum with his replicas and a UK Victoria Cross. I donated a set of replicas which are in the Long Tan display there; the originals being kept in the safe. I have donated two Long Tan prints by Fletcher and Ian Grieves and loaned my cigar box presented by the Vietnamese Government in 1966. Bob Buick MM, Dave Sabben MG and Ron Eglinton MM have done similar things with their medals and other memorabilia. Bill Roche has loaned his lacquered cigarette box, and Bev Kirby has loaned late husband Jack's replica medals and various items from his time in Malaya. Bob and I have also donated a brass incense burner and candle sticks that we purloined from the ruins of Long Phuoc village which 6RAR destroyed in July 1966.

The director of the local museum is John Meyers, a former timber businessman, who also served some 20 years in the CMF leaving as a Warrant Officer Class 2. With wife Else, they have a wonderful collection of medals and memorabilia, some 7000 items, and the Gallipoli room display is amazing. The museum is run as a family trust in memory of their two children, one a young girl, the other a young soldier, killed in an accident with a rogue truck near Gympie in 1982. John Meyers's brain is like a computer hard drive with regard to military history and medals. He has 100 volunteers who help run the museum. A visit is highly recommended.

In 2013 the Hervey Bay RSL invited me to be Honorary Patron of the 2015 Anzac Memorial Park project worth over $700,000 to provide a larger area for the increasing Anzac Day crowds. Humbled and honoured to accept, Felicia and I donated $5000 to the project to set an example so that in my lobbying of local business and the community I was able to seek donations. My Army modus operandi was not to ask anyone to do something that I would not do myself. My wife Felicia's uncle was killed on the beach at Anzac Cove. To remember him and the 23 soldiers I lost in Vietnam and all the others who sacrificed their lives or health in war we were happy to donate to commemorate them in this local Anzac project and it was completed in time for the 100th commemoration.

The centrepiece costing $400,000 is a 3-m bronze statue of a World War I light horseman jumping over enemy trenches at Beersheba and would be one of the best memorials in Australia. In October 2014 it was finished and mounted on the plinth. It was made at Brendale near Strathpine; the wire and clay model converted to fibreglass moulds which were converted to ceramic into which a thin 6-mm layer of bronze was poured and then all parts were welded together and polished. The dedication ceremony took place on 11 October with Rear Admiral Ken Doolan AO, National President RSL, Presiding.

3-m bronze statue of a World War I light horseman at Anzac Memorial Park Hervey Bay Queensland.

WWI hospital ship Maheno wreckage on Fraser Island, Queensland.

In late 2013 local MP Paul Neville enlisted me as Chairperson of the Hinkler Electorate 2015 Anzac Committee in Bundaberg to adjudicate on the Commonwealth grant of some $140,000 to each electorate. After a number of meetings we submitted our recommendations to DVA (Commem) early 2014 and it was gratifying to see our new MP Keith Pitt present a $50,000 cheque to the RSL to help with the statue which was erected for the anniversary of the fleet sailing from Albany to Egypt on 1 November 1914. All other work, like the granite wall with 1200 pavers with names engraved, including those for Long Tan, Buddy Lea, Bill Roche, Felicia's uncle and myself, was completed in time for Anzac Day 2015.

Adding my support to this project involved much of my time and continued to the Centenary on 25 April 2015. Then, in June 2015 I was asked to be Patron of the Fraser Coast 'Heritage War Tracks' Committee which will link all War Memorials, Museums and RSLs plus the former Z Special Commando camp and WWI hospital ship 'Maheno' wreckage on Fraser Island. A week later I was asked to attend a DVA (Commem) conference in Canberra relative to the 2016 50th anniversary of Vietnam Veterans on 22 July, three days before my 82nd birthday. Never get a day off when retired! But with my sailing it keeps my body and mind active and I am happy to contribute. The 2016 Vietnam War Commemoration is to be based around Long Tan Day at the Canberra National Vietnam Memorial and a function in the Great Hall as for the 40th in 2006, but could also include a delegation to Vietnam to accept the invitation of former enemy we fought at Long Tan to meet and cement ties as has been done with the Anzacs and Turks who fought at Gallipoli.

In June 2014 my regular PSA blood test revealed another problem – a very low iron count – a red flag for internal bleeding. After two colonoscopies and an endoscopy clearing the stomach and colon, I had to have a capsule endoscopy (pill camera) to check out the 8m of small intestine for possible lesions. The result was a perforated small intestine caused by bacteria, most probably from untreated drinking water in Vietnam.

In October 2014 my medals, along with my father's OBE and World War II medals, were presented to the Australian War Memorial National Collection to be displayed in the Long Tan area of the Vietnam Gallery at the request of Director Dr Brendan Nelson. They will be on display for my former soldiers, my children and their families, the public, and veterans to see. It is a colourful medal group with the Star of Gallantry, the Military Cross, an original National Order of Vietnam 5th Class (Knight), a Vietnamese Cross of Gallantry with Palm, plus my service medals and three gallantry citations, our UCG, the US PUC and the GRVN CGCP. I am very proud and pleased to see my medals in the AWM. My decorations come from our victory at Long Tan and were earned for me by the gallantry of my officers and soldiers and the units which supported us, especially the Artillery, APCs, A Company 6RAR, B Company 6RAR and RAAF helicopters.

Unlike most of the past 34 years we will not be venturing north on the water this year. However, I am still sailing and now racing with the local Hervey Bay Boat Club Sailing Squadron. With our six-person crew, we were placed second in the 10-race 2014 Winter Series, and also second in the 2014–15 Summer Series. The 11m Sydney 36 yacht is named *Mayhem* and it sure is mayhem when setting or recovering the spinnaker goes wrong. It is a battle to get good foredeck crew. But while second last in the first race, we won the second race and took second place overall in the nine races. We are looking at racing offshore Mooloolaba in the SCOR Series in August and perhaps the Brisbane to Gladstone race in 2016.

Sydney 36 Yacht Mayhem.

EPILOGUE

At 82 years of age in July 2015 I can look back on my life and say it has been very diverse, adventurous and, overall, wonderful, despite the misgivings I have about my personal family life; the sadness at losing so many soldiers in Vietnam and my second wife to cancer; the battles with the bureaucracy and the Generals Club and, in more recent years, all those jealous detractors who have tried hard to 'cut down the tall poppies' and have really only put themselves down in the eyes of the veteran community, but still remain a nuisance to us. It remains an ongoing battle with these people.

I have battled injury from parachuting and then prostate cancer, and at times very rough seas and many skin cancers, with excision number 23 last month. But I still enjoy yachting life on the water, which has been my largest single sporting interest since childhood. I am battling a recurrence of prostate cancer and internal bleeding in the 8m of perforated small intestine which has been diagnosed by a capsule endoscopy (pill cam). What an amazing device this is, complete with flashlight, camera, transmitter and battery, taking some 60,000 images in the nine hours it took to travel though the intestine. The specialist told me it was developed in Israel to check the innards of suspected spies who may have swallowed secrets on notepaper.

My bleeding problem was diagnosed from the video of the many images as pinhole bleeds which medication should have healed, and along with iron tablets should restore my former fitness and improve my outlook on life. So life on the water can continue. It is interesting that it appears I have had the bacterial infection for 48 years, and it is common in World War II New Guinea and Vietnam Veterans, and can live for 65 years. Drinking untreated water in Vietnam which may have been contaminated by sewage from a local village upstream is quoted as the probable cause. I recall we mostly used purification tablets, but where the water was free-running and clear in creeks I usually drank that. I gather Veterans'

Affairs newsletters have mentioned this matter in past years although I admit I was unaware of the problem.

Since 1978 when I set sail from Sydney for a once-only trip to 'the reef', I continued to sail or cruise for most of the next 35 years, mainly along the north Queensland coast to Thursday Island and down into the Gulf, logging 150,000 nautical miles at sea, which is about the same as six times around the earth on the 25,000-mile Equator. We have met some wonderful sincere people on other boats, many who remain close friends, explored most of the coast and reef up to Cape York and into the Gulf, walked most of the beaches between Cooktown and the Cape, seen lots of crocodiles and feral pigs, found hundreds of glass floats, caught heaps of fish and eaten lots of oysters.

I apologise to the relatives of former commanders in Vietnam in 1966–67 for my criticism of those in power at the time who were unable to ensure the fighting soldiers were given all the available intelligence about the enemy, and who were unable to make appropriate decisions and who thus caused the unnecessary loss of life at Long Tan. Their excuses about withholding the intelligence to preserve the secrecy of the sources do not hold water with me. Those in combat should have been given all the available information and provided with all the support they required. Then to downgrade gallantry awards for officers and soldiers who fought in close combat and defeated the enemy while accepting high awards themselves on questionable citations simply adds insult to injury.

All those who are or were in the military and civil bureaucracy and are unable to comprehend my need to properly recognise my men who fought and died at Long Tan for the government of the day and continually invent excuses to reject my overtures for awards justice may feel I have maligned them. If the cap fits wear it, but the facts need to be told in the hope that the abysmal awards system which applied in Vietnam is never again allowed to tarnish the gallantry of our soldiers' service in action in future conflicts, although I wish no further wars and loss of life.

And if the few unresolved Long Tan awards and unit awards for other units who fought gallantly have still not been approved by the time this book is published, I trust that people will understand my fight for justice will continue until successful, even after I have left the planet. My loyal colleagues will fight on.

I am very pleased to see more liberal recognition in Afghanistan. I note from awards statistics four Victoria Crosses, six Stars of Gallantry, and some 50 DSCs and 800 Conspicuous Service Crosses (CSC) have been awarded since the new 1991 awards system was introduced. While the DSC is available to all ranks it seems to be reserved for senior officers and being in action with the enemy is apparently not required. I am aware of one young Commando officer who told me he was recommended for the DSC in 2010. It was then downgraded to a lesser DSM award while the DSC went to a General sitting in an office, almost a copycat situation of what took place in Vietnam after Long Tan and, overall, where more awards went to officers far from the action than those soldiers who fought in close combat with the enemy.

I am of the opinion that our awards system needs to follow the US Army Honours Units' system which investigates actions and battles and recommends appropriate awards, thus removing the often demeaning opinion of senior officers who were not in action but who are allowed to moderate awards submitted by the officers in the field who observed the acts of gallantry.

The Long Tan awards battle continues, with my local MP Keith Pitt proposing a Private Members' Bill to enact legislation that might lead to approval of the few unresolved awards. The US Congress passed legislation in 2010 that finally approved appropriate awards for the Battle of Ia Drang Valley in 1965.

In August 2014 the Private Members' Bill was lodged in the House of Representatives requiring the government to expedite the Valour Inquiry Part 2 which includes 13 unresolved awards from Long Tan, being 10 for Delta Company, two for Alpha Company, one for 3 APC Troop, plus the proposed Victoria Cross for 'Big Jack' Kirby.

The Bill was moved by my local MP Keith Pitt and seconded by Alan Griffin MP, who generated the ALP's 2009 Long Tan Review which failed because it was flawed by the requirement for documentary evidence known not to be on file, rather than accepting testimony the awards were recommended in 1966 as permitted by a principle of the 1994 (CIDA) Inquiry into Defence Awards. Keith Pitt stated in the House that those who were involved in this Review and other flawed award decisions had never before met me, and that I am the definition of 'tenacious'. He said that words like 'stubborn', 'obstinate', 'resolute', 'firm', 'persistent', 'dogged', 'determined' and 'steadfast' are close to the mark. I guess that is me, and I am determined to continue the fight for justice. But I have to say Private Members' Bills have a legacy of not obtaining action.

However, despite all the addresses in the House in recent years and the 2014 Private Members Bill, Defence advised in January 2015 that the Long

Tan awards have been the subject of two previous Reviews, that no maladministration has been uncovered and thus no further Review is to take place. Apart from the maladministration in 1966, with two flawed Reviews in 2008 and 2009, what a ridiculous statement. That resulted in a very prompt reply to Defence's Darren Chester MP to forget what is said by advisers and look at the facts. Here we go again. In late March 2015 Chester confirmed Defence would not review the awards which then allowed me to request the Honours Tribunal overturn that decision, permitted in the 2010 Amendment of the Defence Act. In early May 2015 the Tribunal Chair agreed to review the Defence decision and we await the outcome of the review process, which will obviously not happen overnight.

In my spare time I intend to continue to try and enjoy life. Luckily, my wife Felicia and I are usually still fit enough to continue sailing, although right now she is recovering from a fractured pelvis, back ala wing and a lower vertebrae from a horse accident at her daughter's Eudlo home in January 2014 and it may be another few months before she regains her former fitness. She was initially confined to resting and getting around in a wheelchair, but she is now driving again after a year of yours truly having been a cook and bottle washer. In April 2015 it appears all the fractures had healed but she suffers pain from labral and tendon tears in the right hip joint recently diagnosed by MRI. Given her perseverance I have no doubt she will eventually recover to sail with me again.

Should you spot me on our 2005 Sydney 36 yacht *Mayhem* give me an Ahoy on the radio if out of voice range. As outlined in previous chapters I fight on for my men and I fight to win races. As the America's Cup's most unremitting warrior Dennis Conner so rightly once said, 'My goal in sailing isn't to be brilliant or flashy in individual races, just to be consistent over the long run.'

Apart from all the derogatory crap from our detractors trying to cut down the tall poppies, stemming from jealousy over the awards we have been given, with my former company being the most decorated in the Royal Australian Regiment, I remain very proud of all my officers and soldiers who fought and sacrificed in Malaya and especially Vietnam. I am also proud of having served with 1 and 2 Commando and the Parachute Training School.

And while the Long Tan battlefield was cleared again in April 2014, as in 1992, I understand new rubber trees have been planted and the greenery will add a better atmosphere to the 50th Anniversary Commemoration in 2016. I am hoping the government will agree to a delegation of my former soldiers and partners along with other Vietnam Veterans being taken back to the Long Tan Cross and to meet up with former enemy who have had a change in policy and indicate they wish to have a reunion in Vung Tau.

The cleared rubber plantations at Long Tan 2014.

My initial request to DVA (Commem) in 2014 resulted in a reply which suggested a new system in which only six to seven medically fit male former soldiers would be sponsored. I am sure the Vietnam Veterans Association and Federation will bring pressure to bear on Canberra that will obtain a proper commemoration in 2016 representing most of the units which fought during the war, not just at Long Tan. I also hope ambassadorial work behind the scenes might see the Socialist Government of Vietnam let the Long Tan Cross come back permanently to the Australian War Memorial to commemorate the 50th Anniversary, even if only on permanent loan.

This photograph was taken at the 2015 Anzac Dawn Service with 500 people in attendance.

This book might help our families, friends and other veterans, and those in power, to better understand what we have done and why. I try to put all the detractors out of my mind and get on with life with my lovely wife in our twilight years, but some of them keep at it.

To all those who continue to try and vilify me and some of my gallant men and other veterans so long after Vietnam – almost 50 years – I say go and take a good look in the mirror and ask yourself if you were involved in close combat with a well-armed experienced enemy which numbered 20 times our company strength. With wonderful artillery support we defeated them and they lost upwards of 500 killed while, sadly, we lost 17 young soldiers killed in four hours.

An honest answer will be a negative, so go jump, and let me and my former officers and soldiers and our loved ones get on with life and enjoy what years we may have left without being harassed by those who are jealous of our achievements. We did what we had to do and did it well, and should not be harassed after all these years.

As mentioned earlier, in October 2014, my medals were presented to the AWM Canberra by my family to whom I had given my medals ahead of my passing. Director Dr Brendan Nelson suggested he would like to have the medals displayed in the Vietnam Gallery to honour my soldiers and the units that supported us during the battle and, indeed, all Vietnam Veterans, given the battle was chosen by them as the iconic action of the war. The presentation took place on 23 October 2014 and the medals are now in the Long Tan display in the Vietnam Gallery.

Presentation of my medals to the Australian War Memorial, Long Tan Display, Vietnam Gallery with son Brett and daughters Deborah and Sharon.

To all my former soldiers I say walk tall and always remember those we lost, those who were wounded, and those who have become affected by the sacrifices we made for the government of the day. And remember the families and loved ones who have to put up with us and often care for us. And spare a thought for the families of all those we killed.

Lest we forget.

ACRONYMS AND ABBREVIATIONS

1ATF	1st Australian Task Force
2IC	second-in-charge
2RAR	2nd Battalion, Royal Australian Regiment
5RAR	5th Battalion, Royal Australian Regiment
6RAR	6th Battalion, Royal Australian Regiment
AATTV	Australian Army Training Team Vietnam
AD	Accidental Discharge of Weapons
AF	Army Form
AFP	Australian Federal Police
AFV	Army Force Vietnam
AHQ	Army Headquarters
AIF	Australian Imperial Force
ALP	Australian Labor Party
AM	Member of the Order of Australia
ANZMI	Australian & New Zealand Military Imposters
APC	Armoured Personnel Carrier
ARVN	Army of the Republic of Vietnam
ATF	Australian Task Force
AWOL	Absent Without Leave

BCFESR	British Commonwealth Far East Strategic Reserve
BOQ	Bachelor Officer Quarters
CAP	company aid post/combat air patrol
CARO	Central Army Records Office
CASEVAC	casualty evacuation
CB	counter bombardment/Companion of the (Order of the) Bath
CBE	Commander of the British Empire
CDF	Chief of the Defence Force
CGCP	Cross of Gallantry Citation with Palm
CGS	Chief of General Staff
CHQ	company headquarters
CIDA	Committee of Inquiry into Defence Awards
CMF	Citizens Military Force
CO	Commanding Officer
COMAFV	Commander Australian Force Vietnam
COMATF	Commander Australian Task Force
CP	command post
CQMS	company quartermaster sergeant
CSC	Conspicuous Service Cross
CSM	company sergeant major
CTs	Communist Terrorists
DCM	Distinguished Conduct Medal
DFs	Defensive Fire tasks
DFAT	Department of Foreign Affairs and Trade

DFC	Distinguished Flying Cross
DFRDB	Defence Forces Retirement and Death Benefits Scheme
DHAT	Defence Honours and Awards Tribunal
DHAAT	Defence Honours & Awards Appeal Tribunal
DSC	Distinguished Service Cross
DSO	diving instructor/supervising officer OR Distinguished Service Order
Dustoff	Dedicated Unhesitating Service to Our Fighting Forces (callsign for medical evacuation)
DVA	Department of Veterans' Affairs
DZ	drop zone
FAC	Forward Air Controllers
FE	Fit Everywhere
FFV2	Field Force Victor 2
FN	Fabrique Nationale de Herstal
FO	Forward Observer
GLO	Ground Liaison Officer
GRVN	Government of the Republic of Vietnam
HQ	headquarters
IED	improvised explosive device
IO	Intelligence Officer
JW	Joint Warfare
KIA	Killed in Action
LTVA	Long Tan Veterans Association
LZ	landing zone

MACV	Military Assistance Command Vietnam
MBE	Member of the British Empire
MC	Military Cross/Imperial Military Cross
MCP	Malayan Communist Party
MFC	Mortar Fire Controller
MG	Medal for Gallantry
MID	Mentioned in Despatches
MM	Military Medal
MMG	Medium Machine Gun
MNLA	Malayan National Liberation Army
MPLA	Malayan People's Liberation Army
MRLA	Malayan Races Liberation Army
MTF	Mentoring Task Force
MUC	Meritorious Unit Citation
Nasho	National Serviceman
NATO	North Atlantic Treaty Organization
NCO	non-commissioned officer
NLF	National Front for the Liberation of South Vietnam (also known as Viet Cong)
NS	National Service
NVA	North Vietnamese Army—see VPA
OBE	Order of the British Empire
OC	Officer Commanding
OCS	Officer Cadet School
PC	Para-Commander
PJI	Parachute Jump Instructor

PM & C	Department of the Prime Minister and Cabinet
PT	physical training
PTSD	Post-traumatic Stress Disorder
PUC	Presidential Unit Citation
R & R	rest and recreation
RAANC	Royal Australian Army Nursing Corps
RAAF	Royal Australian Air Force
RAN	Royal Australian Navy
RAP	Regimental Aid Post
RCL	Recoilless anti-tank guns
RDF	Radio Direction Finding
RMC	Royal Military College
RMO	Regimental Medical Officer
RPG	rocket-propelled grenade
RTA	returning to Australia
SAS	Special Air Service
SEATO	Southeast Asia Treaty Organisation
SG	Star of Gallantry
SIGINT	Signals Intelligence
Sitrep	Situation Report
SLR	self-loading rifle
SOPs	Standard Operating Procedures
SWD	shallow water diver
TEWTs	Tactical Exercises Without Troops
TOR	Terms of Reference

UCG	Unit Citation for Gallantry
USAF	US Air Force
VC	Viet Cong
VD	venereal disease
VMR	Volunteer Marine Rescue
VPA	Vietnam People's Army (also known as the North Vietnamese Army)
VVAA	Vietnam Veterans Australian Association
WIA	Wounded in Action
WRAAC	Women's Royal Australian Army Corps

BACK COVER MATERIAL

"A MUST READ FOR EVERY AUSTRALIAN"
"A TRULY REMARKABLE STORY"

On the afternoon of 18 August 1966, just five kilometres from the main Australian k Force base at Nui Dat, a group of Vice Cong soldiers walked into the right flank of Delia Company, G RAR. Under a blankei of mist and heavy monsoon rain, amid the mud and shattered rubber trees, a dispersed Company of 108 men held its ground with courage and grim determination against a three-sided attack from a force of 2,500 Viet Cong and North Vietnamese Army troops.

When the battle subsided, 17 Australian soldiers lay dead, 24 had been wounded of which one died 9 days later. Battlefield clearance revealed 245 enemy bodies with captured documents later confirming the count at over 500 enemy killed and 800 wounded.

These men were led by a gruff and gutsy perfectionist, Major Harry Smith.

Now, some 49 year after the battle, Harry tells his story for the first time. But this book is more than just an account of a historic battle. Harry Smith takes his readers on an extraordinary journey—one that ultima rely reveals a remarkable cover-up at the highest military and political echelons.

Long Tan is also Harrys lite srory and portrays his many personal battles, from railed marriages to commando-style killing; from a horrific parachute accident through to his modern-day struggles with bureaucracy for recognition for his soldiers. Harrys battles arc tempered by his love of sailing, where he has at last found some peace.

Long Tan the start of a lifelong battle portrays the wrenching, visceral experience of a man who has fought lifelong battles, in a story that he is only now able to tell. Harry can still hear the gunfire and smell the blood spilt at Long Tan. For him, the light continues.

www.ingramcontent.com/pod-product-compliance
Ingram Content Group UK Ltd.
Pitfield, Milton Keynes, MK11 3LW, UK
UKHW040237250426
12048UKWH00041B/1557